COLLINGWOOD STUDIES
VOLUME 4

COLLINGWOOD STUDIES

Volume Four

Variations: themes from the manuscripts

Edited by
DAVID BOUCHER
and
BRUCE HADDOCK

Published by the R. G. Collingwood Society
Registered Charity No. 1037636
Department of Political Theory and Government,
University of Wales, Swansea SA2 8PP

ISSN 1356-0670
ISBN 0 9524393 2 8

British Library Cataloguing in Publication Data.
A catalogue record of this book is available from the British Library.

Printed in Wales, UK, by Dinefwr Press, Llandybïe

ERRATUM

The first sentence of endnote 6 on p. 214 of *Collingwood Studies* vol 3 should read:

The reader will observe that I do not accuse the psychoanalysts of having *no* normal psychology; they have a normal psychology, but no normal psychology of *the imagination*.

COLLINGWOOD STUDIES
VOLUME FOUR

TABLE OF CONTENTS

The Manuscripts

Collingwood Corner

Obituary

THE MANUSCRIPTS

Broadening the Historian's Subject-Matter in The Principles of History

WILLIAM H. DRAY

University of Ottawa

I

In this paper I want to look critically at some apparent revisions of Collingwood's view of what constitutes a proper subject-matter for history which are found in Chapter 2 of the newly-discovered *Principles of History*.[1] Collingwood's chief purpose in that chapter is to argue, as he did in earlier writings, that what historians should be concerned about is human action. He makes it clear that, in the admittedly narrow sense of 'action' he has in mind, to act is necessarily to express thought.[2] This leads him to reiterate a familiar slogan: that all history is history of thought – adding, more explicitly than he ever did before, that this makes it a study of human rationality. He supports this position with a rather curious argument that, in all spheres of inquiry, method determines subject-matter,[3] and that an examination of historical method (which had been his theme in Chapter 1, and is redescribed in Chapter 2 as 'reading' what 'relics' say) will show that *action expressing thought* is what historical method is distinctively equipped to deal with. It is one of the puzzles of the rediscovered manuscript that, although the terminology Collingwood uses at this point, and at some others too, suggests a connection with his well-known theory of historical understanding as involving a re-enactment of expressed thought, the word 're-enactment' is never mentioned in it. Despite this, I shall assume in what follows that, when Collingwood wrote *The Principles of History*, he still held a re-enactive theory of historical understanding, adducing in a final section of the paper some considerations which seem to me to support that assumption. What the paper itself will be chiefly about, however, is not Collingwood's idea of re-enactment but the companion doctrine that all history is history of thought, focusing particularly upon certain emendations and clarifications of that doctrine which he offered in *The Principles of History*, apparently with a view to shoring it up against likely attack.

Critics of Collingwood have often seized upon earlier statements of his claim that history's concern is with thought as excluding from its subject-matter far too much of what it has been traditional for historians to investigate. And Collingwood himself may sometimes seem to waver on the point. Thus although, in the *Autobiography*, he states unequivocally: 'there is nothing else except thought that can be the object of historical knowledge', and in *The Idea of History* even insists that historians should limit their interests to 'reflective' thought, in the Lectures of 1928 he describes the object of historical study as past thought 'in the widest sense of the term', adding that, so understood, it includes 'all the conscious activities of the human spirit'.[4] In Chapter 2 of *The Principles of History*, he makes what looks like some further moves in the same direction in the responses he offers to three specific forms of the complaint that his position on subject-matter is too restrictive. The first is that, to regard history as a study of human rationality simply because it is concerned with past thought, is to ignore the extent to which human thinking is often far from rational; the second, that limiting it to a study of thought, whether fully rational or not, quite arbitrarily excludes from history other important regions of human experience, especially emotions; the third, that, since only individuals can think, the present doctrine in effect reduces history to an 'aggregate' of individual biographies, this excluding what unidentifiable historical agents may have thought and done, whether individually or collectively.

As will appear, I do not think that the responses offered by Collingwood to the three criticisms are entirely adequate. They seem to me to remain inadequate even when supplemented by what he maintains on the same issues elsewhere. That isn't to say, however, that the idea that human history is in some essential way history of thought can simply be dismissed. What Collingwood's responses usefully do, I shall argue, is direct our attention to certain limits to the applicability of that notion, this setting philosophers of history the task of identifying what else it may be reasonable to say history is or should be about, and how that, too, is to be understood. From which it follows, I shall suggest, that one should be wary of embracing too quickly or too uncritically Collingwood's principle that the proper subject-matter of history can simply be read off what may be distinctive about its method.

II

To the complaint that his well-known slogan limits the subject-matter of history inappropriately to what is rational in human life, Collingwood's initial and perhaps surprising response is that he had no intention of excluding the irrational from the historian's concerns, only the non-rational.[5] He intended, certainly, to exclude what can be said of human beings simply as natural objects or as living organisms (he mentions changes in skin colour, or rate of sexual maturation); and also what they experience at the level of psyche rather than of mind: the level of sensation, appetite, or feeling, the latter, in his view, being proper subject-matter for a naturalistic science of psychology. But it is an 'obvious fact', he says, that human reason includes unreason: that actions are often done for bad reasons as well as for good ones; and that the presence of bad reasons is not at all the same as an absence of reason. As he puts it: only a rational creature can make a fool of itself, this being quite beyond the capacities of 'brutes'. He supports this stance with some eloquent talk about historians' interest in reason triumphant or frustrated, wise or foolish, in high or low degree.

In thus stressing how imperfect, precarious and intermittent the life of human reason really is, Collingwood is, of course, himself declaring what his critics have so often reproached him with forgetting. Nor is his doing this in *The Principles of History* evidence of some late conversion on his part. In *The Idea of History*, human beings were said to be rational only in 'a flickering and dubious manner'; the Greeks were described as 'naïve' to think that man is 'essentially a rational animal';

Kant was praised for finding irrationality as well as rationality in human history; Hegel was commended for seeing that people act, at most, as rationally as their situations permit.[6] The question, however, is not how rational Collingwood believed human nature to be, but what follows for his view of history as a study of past thought from his admitting the presence of a good deal of irrationality in human life. We need to know, for example, how far he considered irrational actions to be a legitimate historical subject-matter because understandable in a properly historical way – in other words, how far he considered thoughts expressed by irrational actions to be re-enactable.

In Chapter 2 of *The Principles of History*, Collingwood points to three kinds of actions which, although done for what he would call bad reasons, he still considers to fall within the subject-matter of history. In acting for a reason, he says, an agent must conceive his situation in a certain way; but he may be quite mistaken to conceive it that way. He must be discontented with his situation in certain respects; but he may be foolish to be thus discontented. He must believe that, by acting in an envisaged way, he will improve his situation; but he may be quite wrong in believing this. Collingwood does not discuss such cases; he only points us towards them. But we could say of them that they are all cases in which the unreasonableness of an agent consists in a bad choice of considerations upon which to act, whether this is due to misinformation about the way things are, or to an unrealistic view of how tolerable this is, or to a mistake about how changes can be made for the better. In none of these cases is the agent represented as acting irrationally in the sense of failing to do what is rationally required by the considerations he did take into account. Or, to put it in a perhaps more familiar way: in none of the three cases is there any suggestion that what the agent did expressed an invalid practical argument, given what he regarded as the relevant data. The foolishness is located outside the implicit argument in his perception of his situation, or in his idea of desirable ends, or in his capacity to foresee consequences.[7] The only example which Collingwood gives of the sort of thing he has in mind (and even then in a passage of the manuscript which is struck out – although, I think, for stylistic, not substantive reasons) is that of Ethelred the Unready paying blackmail to the Danes.[8] Although this, in Collingwood's view, was action for a bad reason, there is no suggestion that it should be regarded as expressing bad *reasoning*, once one takes into account the limited possibilities of the king's situation as he saw it.

As Boucher has noted, I dealt with cases like these in *History as Re-enactment* by distinguishing between objective and subjective rationality, meaning by the latter what was rational from the agent's point of view.[9] This terminology, however, may invite misinterpretation. By subjective rationality I do not mean simply what the agent happened to think was action in accordance with a valid practical argument, but action which really was in accordance with one – with the proviso that the premises and assumptions of that argument, although attributable to the agent, need not be ones which the historian himself judges to be correct, or even right-minded. It is nevertheless the historian, not the agent, who must determine, after taking the agent's own data into account, whether a given action was done in accordance with a valid argument or not, and is therefore subjectively rational. Interpreted in the light of this distinction, what Collingwood has to say about the admissibility into history of actions for bad reasons does not seem to me particularly controversial.[10] What is less clear, and much more problematic, is the view he would have taken of actions deemed irrational in a more extreme sense: ones not even subjectively rational, although still genuinely actions in his narrow sense, since still expressions of an agent's will and beliefs, and, as such, still quite beyond the capacities of physical objects or 'brutes'. Let me look briefly at two such cases.[11]

The first is action which, although unquestionably an expression of an agent's will, cannot be said to be in accordance with a valid argument, even one using only data correctly attributable to the agent, because the agent was in this case just confused, misconceiving the connection between what he took as premises and the way he chose to act. In other words, if we are to gauge how much irrationality Collingwood is really prepared to allow into the subject-matter of history, we need to ask what his theory implies about sheer miscalculations – errors not of perception, or of prediction, or of value-judgment, but of reasoning. What he says in *The Principles of History* gives no indication of his position on this matter, although elsewhere he sometimes exhibits a rather dismissive attitude towards sheer error. In the Lectures of 1926, for example, he insists that there is always a 'reason' for an error; and by this he doesn't appear to mean simply an explanation of some sort (e.g. 'He was distracted by a noise'), but rather a hidden rationalising consideration.[12] Similarly, when, in *The Idea of Nature*, he finds contradiction in doctrines attributed to Anaximander, he observes that there must have been a reasoned basis for what was said, although we can only guess at what it was.[13] The problem here is that Collingwood leaves no room in his theory of understanding for the making of a logical mistake.[14] He insists at a number of points that, if re-enactment is to be explanatory, it must be critical; and this appears, among other things, to mean that the historian must test the thought attributed to the agent and find it sound. Collingwood sometimes gives the impression that he accepted it, at least as a working hypothesis, that all genuine actions, if investigated thoroughly enough, will be found to pass such a test, and thus be classifiable as subjectively rational. But a working hypothesis is not a metaphysical principle; and Collingwood himself admits into history from time to time genuine instances of this kind of irrationality.

A second sort of action that appears to raise difficulties for Collingwood's idea of historical understanding – although, once again, a sort only possible to rational beings – I will call arbitrary. What I have in mind is actions done quite deliberately, perhaps even after great reflection, but not done for reasons, whether because the agent could discern no reasons for acting in the chosen way, or because he brushed aside acknowledged reasons for acting otherwise. The possibility of such action has sometimes been denied. Collingwood himself may seem implicitly to deny it when, in *Speculum Mentis*, he declares that even changes of Paris fashions always occur for some reason.[15] At other points, however, he talks about arbitrary action as a real possibility: in the Lectures of 1926, for example, when he contrasts 'appeal to blind caprice' with the 'rational solution' of a conflict; or in the Lectures on Moral Philosophy of 1940, when he dismisses action for which an agent had no reason, not as impossible, but as 'goatish behaviour', for which we can seek only nomological explanation.[16] It might be argued, further, that there is at least an element of arbitrariness in more action than immediately appears, since even when taking reasons into account, people quite often act for ones which they recognise to be insufficient.[17]

The point is that, to the extent that such action occurs, there will be a range of human activity which Collingwood's theory still excludes from the historian's subject-matter, if not as irrational, then at any rate as non-rational – and in a sense of non-rational quite different from the one he applies to mere psyche or to 'brutes'. For ex hypothesi, an arbitrary action cannot express a valid practical argument, and therefore cannot even be subjectively rational.

III

I turn to the second of the three issues. Collingwood's theory of history has long been criticised for excluding from its proper subject-matter not just mere feelings, purely animal activities, and irrational actions, but also emotions. In *The Idea of History*, these are lumped together with feelings and sensations, contrasted with reason and thought, and said to be beyond the range of the historian's interests and techniques because bound up with bodily life.[18] In the *Essay on Metaphysics*, they are said to pertain to psyche, not to mind proper; and are handed over to psychologists for nomological treatment.[19] And as early as the Lectures of 1928, Collingwood had stressed that, although historians are able to re-think the thoughts expressed in past actions, they cannot share the 'emotional heat' with which those actions were performed.[20] Not that his position on this issue is entirely without ambiguity. For example, his observation in the same Lectures that thought in the relevant sense includes 'all the conscious activities of the human spirit', seems to leave it open that it might include emotion.[21] And in *The Idea of History*, he is far from implying that emotions should be entirely ignored, witness his commendation of Hegel for insisting that, while history may be a story of passion, it is a story of passion in the service of reason – as if there could be reasons (not just natural causes) for people having the emotions they have.[22]

It is therefore of some interest that, in the second chapter of *The Principles of History*, Collingwood explicitly declares that emotions of a certain kind belong to history's subject-matter. Although he repeats the slogan, 'all history is the history of thought', he now adds that 'this includes the history of emotions so far as these emotions are essentially related to the thoughts in question'.[23] He explains what this means as follows. If a military officer, in the course of a campaign, builds a fort with a view to providing protection against an enemy, we can infer, he says, that the officer felt a certain emotion in acting for such a motive. He may, of course, have felt many emotions. But most of these will be of no concern to an historian, since they had 'nothing to do' with the building of the fort.[24]

Unfortunately, although Collingwood thus indicates one reason why an historian might regard an emotion as an inessential one, and although he sketches circumstances in which he believes an essential emotion would be felt, he offers no actual example of such an emotion. What might seem the most plausible candidate in the case of the fort-building officer – fear of a threat posed by an enemy – he explicitly rules out as inessential.[25] We can no more conclude from the precautions the officer took that he was afraid, he says, than we can infer from a man's taking out insurance on his house that he fears it will burn down, or from a woman's insisting on a marriage contract that she fears her prospective husband. Such remarks cannot but make one wonder just how much of a concession Collingwood is really making here to critics who object to his excluding emotions from history's subject-matter. For they leave it in doubt whether there *are* any emotions which can be considered essential in the specified sense, namely, that of being strictly inferable from actions which (to use his own term) they 'accompany'.[26] It is not as if he had shown us, by a general analysis of the concepts involved, that particular emotions are, say, logically or conceptually connected to corresponding types of action, as he might claim to have shown in the case of the relationship of action and thought. If one person cheats another, he necessarily intends that his victim lose some assets, and necessarily believes that he has some. But what emotion does he necessarily feel in so acting?

Even if Collingwood had been able to demonstrate that certain emotions are strictly inferable from a person's acting in certain ways, and are thus essential in the sense indicated, we should still need to ask just how he conceives the role of these emotions in historical accounts, and thus just how far his new doctrine really opens the door to emotions as properly belonging to the historian's subject-matter. There is no suggestion that he sees them as having any explanatory function in relation to the actions to which they are said to be essential, as he apparently did fury at Roman breach of faith in relation to the revolt of the Iceni, or fear of rebellion in Gaul in relation to Caesar's repression before leaving for Britain, or hostility towards Caratacus in relation to the refusal of the British tribes to follow him after Medway.[27] They do not indicate reasons for which the actions were performed; they are said merely to occur along with them, although necessarily. Nor is there any suggestion that essential emotions might sometimes provide historians with a legitimate object of study in their own right. Their admissibility into history is represented as deriving entirely from their relationship to the actions with which they are associated. Nor does Collingwood even hint, in the passage I have been considering, that essential emotions, or indeed any emotions, can be regarded as themselves explicable in the distinctively historical way – i.e. re-enactively – which, if they were indeed to be admitted into history as a study of rational mind, one might have expected to be part of their admission fee. Thus, if Collingwood, in *The Principles of History*, opens the door at all to the idea that emotion belongs to history's proper subject-matter, he surely opens it no more than a crack.

Could he have opened it further? I think he would like to have done so; but it is far from clear to me that he could have done so coherently. One way of focusing the issue would be to ask, assuming that the re-enactment requirement holds, how the idea of re-enactment can be applied to emotions. Let me try to show why I think that, even if it does apply to some degree, the place of emotions in history would remain even more restricted than the very limited one Collingwood here claims for them.

There is no great problem with the idea that emotions, quite as much as perceptions or beliefs, may afford reasons for acting, and that, as such, may become *elements* in historians' re-enactments of thoughts expressed in past actions – which is to say, in effect, that they, too, can yield premises for explanatory practical arguments attributed to agents.[28] Some authors – for instance, the late Louis Mink – appear to have regarded emotions (and also, for that matter, perceptions and beliefs) as themselves re-enacted whenever they enter into practical arguments in this way.[29] But to say this seems to me very misleading. Understanding actions by re-enacting the thoughts they expressed is a way of answering 'why' questions about them; but answering the question why a certain act was done by reference to the way the agent thought, and also perhaps felt, does not at the same time answer the question why the agent thought and felt that way. Some elements in re-enactments may themselves be found re-enactively understandable upon further inquiry. Some may not.

The situation is quite different if what is claimed is that, at least sometimes, emotions are of interest to historians in their own right – that emotions are sometimes what historical inquiry is about;[30] and that when they are, they can and should be understood in the re-enactive way. In his lectures on moral philosophy and in his writings on Folklore, Collingwood seems implicitly to make both claims – at any rate with respect to what he there calls 'rational' emotions: ones like jealousy or jubilation or remorse which, unlike mere bodily feelings, would often be judged appropriate or inappropriate to the circumstances as envisaged by the agent.[31] More tentative approaches to the same position can be found in *The Idea of History*.[32] This would still not legitimise many expressions of emotion that historians have actually regarded as interesting in their own right: for example, the Great Fear that swept across France in the spring and summer of 1789,[33] or the witch craze in colonial New England. But there are others that seem to exemplify well enough what Collingwood says about rational emotions: for example, the resentment which Collingwood tells us was felt by many Britons at Colchester when their property was expropriated by the Roman authorities for distribution to time-expired legionaries.[34]

There is a fundamental difference, however, between cases in which historians might claim to find reasons why people acted in certain ways and reasons why they felt in certain ways.[35] What is explained in the first sort of case is what an agent decided to do – an expression of will. But there is no expression of will, no decision, where an agent is said to have had reasons for feeling as he did. How important this difference is becomes clearer if one remembers, again, that in explicating his idea of re-enactive understanding, Collingwood always insisted that it required *criticism* of the thoughts attributed to the agent.[36] In fact, in putting forward a re-enactive explanation of an action, an historian must be doubly critical: critical, first, with regard to the adequacy of the evidence adduced for attributing certain explanatory thoughts to the agent; but critical also with regard to the implied claim that the practical argument expressed by those thoughts is sound – or, in other words, that what the agent decided to do was the rational thing to have done. If it makes sense to say that a certain emotion was, in a similar way, the rational thing to have felt – what the agent *ought* to have felt – then ascriptions of emotion as well as of thought can be regarded as critical in the second sense. But emotions cannot be felt on purpose, as actions expressing re-enactable thoughts must be done on purpose.[37] Thus, if the idea of re-enactment is to be applied to understanding emotions, it will have to be given a meaning which is radically different from the one it bears when applied to understanding thoughts.

Collingwood sometimes gives the impression in *The Principles of History* that anyone needing further light on the theory of historical understanding he sketches there should find it easily enough in the more extensive theory of mind and understanding that he set forth two years earlier in *The Principles of Art*. But there are only two specific references to this earlier work in the recovered parts of *The Principles of History*; and neither of them has any bearing on the way emotions are to be historically understood.[38] We are thus left to find out pretty much on our own what significance, if any, *The Principles of Art* has for our present problem. I can hardly attempt in the present context any systematic review of doctrines found in the latter work which might conceivably be relevant to it. I'll just single out four ideas that some may well consider so, and indicate briefly why I think they do more to complicate the problem than to solve it.

The first is what might be called Collingwood's principle of the joint expression of thought and emotion. At more than one point in *The Principles of Art*, we are told that the very same linguistic act that expresses a thought also expresses an emotion: that there are not two expressions, but only one. That may suggest a variation on Mink's position on the re-enactability of perceptions and beliefs, namely that in re-enacting a thought, one necessarily re-enacts the emotion as well.

But as a contribution to a theory of how a properly historical subject-matter is to be understood, such an idea of emotion being re-enacted piggy-back, as it were, seems to me to leave much to be desired. A main difficulty has already been touched on in considering what Colling-wood said about essential emotions: that it is not enough to believe on general grounds that emotions are necessarily connected to thoughts; one needs to be able to say, in particular cases, what the emotions are – which, in his example of the fort-building officer, Collingwood con-spicuously failed to do. The plot thickens when we read, in *The Prin-ciples of Art*, not that one first discovers an expressed thought and then infers a connected emotion from it, but that one first discerns an emotion and then 'thinks out' the thought implicit in it.[39] To say the least, it is not easy to relate this to anything historians actually do.

A second idea which may seem promising is Collingwood's talk of art, and thus of all language, and by further extension of all activity, not just as expressions of emotion, but as *controlled* expressions of it.[40] Boucher has pointed to this as evidence that Collingwood sees emotional as well as intellectual experience as proper subject-matter for what he calls criteriological science: a type of inquiry which takes seriously the self-critical nature of human activity, and which is presumably exemplified by history to the extent that historians critically re-think agents' thoughts.[41] Now it is true that the way emotions are expressed, once one passes beyond blushes or nervous stammers, can to some extent be controlled, even if we exclude from consideration, as we should, merely simulated emotions, like those displayed on the stage.[42] One might choose, for example, to vent one's anger against someone by shouting rather than by writing a letter to the *Times*. To the extent that expressions are thus controlled, they are, of course, themselves actions, which can be done for better or worse reasons, and which it makes sense to try to understand re-enactively, and therefore criteriologically.[43] But that doesn't mean that the emotion itself is something under one's control, something that one chooses to feel. There is a parallel here with what can be said of belief. Belief, too, is not something chosen, something subject to an agent's will – although expressing a belief one way rather than another may be a matter of choice, and, as such, under-standable by reference to the agent's purposes, i.e. re-enactively.

Still a third idea found in *The Principles of Art* which may be thought significant for Collingwood's philosophy of history is the idea of criteriological inquiry itself,[44] and especially the directive that comes with it that there be judgements of success and failure. In fact, even as applied to understanding actions there is some looseness about the latter idea. Sometimes what is at issue seems to be the internal structure of the thought which an action expresses: for example, whether it constitutes a valid argument, in which case a successful action is presumably one that makes a truly rational response, if only subjectively, to an envisaged situation. At other times, what is in view seems to be a more external kind of success, as when Collingwood, in the *Autobiography*, calls upon historians to take note of the fact that by rowing around the Corinthians Phormio in fact beat them.[45] There are further complications if one asks how the idea of success and failure is supposed to apply where what is to be understood is having certain emotions. Collingwood tells us that, before setting off on his second invasion of Britain, Caesar expressed his suspicion of the intentions of the Gaulish tribes by taking hostages. Since no revolt occurred during his absence, presumably Caesar's expression of emotion should be judged a success externally speaking.[46] But how, in such a case, is internal success to be judged? Would it be enough that the suspicion expressed by Caesar's hostage-taking can be seen as a rational response to the situation as he saw it? Or would we need to go further, and ask whether the act of hostage-taking adequately – i.e. successfully – expressed the precise nature of the suspicion Caesar felt? The latter, I think, would take us rather closer to the concerns of *The Principles of Art*; but to expect historians to answer such a question would surely lay an unreasonably heavy burden upon them. Indeed, it would seem to demand from them precisely what, in the Epilegomenon to *The Idea of History* entitled 'The Subject-matter of History', Collingwood expressly (and I think correctly) said was beyond any historian's powers – this because it involved an interpretation of immediate experience.[47] One can hardly assign to historians the task of critically re-interpreting such experience.

A fourth idea found in *The Principles of Art* that may seem relevant is the idea that grasping another person's emotions requires a 'reconstruction' of that person's experience in one's own mind.[48] This may look like a version of Collingwood's idea of understanding as re-enactment. But there is a great difference between the way the reconstruction of emotional experience is characterised in *The Principles of Art*, and the way the re-enactment of thought is characterised in *The Idea of History*. In *The Principles of Art*, Collingwood tells us that coming to understand another's emotion is achieved by *projecting* upon that person the experience which his expressive behaviour produces in oneself, and that conveying an emotion to him is a matter of *causing* him to have an experience similar to one's own.[49] Even when not depicting emotional understanding in such a crudely causal way, Collingwood often, in that work, stresses a need for sympathetic identification and a commonality of experience when one person seeks to understand the emotions of another.[50] In other words, in *The Principles of Art*, understanding emotions appears to be characterised as intuitive, not ratiocinative, and certainly not critical. Given the warnings that Collingwood himself issued in previous writings against viewing historical inquiry as intuitive – not to mention the efforts of so many of his commentators to clear him of any suspicion of holding such a view – it would surely be ironical if the price he paid for admitting emotion into history were the acceptance of a directly empathetic view of how it is to be understood.

IV

Further study of the relationship between *The Principles of History* and *The Principles of Art* may perhaps make plainer the conditions under which a Collingwoodian theory of history can plausibly regard emotion as part of history's subject-matter. Here I must go on to consider the third way in which, in the final section of Chapter 2 of *The Principles of History*, Collingwood cautioned against conceiving his idea of history as history of thought too narrowly. Besides there being room in it for knowledge of the irrational and the emotional, he there maintained, it can also accommodate knowledge of what was thought by anonymous individuals, and thus also – although he does not stress the connection – for knowledge of group phenomena.[51] As in the case of the subjectively irrational, it does not seem to me that Collingwood really needed to argue in *The Principles of History* for the admissibility of the anonymous. For his previous writings, and especially the constant stress he placed in them on the likeness between history and archaeology, had, I think, made his position on this point clear enough.[52] However, his reiteration of it in the second chapter of *The Principles of History* has the special interest of being embedded in a critique of biography, the paradigmatic study, some might feel, of *non*-anonymous individuals – a critique which is quite as slashing as the one he is notorious for having mounted against psychology conceived as a science of mind.[53] I'll look first at the way he contrasted biography with what he regarded as history proper, and then at some of the conclusions he drew from this about the place of the anonymous in history.

In the Epilegomenon of *The Idea of History*, entitled 'The Subject-matter of History', Collingwood had already contrasted biography with history on the ground that its structure is determined by biological considerations. What a biography is about, he reminds us, is the birth, life and death of some human organism. Unlike historical movements or institutions, it has a natural rather than a mental framework. It is non-historical, too, according to Collingwood, because it tends to stress human experiences, and especially human emotions, which are bound up with the bodily life that sets its limits.[54] In *The Principles of History*, he returns to the subject to offer a more extended and also more controversial account of how biographies differ from history. Much of what they typically include, he declares, is in no sense expressive of thought; and even what does express thought is not typically included for that reason.[55] The principle of selection into a biography is 'gossip-value'; or, more specifically, it is what best serves a common purpose of biographers: arousing the emotions of readers, especially sympathy or malice, these being feelings which Collingwood sees as closely bound up with a subject's animality.[56] To complete the deflation of any claim by biographers to be writing history, he adds that their typical method is that of scissors-and-paste. Like pre-scientific historical writers, biographers are said merely to organise ready-made materials found in memoirs, diaries, supposed reports of eyewitnesses, and the like.[57]

In arguing that the aim of biography is to arouse emotion, Collingwood makes a connection – his second in *The Principles of History* –

with ideas he had worked out in *The Principles of Art*.[58] The way biographers dwell on trivial family connections, or indulge in exhortation and moral-pointing, he declares, invites a comparison with what, in the earlier work, he had called amusement art and magical art, depending on whether its purpose is to stir emotion in a reader or an audience with a view to discharging it in the aesthetic experience itself, or to conserve it for the fuelling of practical life. Among his examples of amusement art are the modern detective story and snobbish novels of upper-class life; of magical art, the rain dance, hymn-singing, and imperialist poetry. He claims that one can draw a similar distinction by reference to purposes between amusement biographies and magical biographies. The first sort he finds exemplified in works by Lytton Strachey; the second, in certain kinds of biographies of Mussolini and Hitler. He does express doubt that anyone ever 'ploughed through' such monumental tomes as Morley's *Gladstone* or Buckle's *Disraeli* for the sake of either their magical or their amusement value. A more likely motivation, he suggests, is a quite false assumption by their readers that, in reading them, they were reading history.

One can hardly complain that Collingwood has characterised incorrectly either the kind of content often found in biographies, or the motives of many biographers. However, his implicit claim that the account he gives of biography has universal application raises some questions about the philosophical status of what he has to say. In earlier works – for example, in the lectures of the 1920s – he had insisted that the business of philosophy is not merely to report facts, however true or interesting, but to make clear what is universally and necessarily true of certain kinds of enterprises or subject-matters.[59] When he points out that the overarching structure of a biography, determined as it is by biology, is not that of a work of history, he clearly remains within that conception of the philosopher's task. But when he describes biography as something structured by gossip-value, aimed at arousing emotion, and only loosely related to evidence, he passes well beyond it. And if he wants to say, as he apparently does, that biography is *necessarily* that way, this can only be taken, with any plausibility, as a rather dubious psychological claim about characteristic weaknesses of those who write biographies, not as something following from the very concept of writing one – as what Collingwood tells us about history is presented as following from the very concept of the enterprise. The idea that a prime task of a philosopher 'of' is to analyse the basic concepts or conceptual framework of a given field has become a familiar one in English-speaking philosophy since Collingwood; but it is already present in his own writings: for example, in the 'Preliminary Discussion' of the lectures of 1927, in the opening section of *The Idea of History*, and also in the *Autobiography*, where the task of the philosopher of history is said to be, in part, the elucidation of concepts like progress, civilisation, and so forth.[60] If philosophical claims are to be made about biography, the concept governing it surely deserves the same respectful attention that is accorded the concept of history.

A related way of coming to grips with Collingwood's contrast between biography and history is to ask just how well his complaints about the one really mark it off from the other. I have conceded that the attribution of a biological framework to biography does this in a significant way.[61] But with regard to the alleged tendency of biographers to select materials for their gossip-value, two things should be remembered. First, as is made especially clear in a paper of 1935 entitled 'Can Historians be Impartial?', Collingwood readily concedes that the reconstructions of historians, too, are often highly value-judgmental.[62] His complaint therefore can only be against the particular values he finds implicit in the particular biographies he has in view – although he has no difficulty at other times in taking seriously historical works which express values with which he disagrees. Second, since he allows that biographies may express interests which are genuinely historical in what he calls their 'embroidery', his claim that in biographical writing gossip-value must still prevail seems rather arbitrary. With regard to the further charge that the works of biographers have the pragmatic motive of arousing emotion rather than the purely theoretical one of discovering past thought, it might be noted, too, that, in his paper of 1935, but elsewhere as well, Collingwood displays a toleration not only of value-judging histories, but of emotion-evoking ones as well – for example, histories of a frankly nationalistic kind – even declaring that, without some such motivation, many of our most treasured historical works (he thinks particularly of ones by Grote, Macaulay, and Rostovtseff) would never have been written.[63] Emotional goals, he declares, not only add a welcome spice to what historians write, but also, in many cases, provide the head of steam that may be needed for writing about the past at all.[64]

As for the charge that biographers are condemned to using the method of scissors-and-paste, I find this positively mystifying. No doubt many of the biographies that are actually written are constructed, at least partly, on such principles; but, as Collingwood himself repeatedly pointed out, so is much so-called history.[65] It will not be enough for him to respond that this is a mode of historical thinking which should be discouraged. For if the fact that scissors-and-paste histories exist at all is not considered to show that historical inquiry cannot be a recon-struction of past thought based on evidence rather than on testimony, the fact that scissors-and-paste biographies exist can hardly, with con-sistency, be held to show that biographers cannot make respectable use (as many of them claim to do) of archives, or even of digs.

One cannot but wonder, too, what Collingwood would have felt obliged to say, in the light of his present analysis, about the status of his own *Autobiography*. For although this depends heavily on memory, contains many deliberately provocative statements, and clearly has the practical aim of improving the world in certain respects, it hardly corresponds to the dismal picture of the genre which is presented in *The Principles of History*.[66] It is of interest to note, in this connection, that when Collingwood wanted to argue, in the British Academy Lecture, that the methods of scientific history are now the secure possession of a far broader section of the population than the guild of professional historians – indeed, that we all constantly use versions of it in our daily lives – one of the things he pointed to was the historicity of auto-biography. As he put it there, autobiography has two stages: first, searching memory with a view to conjuring up a 'spectacle' of past experience; and then subjecting the result to the test of argument from evidence.[67] He insists that there is nothing done by the autobiographer in the second part of his task, that the historian cannot do for other people. On this point, as well as some others, his first thoughts seem to me better than his second.

But let me return to the ostensible topic of the section on biography, the place of the anonymous in history, from which much of Collingwood's lament about the vulgarity of biographers is really a digression. In his view, history can only benefit from what he sees as a progressive decline in the prestige of biography as a serious intellectual pursuit. For he believes it will render less tempting the widespread illusion that, in the last analysis, history is simply a sum of many biographies, a composite account of what particular individuals thought and did in the past. In repudiating the latter view, he declares roundly that, although concerned with past thought, history has 'nothing to do with the names of the people who think it'.[68] As he had said earlier in *The Principles of History*, what interests historians most is the thought implicit in customs and practices developed not by particular individuals, but by populations at large. Much the same view can be found in other writings of Collingwood's, for all the tendency of some of his critics to represent him as an extreme individualist: for example, in his commendation of Vico, in *The Idea of History*, for being one of the first to achieve a view of history as concerned with the 'genesis and development of human societies and their institutions'.[69] This conception of it is, of course, well exemplified in Collingwood's own *Roman Britain*,[70] with its description and analysis of town and country life, agricultural systems, military organisation, and styles of art.

But while this may be acceptable enough as a reminder that history can be about what unnamed individuals thought – the members of a trade union, for example, or the courtiers of Queen Elizabeth – what Collingwood actually says, in the heat of his attack on biography, runs some danger of promoting an error equal and opposite to the one he wishes to quash. For, as his own histories of Roman Britain also so splendidly show, it is quite normal in history, and it is sometimes important, to be able to assign thoughts to named individuals: the intentions of Caesar in invading Britain, for example, or those of Hadrian in building the Wall. Furthermore, besides being at odds with Collingwood's historical practice, his saying that, as a study of past thought, history has 'nothing to do with' the individuals who thought them, is in flagrant conflict with positions he took at various times on theoretical grounds. An interesting example is his welcoming observation, in *Roman Britain and the English Settlements*, that, by the first half of the fifth century, 'British Christianity had ceased to be anonymous.

Its leaders,' he says, 'are no longer mere figure-heads of shadowy congregations: they stand out in all their individuality as living men'.[71] A perhaps more eccentric, but even stronger expression of the same tendency to dissociate historicity from anonymity appears in an essay of the 1920s on Spengler, in which Collingwood declares that the latter's prediction of a new Caesar arising at a certain stage in our civilisation would be brushed aside by any self-respecting historian on the ground that Spengler was unable to tell us who that person would be.[72]

For what sorts of reasons might historians want to breach anonymity from time to time, and make reference to named individuals? Sometimes, no doubt, as a way of showing how larger trends and movements worked out, as when Collingwood, *qua* historian, catalogues the misfortunes of the sons of a British king in order to illustrate concretely the way British society was breaking down under Roman pressure.[73] At other times, perhaps as a convenient way of identifying some larger social entity, as when historians refer to the Theodosian Code, or to the foreign policy of Ferdinand and Isabella. But reference to named individuals is also sometimes required because of the crucial role they played in the social developments which may still be the prime focus of the historian's attention: Cromwell or Charles I in the case of the English Civil War, for example, or Napoleon in the case of French imperialism.[74] There are theories of history which have denied that particular individuals can play unique and indispensable roles in social movements, but Collingwood's is not one of them. It may seem inconsistent with such a view that, in a review of recent trends in English historiography, he should have attacked J. B. Bury for accepting an idea of crucial causes in history, using against him the story of Cleopatra's nose.[75] His argument against Bury, however, is not that particular historical agents cannot be indispensable, but that they cannot in themselves constitute sufficient conditions of large-scale historical events.

An important point that emerges out of Collingwood's contrast of biography with history, and more particularly out of his denial that a history is to be conceived as a sum of biographies (although not, perhaps, as clearly as one might have wished), is that, even when historians draw upon biographies, which Collingwood comes close to denying they ever ought to do, they do not assimilate them as such. By this I mean that, while some of their contents may be found relevant to problems on which particular historians are working, it is unlikely that the whole of any biography will ever be found so.[76] For example, although many details of Bismarck's life, details which his biographer could not ignore, may be of importance for understanding his role in the unification of Germany, many others, quite as relevant to a serious, and not at all trivial or popular biography of Bismarck, will not be. This is an important implication of the fact, rightly stressed by Collingwood, that biography is different from history as a genre of inquiry. Although a cousinly sort of inquiry, sometimes unearthing details that may contribute to given historical accounts, differences of scope and mode of organisation make it non-assimilable as such. Biographical studies can nevertheless be a support to certain kinds of history, and historical studies to certain kinds of biography. And there are perfectly respectable hybrids: political biographies aimed at rounding out our knowledge of the historical background of an individual's life, for example, or scientific ones aimed at illuminating certain developments in the history of inquiry.

V

The conclusion I reach is that what Collingwood has to say in *The Principles of History* about the admissibility of irrational actions and the anonymous in history, although less a broadening of an existing view than a clarification of views he had already expressed, is in the main acceptable. By contrast, what he tells us about the historical relevance of emotions, although going well beyond his previous treatments of the subject, leaves the whole question of the place of emotion in history in some obscurity. Clearly there is need here for further analysis and discussion. In concluding the paper, however, what I want to do is to return briefly to the assumption I stated at the beginning and held to throughout: that, for Collingwood, the test of admissibility into an historical subject-matter is still re-enactability – this despite the puzzling fact that neither in the rediscovered parts of *The Principles of History*, nor in the parts which were incorporated into *The Idea of History*, did he ever mention the word 're-enactment'.

This fact can hardly fail to send Collingwoodians scurrying for an explanation. One with considerable plausibility has already been proposed by David Boucher.[77] He suggests that Collingwood's determination, in *The Principles of History*, to defend his doctrine that all history is history of thought by broadening its meaning, and, in particular, by breaking down any absolute distinction between thought and at least certain kinds of émotion, pitched him into a difficulty from which he was unable to extricate himself. For, as we have seen, it is at least doubtful that emotions meet the test of re-enactability – at any rate, as thoughts expressed in actions do. Collingwood was therefore confronted with a dilemma. He could either repudiate the idea that re-enactability is a test of historicity, or revise the idea itself in such a way that it clearly applies to understanding emotions. Shrinking from the first alternative, and failing to find an acceptable way of proceeding with the second, he tried to work around the problem, perhaps with the hope of returning to it at some later date. By the time he reached the last chapter of Book I, however, this attempt had broken down. And so had the writing of *The Principles of History* – which is hardly surprising, since the plan for the whole work which he had sketched before beginning to write called for extensive use of the idea of re-enactment not only in Book I, but also in Books II and III.[78]

Boucher's suggestion may, in the end, come to be regarded as the most likely explanation of the absence of the idea of re-enactment from *The Principles of History*. In considering it, however, one should not forget that there is no direct evidence for it, no explicit rejection of the idea by Collingwood. The evidence is all circumstantial; and it doesn't all point the same way. Let me illustrate what I mean by noting briefly some conflicting considerations.

One which makes it difficult to believe that Collingwood would even entertain the idea of abandoning the notion of re-enactment is, of course, the fact that it had appeared so frequently in his writings since he announced his discovery of it in his Lectures of 1928. The idea bulks large in the British Academy Lecture, and in two of the original Epilegomena to the lectures of 1936 which became *The Idea of History*; and there are many references to it throughout the historical parts of that book as well, references which evidently survived the changes Collingwood made to the manuscript in 1940, when he began revising it for publication. The idea is prominent also in the *Autobiography*, a book which Collingwood revised, and for which he rewrote the last chapter, on the very same voyage to the Dutch East Indies that he wrote *The Principles of History*.[79] It is very much present, too, in the Scheme for *The Principles* which he composed just the day before he began writing out the text, and only ten days before he reached the part of Chapter 2 in which he is supposed to have encountered insuperable difficulties about applying the idea of re-enactment.[80] I do not find it easy to believe that he could have been so confused that he completely failed to see such a potentially explosive problem coming. As for the complete absence of the idea from what was completed of *The Principles of History*, it should be noted that, although the word re-enactment never appears, it is less clear that the idea does not. There seem to be hints of it at least in what is said in Chapter 2 about historical understanding, especially where it is clearly action that is being considered; and some of the examples offered in that chapter closely resemble those used in *The Idea of History* and in earlier writings to illustrate understanding of the re-enactive kind – for example, that of the promulgation of the Theodosian Code.[81]

On the other hand, it is true that Collingwood stopped writing very soon after the point at which his Scheme called for a further development of the re-enactment doctrine. And although he does not say so, some of his arguments for the admissibility of irrationals, and even more of emotions, do put some strain on the notion of re-enactment. The vagueness with which he refers readers to *The Principles of Art* for further enlightenment might be seen as betraying some uncertainty on his part about how well the view of re-enactive understanding he offered previously survives its doctrines. And it could be regarded as significant, too, that, apart from the *Autobiography* and some of the piecemeal 'Notes on Historiography' recorded in 1939, other late works of Collingwood's also fail to mention re-enactment. Indeed, two of them raise problems for the idea that all history must be re-enactively understandable which are quite additional to ones we have already noted. The *Essay on Metaphysics*, for example, written just before *The Principles of History*, sketches a view of one level of the history of ideas to which re-enactment theory does not seem to be applicable at all. For, if there can be no reasons for holding absolute presuppositions, any changes in them which an intellectual historian might want to trace would be beyond re-enactive understanding.[82] Collingwood's lectures on moral philosophy of 1940, now appended to *The New Leviathan* under the title 'Goodness, Rightness, and Utility', also appear to pose a serious problem for re-enactment theory, although, again, there is no acknowledgment of this by Collingwood. For the similarity which is there said to hold between historical thinking and a recognition of duty individualises both so radically that it is difficult to see how any mode of understanding in terms of bringing under kinds would apply; and re-enactive understanding is such a mode. In *The New Leviathan* itself, Collingwood's last book, there is also silence on re-enactment.[83]

Thus the evidence is ambiguous in the sense that one can find reason for saying that Collingwood was in trouble (although he never admitted he was) and for saying that he couldn't possibly have abandoned one of his most cherished ideas without so much as a good-bye (although that is just what he appears to have done). I think it is possible that, in the end, we may have to write off the problem as insoluble. But even if we do, we shall still want to ask what can be made of the idea of a specifically historical kind of understanding in Collingwood studies; and in addressing this question, I don't see why we shouldn't exploit whatever we find useful in Collingwood's dicta on the subject, early or late. It shouldn't be necessary to apologise for treating an idea of his in this way. Collingwood is a fertile and immensely stimulating writer, but he is not to be valued simply as (to use one of his own terms) a purveyor of ready-made ideas. What one finds him saying at a given moment often has to be re-thought critically, as was his own practice when considering the thoughts of others; and this may sometimes take one well beyond anything he himself says.

Let me therefore go back to the dilemma apparently facing the Collingwood of *The Principles of History*: either to abandon re-enactment or to enlarge the idea so that it somehow covers other things judged to be appropriate subject-matter for historians. The best response to this dilemma, I suggest, is to refuse it – to insist on going between its horns. Re-enactment theory as Collingwood originally expounded it can and should still be applied strictly to claims to understand actions done for reasons (perhaps allowing for certain classes of exceptions), while other theories of understanding may have to be sought for other kinds of subject-matter which historians may be expected to treat, beginning with emotions. Dealing with the dilemma in this way may have the further and (in my view) salutary effect of encouraging an avowedly eclectic approach to the problem of historical understanding, one prepared to recognise as many varieties of it as are required to accommodate the different kinds of subject-matter historians treat. And, in fact, despite the narrowly monistic position he adopted officially on this matter, Collingwood does not entirely renounce, either in his theoretical pronouncements or in his historical practice, the idea that historians will have to seek understanding of some things in a non-re-enactive way. To take an obvious example: his insisting, both in earlier writings and again in *The Principles of History*, that they must ask not only why actions were undertaken, but also why they succeeded or failed,[84] by itself introduces the possibility of having to call upon other kinds of explanation than the re-enactive. This is most easily seen where physical conditions themselves, and not just agents' ideas of them, are allowed to have played a role (as Collingwood himself sometimes, if not always, concedes that they do[85]). Nor are purely physical conditions the only ones to raise this possibility – as, again, Collingwood implicitly concedes when, in a section of *The Principles of History* that was incorporated into *The Idea of History* as 'History and Freedom', he depicts the problem of acting as, in part, that of determining how a proposed initiative of one's own can be fitted into the gaps between the actions of others.[86] For actions, although expressions of thought, are at the same time (as Collingwood himself repeatedly says) events in the physical world.

In challenging Collingwood's monism about historical understanding in this way, I am also, in effect, bringing into question the principle which, as I noted at the beginning, he calls upon in defending it both in *The Principles of History* and, less obtrusively, in some earlier works: the principle that method should determine subject-matter, or that history *a parte subjecti* should determine history *a parte objecti*.[87] It is in conformity with this principle that he argues that the subject-matter of history must be actions expressing thought, for that, he maintains, is what its technique of interpreting relics for their meaning is alone capable of revealing.[88] Perhaps because I am further removed from the ghostly whisperings of idealist philosophy which sometimes seem to haunt Collingwood's pronouncements, it seems to me just as useful, and in some contexts more useful, to say that subject-matter should determine method, the philosopher first having to decide what human history is, or should be, about, and only then to ask what method or methods historians need to follow if that subject-matter is to be made understandable. It might be better still to say that method and subject-matter are mutually related, so that, when trying to elaborate an adequate philosophy of history, one might quite properly oscillate between asking Collingwood's question and asking mine. Of course, if a prime task of a philosopher of history is to elaborate a theory which illuminates what historians actually do, the question arises: which historians? My reply to that would be: why not begin, at least, with the historical writings of Collingwood himself, in which a good deal more than a re-enactment of past experience goes on.

NOTES

1 To a considerable extent I shall be following in the footsteps of David Boucher in 'The Principles of History and the Cosmology Conclusion to The Idea of Nature', *Collingwood Studies*, 2 (1995), 140-74 (abbreviated hereafter as 'Principles'), and 'The Significance of R. G. Collingwood's *Principles of History*', *Journal of the History of Ideas*, 58 (1997), 309-30 (abbreviated hereafter as 'Significance'), and Jan van der Dussen in 'Collingwood's "Lost" Manuscript of *The Principles of History*', *History and Theory*, 36 (1997), 32-62 (abbreviated hereafter as '"Lost" Manuscript'). While I have learned much from both authors, however, my conclusions are in some respects different from theirs.

2 Much the same distinction between historical and non-historical actions is drawn in *The Idea of History* (Oxford, Clarendon Press, 1946), 216 (abbreviated hereafter as IH: the lectures of the twenties which are appended to its revised edition will be abbreviated as L26, L27, L28, with page numbers from IH rev.).

3 The principle that history *a parte subjecti* determines history *a parte objecti* appears also in Ch. 4 of *The Principles of History* (abbreviated hereafter as PH), where it supposedly underpins the claim that history is about past actions.

4 *An Autobiography* (abbreviated hereafter as A), 110; IH, 308; L28, 445.

5 PH, 37-8 (page numbers for PH are those of the ms. in the Archives of The Clarendon Press).

6   IH, 227, 41, 116.

7   Throughout his discussion of rationality in PH, Collingwood appears to have in mind only the kind of action which in Ch. XV of *The New Leviathan* (Oxford, Clarendon Press, 1942), he called utilitarian (abbreviated hereafter as NL). Bad reasons in e.g. rule-governed actions, which also sometimes need explanation by historians, would be somewhat different, but a distinction between subjective and objective rationality would still need to be drawn.

8   PH, 38.

9   Boucher, 'Significance', 322.

10 In *The Principles of Art* (Oxford, Clarendon Press, 1938), 60 (abbreviated hereafter as PA), Collingwood maintains, in effect, that the supposed irrationality of the savage, when properly investigated, turns out to be subjectively rational. Historians' or anthropologists' misconception of the savage as irrational could also, of course, be subjectively rational.

11 These are treated in a similar way, along with others, in *History as Re-enactment* (Oxford, Clarendon Press, 1995), 119-22. Such cases need to be weighed against Collingwood's tendency to universalise subjective rationality: see e.g. IH, 116, 77-8, 218, 310; L28, 47.

12 L26, 345.

13 (Oxford, Clarendon Press, 1945), 34.

14 One needs to cavil a little therefore before accepting van der Dussen's conclusion that in PH Collingwood holds that, by historical thinking, 'unreason . . . can itself be understood' ('"Lost" Manuscript', 44).

15 (Oxford, Clarendon Press, 1924), 227.

16 L26, 375; 'Goodness, Rightness, Utility', NL rev., 430.

17 In NL, 96, Collingwood remarks that no one can set out to do an action characterised to its last detail; and in NL, 108, he declares that there is an element of caprice in all utilitarian actions (this would be true also of rule-governed ones).

18 IH, 205, 297, 304.

19 (Oxford, Clarendon Press, 1940), 267, 141 (abbreviated hereafter as EM).

20 L28, 446.

21 L28, 445.

22 IH, 116.

23 PH, 54-5. The discussion is tantalisingly brief, but even so, more extensive than Collingwood's discussion of irrationals.

24 Collingwood says similarly that Wolfe's preoccupation with Gray's *Elegy* during the early stages of his assault on Quebec has no place in English military history because it did not interfere with either the assault or its aftermath. (In fact, he lumps together emotions which were irrelevant in this sense and ones which fall outside the story because historians have no evidence for them.) A good example of a merely accompanying, but presumably inessential, emotion is the 'malicious sense of humour' with which, according to Collingwood, Augustus always produced some variant of the old excuse 'trouble in Gaul' whenever he was expected to implement the plan for invading Britain which he inherited from Julius Caesar (RBES, 72).

25 Boucher takes it that, in this case, Collingwood regarded fear as an inferable essential emotion ('Significance', 325); but I think this misreads the example.

26 I cannot myself think of a single emotion that would *necessarily* accompany an action like building a fort. It has been suggested to me by Rex Martin, however, that in

equating 'essential' with 'necessary', I may have misunderstood Collingwood's intention. Since the equation seems to me natural, in context, I can only record this as an idea that may deserve further consideration.

27 RBES, 99, 32, 88.

28 Emotions can also, of course, explain actions without being reasons, but not actions in Collingwood's narrow sense (fright can make one jump; sympathy can make one wince involuntarily). There is also, as noted in NL rev., 400, such a thing as emotions 'taking charge'. Collingwood does not always distinguish clearly between explanations of and by the emotions (see e.g. his ms. on Folklore, 1936-7, Collingwood Mss., Bodleian Library, IV, 6, 8, 12, 14, 17).

29 *Historical Understanding*, ed. Fay, B., Golob, E. O., and Vann, R. T. (Ithaca, N.Y., 1987), 259-60. Somewhat analogous is Boucher's notion that absolute presuppositions are re-enacted along with what presupposes them (NL rev., xxx).

30 Or are partly constitutive of what it is about, as in a patriotic war or a vendetta.

31 'Lectures on Moral Philosophy', 1933, Collingwood Mss., Bodleian Library, 120-1; Folklore, IV, 15-18. Boucher usefully calls attention to such cases in NL rev., xxxv.

32 IH, 116, 293.

33 See e.g. Crane Brinton, *A Decade of Revolution* (New York, 1934), 35. Like other 'blind' emotions, these might have to be explained naturalistically.

34 RBES, 95, 291.

35 A matter also discussed in *History as Re-enactment*, 131 ff.

36 IH, 215, 301. This point will be considered further when examining what Collingwood, later in PH and also in EM, called a criteriological type of inquiry.

37 One cannot say: The situation being as it is, what should I feel? For although an emotion may be expressed by purposive acts, it is not itself felt on purpose. One can sometimes, however, choose to express it by one act rather than another. And it may be possible to exercise indirect control over some emotions by submitting to a process of conditioning, in much the way that Pascal thought we could control some of our beliefs. Collingwood may have something like this in mind when, in 'Goodness, Rightness, Utility', he speaks of our being able to 'cultivate' emotional 'habits' (NL rev., 424). But none of this would justify concluding that specific feelings (by contrast with the controlling procedures) can express a subject's purposes, and thus be critically re-enactable.

38 One concerns the understanding of documents generally (which may include the understanding of emotions, although this isn't explicitly said), and the other divides biographies into magical and amusement varieties (PH, 43, 56).

39 PA, 266, where Collingwood writes: 'Expression of thought in words is never direct or immediate, but is mediated through the emotional charge. A expresses the emotion with which he thinks a thought to B, and invites him to think out the emotion and thus rediscover the thought'. In a passage of NL to which Boucher draws attention (NL rev., xxxvi, 344), Collingwood blurs the relationship between thought and emotion in still another way. Here the close connection between the two is illustrated by insisting that, in the development of consciousness, emotions *turn into* thoughts – a sentiment, e.g., being described as an emotion on the way to becoming a thought. However, if our interest is in how and what historians can claim to understand rather than in a general philosophy of consciousness, we will surely need to ask, with regard to particular agents at particular times, how far such a 'turning into' process had gone. If it had not yet reached the stage of thought, it had better not be explained as if it had.

40 PA, 266.

41 'Significance', 324.

42 PA, 121. In weeping real tears, Collingwood observes, an actress does not feel the emotion of grief, but represents it, and does it well to the extent that she shows what the tears are about.

43 We can ask: Was it wise to express your anger by shouting? but not (at any rate in the same sense): Was it wise to feel angry?

44 The idea is also present in both PH, 66-8, and EM, 109-11. In discussing it, however, there is a point of nomenclature that I think needs to be insisted upon. Boucher sometimes locates the importance of PA for the theory of history in its showing emotion to be criteriological ('Significance', 325), and van der Dussen sees Collingwood as objecting to a natural science of man because it refuses to recognise 'the criteriological nature of its object' ('"Lost" Manuscript, 55). In fact, although he may not be entirely consistent himself on the point, what can be criteriological for Collingwood is not a certain kind of subject-matter but a certain kind of inquiry. It is thus history which is to be considered criteriological, not the actions historians study. What those actions must be, if history is to be criteriological, is self-critical. What PA may similarly claim to show is that aesthetics, not art, is criteriological, depending upon whether it can also be shown that artistic expression, like historical action, is self-critical (in a way that can be 're-thought'). It may help to highlight the importance of being strict on this point to note that, while Collingwood denied that psychology was a criteriological sort of inquiry, he did not deny that it was a self-critical activity - as, one would hope, are physics or mathematics or geology. Indeed, it was because he regarded psychology as itself self-critical, that he was able, in PH, to castigate it as implicitly self-contradictory, charging that it failed to recognise in what it took as its subject-matter the self-critical rationality that it claimed for itself.

45 A, 72.

46 RBES, 32, 43.

47 IH, 313-14. Van der Dussen puts the problem more generally when he questions whether emotions can have the 'mediacy' which Collingwood ascribes to thoughts as a condition of their being historically knowable ('"Lost" Manuscript', 51 n.). Boucher argues, in a very interesting passage that deserves more attention that I can give it here, that the theory of imagination developed in PA shows how emotion can be 'experienced in its mediacy' and therefore re-enacted ('Significance', 330)

48 PA, 250. This is the message Collingwood beams at anthropologists.

49 PA, 250, 118. As van der Dussen wryly but justly observes, what is strikingly absent from what is said about historical understanding where PA is alleged to make contact with PH is any 'critical study of sources' ('"Lost" Manuscript', 46).

50 Collingwood may seem to anticipate the position taken here when he says, in IH, 302-3, that whereas we know our own feelings and sensations by memory, we discover those of others 'by entering with sympathy and imagination' into their experience. The idea that emotions may be known directly through sympathy is also found in Folklore, IV, 2, 26, 37. Such an empathetic view meshes comfortably with Collingwood's observation, in PH, 42-3, that there is always an aesthetic, non-inferential, element in historical understanding – an idea which he stresses there for the first time (although not specifically mentioning emotions).

51 I'll not go into the latter issue as such; I merely underline the relationship, and the important fact that history could be said to be *about* the social. As Boucher has noted,

Collingwood represents this whole section as triggered by a brief remark he made about biography when discussing inessential emotions in the preceding section (PH, 56). The connection is too slight, however, to justify the scale of his discussion of biography.

52　In his philosophical work, see e.g. his commendation of Hegel for realising that history deals with objective as well as subjective mind – i.e. mentality displayed by social structures (IH, 121); or his earlier remarks in the present manuscript describing history as about rituals and customs generated by rational activity (PH, 37). In his historical work, see his attribution of reasons to the unknown Romans who built Hardknot Castle (*Roman Eskdale* (Whitehaven, 1929), 38); or his assertion that the Iceni (a whole people) revolted in fury at Roman breaches of faith (RBES, 96). Boucher sees the section on biography as a repudiation of methodological individualism by Collingwood ('Significance', 320); but if so, it falls short of its mark, since merely finding a place for the anonymous entails nothing about how the social, if also admitted, is to be explained. Van der Dussen observes only that it shows Collingwood not to be advocating any 'one-sided attention to individual persons' in history, but that, too, seems to me to ascribe more to it than is warranted ('"Lost" Manuscript', 53).

53　See e.g. A, 92-5; EM, 102-42.

54　IH, 304. There is an earlier, and similar, attack on the pretensions of biography in L26, 398. In some other writings, however, there are remarks which seem more accepting of biography: e.g. references to historians as 'reconstructing' a biography of Caesar ('Inaugural: Rough Notes', Collingwood Mss., Bodleian Library, 13, 2); or to a popular biography of Napoleon as 'linked' to 'previous historical thought' about him (L28, 404).

55　Collingwood's position here might also be put by saying that he regards biographers as concentrating upon inessential emotions. Any emotions Wolfe may have experienced reading Gray's Elegy while preparing his assault on Quebec, he says, belong to that general's biography, not to the history of the Conquest (PH, 55).

56　The connection of biography with animality is taken to the extreme of maintaining that an animal, such as a dog, is a fit subject for biography, because capable of sympathy (and, should one add, malice?).

57　A biographer is said to be 'essentially a person who sticks together ready-made statements about an individual person's life' (PH, 58). Rather mysteriously, Collingwood adds that ready-made statements are 'well-suited' to arousing emotion. He also associates biography with treating a subject-matter as a 'spectacle', which in IH is regarded as typical of scissors-and-paste thinking. The indifferent attitude of biographers to evidence is said to show itself even in a tendency to suppress it when it does nothing to further their practical goals (PH, 57-8).

58　In this case, the connection made with PA is more casual; Collingwood simply enlarges on the idea that biographies aim to arouse emotion, and distinguishes two likely uses of such arousals.

59　See e.g. L27, 347.

60　L27, 347; IH, 7-10; A, 77.

61　A most important conceptual *likeness* between history and biography which Collingwood doesn't deny (in fact, he accuses biographers of trading on it), is that both individualise their subject-matter. However, biography is said to differ from history in the *way* it individualises (e.g. by showing pictures of a subject's house). A more controversial conceptual claim is implicit in Collingwood's apparent position that, while both biographies and their subjects have beginnings and endings (PH, 57), only history books, not histories, can have them ('Notes on Historiography', 1939, Collingwood Mss., Bodleian Library, 10, 12 (abbreviated hereafter as NH); A, 98). There may be a connection worth exploring between this and Collingwood's attack on biological history in NH, 6-9. For social units as well as natural ones are often described as 'being born' and 'dying', or as 'having cancers' and 'suffering relapses', on a kind of biological analogy.

62 Collingwood Mss., Bodleian Library, 8 ff. (abbreviated hereafter as CHBI).

63 CHBI, 4-5. See also L26, 397-8, where it is pointed out that if 'tendentious' history is condemned, we must regard 'almost all biography and certainly all autobiography as historically worthless' - which, at that point, Collingwood seems not prepared to say they are. In both works he also argues that history is always tendentious, unless written by 'bloodless pedants' or moral 'eunuchs' (L26, 398; CHBI, 4).

64 In any case, there is no reason to hold that discovering past thought and, say, promoting democracy by means of admiring accounts of Greek practice, are incompatible goals.

65 An example from Collingwood's own historical writing is his explicit reference to the 'authority' of Claudian on the question of the withdrawal of troops from Britain by Stilicho (RBES, 291). But his general position is made clear enough in IH, 258, 279, and elsewhere.

66 As Boucher argues, perhaps with Collingwood's obscure remarks about essential emotions in mind, the emotional details of his life which he offers in his *Autobiography* may escape his general critique of biography because related for the most part to his philosophical thought rather than to his personal life ('Principles', 160).

67 IH, 295-6. It is interesting to note that autobiography is here called 'a strictly historical account of my own past'. See also IH, 219.

68 PH, 59. He seems to move here from saying that history *may* be about the anonymous, to saying that it *must* be – one of many assertions justifying Boucher's apt description of him as a 'master of overstatement' ('Significance', 320). All Collingwood really needed to argue was that there is no necessary connection between knowing past thought and knowing the identity of those who thought it: that one can have evidence for the former without having evidence for the latter.

69 IH, 65.

70 (Oxford, Clarendon Press, 1934).

71 RBES, 308.

72 'Oswald Spengler and the Theory of Historical Cycles', *Essays in Philosophy of History by R. G. Collingwood*, ed. William Debbins (Austin, Texas, University of Texas Press, 1965), 69.

73 RBES, 82. Another relevant example is Collingwood's assertion (A, 46) that English philosophy is beginning to recover from the 'blight of realism' in the person of Alexander and Whitehead.

74 An historian may need information about Cromwell because he is studying the outbreak of the Civil War; a biographer about the Civil War because he is interested in Cromwell.

75 IH, 80-1.

76 As Collingwood is forever telling us, what historians assert should be relative to a question asked.

77 He put this forward in a paper delivered at Leeds in 1995, and developed it further in 'Significance', 310, 326 ff.

78 See Collingwood's 'Scheme for a Book' in NH, 20-21. Van der Dussen offers a dif-

ferent explanation of why the writing of PH broke down, citing 'fortuitous circumstances' rather than any significant problem of content as the most likely cause ('"Lost" Manuscript', 38).

79 Boucher follows Collingwood in stressing that PH should be read along with PA. It is even more obvious that it should be read along with A: the two are practically simultaneous works on the same subject.

80 Chapter 2 was to have been on action as subject-matter by contrast with mere process or change; Chapter 3 on re-enactment by contrast with a dead past.

81 See e.g. PH, 40-41. The resemblance has been stressed by van der Dussen, '"Lost" Manuscript', 47.

82 Actions presupposing them might, of course, be so understood, but as already argued, that would not amount to re-enactively understanding the presuppositions.

83 As Boucher has noted, the word appears, but in a different sense (NL, 69).

84 IH, 41, 237; A, 128; PH, 65-6.

85 The ebb tide that Caesar's invasion fleet had to wait for; or the physical distance from the main body of his troops that prevented Suetonius from barring Boudicca's path to London (RBES, 36, 101).

86 IH, 316.

87 On this see e.g. PH, 35; L28, 428-9, 434-5. The question whether re-enactment is a methodological idea at all, and if so in what sense, is not one to be gone into here. But on this see e.g. Margit Nielsen, 'Re-enactment and Reconstruction in Collingwood's Philosophy of History', *History and Theory*, 20 (1981), 1-31.

88 PH, 39 ff.

Collingwood's Essay on Appearance and Reality: *Some Contemporary Reflections*

GUY STOCK
University of Dundee

In the Bodleian there is an unpublished essay by R. G. Collingwood on F. H. Bradley's *Appearance and Reality*.[1] It was dedicated to K.F.E. for Christmas 1933. The central thesis of the essay is that Bradley is not to be seen as an apologist for an already discredited Hegelian idealism. On the contrary, as Collingwood puts it, '*Appearance and Reality*, instead of the last word of a decaying Idealism, is the manifesto of a new Realism.' (p. 34) Thus Bradley's one time disciples, Russell and Moore at Cambridge, and Prichard and Cook Wilson at Oxford (having neither a great interest in, nor great understanding of, the history of philosophy) were simply autobiographically mistaken when they saw themselves as the originators of the "new realist" movement which rapidly became dominant on the British philosophical scene in the early years of the 20th century (p. 32). They had in fact, consciously or unconsciously, imbibed their realism from the very man they now understood themselves to be diametrically opposed to.

How plausible is this thesis? Of course the term "realism" has many different applications within philosophy. However, it seems to me that there is in Bradley's philosophy an irreducibly realistic spirit and Collingwood's interpretation, in highlighting this element, provides a way of reading Bradley which locates him as a radically critical yet genuinely creative force *within* the British tradition of analytical philosophy. Collingwood's reading thus provides a plausible historical explanation of Bradley's local reputation for true philosophical greatness which would have been inexplicable – no matter how exceptional his intelligence and literary style might have been – if his thought had been merely derivative from a defunct Hegelianism (pp. 4-5).

The fundamental philosophical point that I take from my reading of Collingwood's essay is this: Bradley's philosophy stands irrevocably opposed to a certain philosophical conception of the human mind, or thinking subject, and of the role that minds or subjects thus conceived are supposed to play in a human being's knowledge of reality. This complex conception of mind, or thinking subject, can be traced within the history of philosophy both in the British Empiricist tradition and in the German Kantian tradition. It thus has a number of different versions originating, in the context of modern philosophy, in the metaphysical dualism of Descartes and manifesting itself in successively modified forms in the work of those subsequent generations of philosophers who were concerned to respond, positively or negatively, to the conception of mind as they inherited it. One thing that holds the different versions of the conception of mind together and makes it the object of Bradley's attack is the consequence that it has for the distinction that is to be drawn within metaphysics between appearance and reality and, thus, for what is to be seen as the central task of metaphysics. This two-pronged consequence for metaphysics, to both of which prongs Bradley stands radically opposed, is then, specifically, (i) that there is an *absolute*[2] distinction to be drawn within the sphere of existence that is available to adult human beings in the contents of their waking sense experiences, and their self-reflective apperceptive experiences, between what is *merely mind*-dependent appearance and what is mind-independent reality, and (ii) that it is the proper task of the discipline of metaphysics[3] (a) to distinguish what, within the sphere of existence in question, is *mere* appearance from what is mind-independently real and (b), in so doing, so far as is possible, to give a determinate characterisation of the ultimate nature of that mind-independent reality.

To illustrate the conception of mind, or thinking subject, in question we need not go back and consider Descartes in isolation. We can kill two birds with one stone by considering it as it emerged in the philosophy of John Locke since Locke's account of consciousness is fundamentally Cartesian. Locke, however, was agnostic in his metaphysics as to the ontological status of the thinking subject conceived as a thing that has the capacity to think of itself as one and the same thinking thing at different places and times. He took it to be a perfectly intelligible metaphysical hypothesis that the thinking subject, or person, should be one in substance with the universe of spatially extended physical things, i.e. that thinking subject and body should be constituted ultimately from identically the same *'substantial stuff.'*[4]

This, as is well known, is precisely the hypothesis that was taken up in the 1960's by J. J. C. Smart.[5] Through Smart's influence, together with that of philosophers like Quine, Armstrong and Davidson, a science based physicalism once again became – as Bradley predicted that it would[6] – the dominant metaphysics within the world of analytical philosophy. Even now (in 1997) metaphysical discussions within the analytical tradition of philosophy gravitate with monotonous regularity to questions relating to the nature of mind and consciousness thus conceived. The central question is as to precisely how an intelligible account of the intentionality of our consciousness can be given if it is accepted that (i) the laws of fundamental physics must be credited with (to use Quine's expression) 'full coverage' within the domain of physics[7] and (ii) the domain of physics is, so to speak, *omnipresent*, i.e. the ontological commitments of theoretical physics are taken in metaphysics to be ultimate in the sense that all concrete modes of being in our universe *ex hypothesi* are *supervenient*, or dependent for their existence, on entities which are in principle identifiable simply in terms of concepts internal to the fundamental theories of physicists.[8]

There are logical difficulties, pointed out by Saul Kripke,[9] that are connected with Smart's original account of the mind-brain identity theory in so far as it took the assertion of that identity, if true, to be *contingently* true. Nevertheless I will sketch Smart's version of Locke's hypothesis. Kripke's objection is irrelevant to the central point to be illustrated: namely that the physicalist conception of consciousness remains fundamentally Cartesian and thus exemplifies in a paradigmatic way the kind of account of mind, or thinking subject, and correlative account of the relation of appearance to reality, to which Bradley's metaphysics stands radically opposed.

In fact Smart presented his hypothesis by claiming that Cartesian dualism could as a matter of logical possibility be true. In other words he held that Descartes' metaphysics is perfectly intelligible. Mind-body dualism could in fact be true but Smart himself firmly believed it to be false. Moreover he predicted that advances in the natural sciences – in neurophysiology and so on – would in time come to prove conclusively that dualism is false.

Quite how the proof would be carried through he did not explain but he suggested, by way of an analogy, that the relation between human beings' momentary conscious experiences and their brain processes was like that between flashes of lightning and electrical discharges. Lightning is not to be thought of as a phenomenon that is *caused* by electrical discharges from clouds to earth: when there is a flash of lightning there are not two kinds of happening in a causal relation to one another. There is just one happening at a determinate position in space – an electrical discharge – which, when an individual sees a flash of lightning, will be causally related to other electro-chemical events in the visual areas of the individual's brain. The latter will constitute a momentary visual experience having the striking phenomenological content that people like ourselves are well acquainted with within our consciousness. However, the phenomenon of lightning *as it is in itself* independently of the conscious events constitutive of our visual experiences is nothing other than an electrical discharge caused in a way familiar to physicists and meteorologists. Despite the difference in Fregean *sense* between the terms 'lightning' and 'electrical discharge' they will be able, when used in given circumstances, to coincide in their *reference*:[10] any flash of lightning will be 'strictly' identical with an electrical discharge.

Obviously at one time in the history of science this identity statement was not known to be true: it had merely the status of a hypothesis which at the time had seemed, even to those scientists who were convinced that it was true, as though it might as a matter of logical possibility turn out false. However, in fact, in the fullness of time within the history of science, it has been incontrovertibly verified. Analogously, Smart held, it will be so with the present-day hypothesis that the sensory experiences that we enjoy at successive moments of our lives are strictly identical with brain processes. Despite the difference in *senses* of the everyday vocabularies that we can use to characterise the inner looks and feels of the intentional objects of our sensory experiences and the vocabularies used by neurophysiologists to describe brain processes occurring at specific areas of the cortex, and ultimately caused by the presence of such objects, those vocabularies will be able to coincide in their references.

Thus conscious experience, within the context of physicalist metaphysics, is still conceived very much on the Cartesian model. *Ex hypothesi* it just happens, as a contingent matter of fact, that the contents of the various modes of conscious experience that at successive waking moments we have immediate knowledge of are 'realised' in the neural activity currently occurring in various spatially locatable centres of our brains rather than in ontologically independent non-spatial individual substances, or mental stuffs, that are contingently causally interactive with our brains. Hence *given* the account of consciousness that goes along with a quasi-Lockean physicalism the brain-in-a-vat hypothesis could conceivably be true analogously to the way in which the hypothesis[11] of the malignant demon would be intelligible if Cartesian dualism – with its posited causal relations holding contingently between substantially independent minds and bodies – were true.

To make a similar point rather differently: for both Cartesian dualism and quasi-Lockean physicalism the immediate objects of knowledge in the waking sense experiences enjoyed by thinking subjects are realised in 'inputs' caused by, and thus never identical with, the mind-independent objects acting on their bodily sense organs – objects which self-conscious apperceptive individuals like ourselves will be able, at any waking moment, to *think* of as currently in determinate spatial relations to specific regions of our own brains and causally responsible for manifold events therein.

Moreover (and this, of course, is again something Bradley stands irrevocably opposed to)[12] for quasi-Lockean physicalism, the theoretical physicist becomes the ultimate authority with respect to which properties are, in metaphysical strictness, properly construed as *primary*. In other words, the theoretical physicist becomes the authority with respect to (i) which properties – if any – of the intentional objects that are available to us in the contents of our self-conscious waking sense experiences, and self-reflective apperceptive experiences, are actually possessed by the mind-independent reality as it is in itself, and (ii) which properties of such objects are merely *secondary* (i.e. are simply mind-dependent) and, in metaphysical strictness, are to be seen as simply *illusory* with respect to the essential nature of the mind-independent reality.

Now let us consider (rather more briefly) the next version, within the history of Anglo-Saxon philosophy, of the conception of mind, or thinking subject, in question: namely, that implicit in Hume's phenomenalism. Although the Descartes/Locke distinction between primary and secondary qualities was rejected by Humean phenomenalism, and with it both the metaphysical mind-body dualism of Descartes and the monistic physicalism envisaged as a possibility by Locke, nevertheless Humean phenomenalism entails as a consequence of its epistemology and fundamental ontology an analogous account of the distinction between appearance and reality. That is, it entails an account according to which the intentional objects of our everyday sense experiences and self-reflective apperceptive experiences are, with respect to their essential properties, mind-relative and fundamentally illusory with respect to the properties of the mind independent reality as *ex hypothesi* it is in itself.

This is so since, as a fundamental principle of Hume's phenomenalism, the human mind operates in accordance with universal psychological principles of association with the consequence that it has an innate and ineluctable tendency to 'spread itself on things'. So, for example, the necessary connections that we ascribe to successive happenings in *nature* when, at waking moments, we experience them as bearing causal relations to one another, or the self-identity which we ascribe to the intentional objects of our sense experiences when we experience them as 3-dimensional bodies of re-identifiable sorts (inanimate or animate) that are subject to movement in space, or the self-identity we ascribe to ourselves as thinking subjects when, in our self-reflective apperceptive experiences, we are aware of ourselves as identically the same agents at different places and times, are *ex hypothesi* ideas which are generated in the contents of our successive experiences simply as a consequence of the psychological principles of association which govern the operations of the human mind.[13] The collocations and successions of momentary manifolds of designatable sense impressions – designata which, for Hume's ontology, constitute the ultimately independent realities[14] from which all our ideas of complex sorts of thing, both self and not-self, must be derived and constructed – have as they are in themselves no properties corresponding to our ideas of causal necessity, or of self-identity through time, or of permanence through change of position in space. Our ideas of these properties, which are essential to the intentional objects of a human being's everyday waking sense experiences and to ourselves as self-conscious agents, are *ex hypothesi* fundamentally mind-dependent and illusory with respect to the momentary manifolds of impressions which are posited in Humean metaphysics as ontologically basic and the ultimate logical subjects of our designations.

Similarly (to continue the historical survey) for Kant's critical metaphysics *appearances* – i.e. the intentional objects of the everyday waking sense experiences, and self-reflective apperceptive experiences, of self-conscious human beings like ourselves – are *ex hypothesi* mind dependent and illusory with respect to *things in themselves*. According to Kant's Copernican epistemology the pure concepts of understanding that we exercise in having knowledge of ourselves and things other than ourselves, animate and inanimate, have their origin in the rules of synthesis[15] governing the exercise of the active faculty of representation. Given the exhaustive classification of judgement forms available to philosophers through the discipline of formal logic[16] we can infer *a priori* that this active faculty must, with strict universality, be possessed by any species of finite thinking subject whatsoever that is capable of representing, either truly or falsely, the properties of things the existence of which is immediately given to it by a passive sensory faculty. Thus the array of phenomenal objects represented in the contents of the waking sense experiences, and self-reflective apperceptive experiences, of any species of finite subject, in addition to their *material* properties knowable through the manifold of sensory inputs contingently received, will of necessity exhibit *formal* properties corresponding to the pure concepts of understanding.

On the other hand, since the logician's judgement forms can only be a source of pure *concepts*, or maximally *generic* active capacities of representation, there can be no corresponding inference (at the level of transcendental reflection) with respect to the nature of the radically passive sensory faculty,[17] i.e. the faculty for immediate cognition of the existence of *particular* things (self and not-self) of general contingently existing sorts. There can be no *a priori* argument to the conclusion that the passive faculties of inner and outer sense must be strictly homogeneous in their natures for finite beings *as such*. Human beings can know that existence at determinate positions in the 3-dimensional space occupied by their bodies is, for the intentional objects of human subjects' outer sensory experiences, at any waking moments, strictly universal and necessary. However, we have no *a priori* ground – of the kind that we have for our active faculty of understanding – to rule out the logical possibility of species of finite subject whose sensible faculties are radically different in nature from those of human subjects. We must, therefore, admit that as a matter of logical possibility there could be species of subject with passive faculties which (universally and necessarily for members of the species) determined *forms* of inner and outer sense radically different from the human. Thus, we must admit, there could be self-conscious finite subjects to whom reality is presented in the contents of their waking sense experiences, and self-reflective apperceptive experiences, as ordered in radically different ways from the temporally successive and spatially arrayed way in which it is presented in the contents of the waking experiences of self-conscious human subjects like ourselves.

Thus, for Kant's critical metaphysics, *things-in-themselves* could as a matter of logical possibility present themselves in the propositional contents of the *veridical* experiences of self-conscious finite subjects as universally orderable, within a unique discursively knowable system of existence, in some *other* totally different way than they do with us in our historically real human world: namely, in some other way than as existing at successive globally simultaneous instants in a single linear time series, in a single Euclidean 3-dimensional spatial arena. On the other hand appearances could not, as a matter of logical possibility, lack features corresponding to the purely formal concepts constitutive of the strictly universal capacity to generate in consciousness representations corresponding to the various forms of complex bi-valent, contingently true or false, representation that are possible. But of course, for Kant, one way or the other, whether the finite subject is human or not, not only will the ultimate nature of *things-in-themselves* of necessity remain discursively unknown to the finite individual, even the strictly universal purely formal properties of phenomenal objects (i.e. the properties of appearances which are correlative to the pure concepts of understanding appropriately schematised according to the subject's species specific sensibility) will be simply *illusory* with respect to the nature of *things-in-themselves.*[18]

Hence to sum up our historical survey we can see that Cartesian dualism, the physicalism inherited by scientific realism from Locke, the phenomenalism and psychological associationism of the Hume-Mill tradition, and Kant's Hume-inspired Transcendental Idealist response to the inadequacy of Leibniz's account of finite sensibility,[19] all in their very different ways portray the intentional objects of our waking sense experiences, and self-reflective apperceptive experiences, with respect to at least some of their properties, as *mere* appearances which are in metaphysical strictness *illusory* with respect to the nature of a variously characterised mind-independent reality as it is in itself.

The above schemas considered as putative metaphysics are, as Collingwood points out, (p. 15) examined in detail (although typically with scant reference to historical figures) by Bradley in Book I of *Appearance and Reality*. Each is shown to be, in various ways, internally self-contradictory, and therefore – given that conformity to the principle of non-contradiction provides (as Bradley insists) *undeniably* a necessary condition of truth and therefore of metaphysical adequacy[20] – each is shown to be unsatisfactory as a way (i) of drawing, for the purpose of metaphysics, a distinction between appearance and reality and (ii) of giving an adequate account of the nature of reality as it is in itself.

However, on Collingwood's view we have not yet located the *proximate* irritating cause of Bradley's metaphysical unrest. This is to be found especially, according to Collingwood, in the corrupt Kantianism of Sir William Hamilton which had, through the writings and teaching of H. L. Mansel, become dominant in the Oxford of Bradley's youth.

(pp. 10-17) This corrupt-Kantianism was utterly abhorrent to Bradley in a way quite different from that in which any of the above sketched metaphysical schemas were.

Accepting the Copernican premise of the relativity of phenomena, outer and inner, to the nature of the human subjects' representative faculties, active and passive, Mansel (according to Collingwood) concluded absurdly that an empirical psychology, investigating the nature of the human mind, will have a special input into metaphysics: that is, as Mansel saw it, it will have a special input into the task of drawing a dividing line within the phenomenal world between appearance and reality. Roughly his vision seems to have been that psychology, by focusing on the workings of the human representative faculties, could fillet out from humanly knowable phenomena those features that are generated *simply* by the workings of the mind, i.e. could fillet out the *mere* appearances. The metaphysician thus could distinguish the merely illusive features from those properties of things in the phenomenal world which are attributable to reality as it is in itself independently of the contributions made to the intentional objects of human beings' sensory experiences by the operations of the human mind.

Hence, as Collingwood presents it, Mansel's philosophy was a confused mish-mash of Kant's Transcendental Idealism and Hume's quasi-empirical psychologistic associationism which construed the task of metaphysics to be that of drawing a line, within the sphere of spatio-temporally locatable phenomena, between mere appearance and mind-independent reality. And, in the style of Hume or Reid, Mansel took not physics but – a suggestion equally repellent to Bradley – a psychological study of the representative faculties of the human mind to hold the key to the central problem of metaphysics.

So Collingwood sums it up: 'My suggestion is that Bradley's *Appearance and Reality* is in the first instance a polemic against Mansel. It is from Mansel that Bradley borrows the antithesis of Appearance and Reality; it is against the project of dividing the one from the other that his book is directed . . .' (p. 14)

I am not interested in discussing whether Collingwood's account of Mansel is accurate or fair in its evaluation. Nor am I much interested in whether Bradley had particularly strong feelings about Mansel and his philosophy. However, I am sure that Collingwood is right in holding that it is essential for a correct understanding of Bradley's philosophy to realise that *for his metaphysics* there is no absolute distinction to be drawn between appearance and reality. For Bradley's metaphysics it is never a matter of appearance *versus* reality. He has no use for the expression *mere* appearance when that is understood to imply that some kind of feature, or sort of thing, identifiable within the phenomenal sphere of things in space and time, is simply illusory with respect to the character of a metaphysically posited absolute reality. In any appearance, apprehended in thought or perception or apperception at any time by a sentient being, reality will of necessity (on Bradley's view) be present more or less adequately or inadequately.[21] Moreover, it is by reference to the historically and geographically real world in which human beings like ourselves, for better or worse, live out their lives and can in self-conscious apperceptive thought locate themselves at successive waking moments of those lives that Bradley erects what can be seen to be a quite general criterion of adequacy for metaphysics. As Bradley puts it: 'Since we all believe in a world beyond us, and are not prepared to give this up, it would be a scandal if that were something which upon our theory were illusive. Any view which will not explain, and also justify, an attitude essential to human nature, must surely be condemned.'[22]

All the metaphysical theories sketched above involve a kind of metaphysical reductionism in which a theoretical construct *not* identical with a historically real human being (namely a *mind* or *thinking subject* or *consciousness-realising-brain* or *monad* or *person* or whatever) is ascribed a kind of 'inner' being within a human being and is construed to have a more or less fundamental explanatory role in the cognitive behaviour of such a being. Sometimes the thing in question is taken to be the true referent of the 1st person pronoun 'I' whenever it is used by an actual historical human being in sentences expressing psychological states and sometimes, moreover, it is taken in metaphysics to be substantial in a way that a human being *ex hypothesi* is not. In all cases the mind, or thinking subject, or whatever, is taken to have an essentially representative or cognitive role distinct from a practical role, i.e. distinct from the role, attributed within such theories, to *the will*. Nevertheless, somewhat paradoxically, in all the accounts it is taken, in different ways, to generate quite generally through its operations a systematic misleadingness in the intentional objects of human beings' waking sense experiences and self-reflective apperceptive experiences. This systematic misleadingness (to emphasise it once more) *ex hypothesi* allows an absolute distinction to be drawn within metaphysics between (i) the way in which the given reality will appear quite generally in the contents of our waking experiences, sensory and apperceptive, and (ii) the attributes of that reality as it is in itself independently of those features that are generated in the intentional objects of our waking experiences, sensory and apperceptive, *simply* by the operation of the mind's representative faculties.

This conception of a mind or thinking subject or consciousness-realising-brain (etc.) in its various forms, as an *inner* organ or mechanism, not identical with the historically real human being, is no doubt framed by abstracting some sub-set of capacities or elements (primarily those connected specifically with cognition, truth and error) from the indefinitely complex concrete experiences that (we very well know) will be constitutive of a normal adult human being's life at successive waking moments. Bradley rejects for the purpose of metaphysics any such reductionist account of a human being according to which the mind or thinking subject or consciousness-realising-brain is portrayed as an inner cognising thing not identical with the historically real human agent. This is not to imply that Bradley would rule out the legitimacy of employing such a theoretical construct within theories falling within the *special* sciences.[23] Bradley emphasises time and time again that the philosopher 'as such' has no right to legislate with respect to the methods or theories of the special scientist. Moreover, in particular, for example, he insists that within psychology (in which, perhaps, he took himself to have some special competence) it can be necessary for the investigator to work within a phenomenalist framework of thought.[24] Yet again Bradley himself, for certain purposes within philosophy, finds no problem in resting on human knowledge drawn from, e.g., neurophysiology, and in referring to the physical basis of mind or in envisaging the *personal* identity of a human being as going along with brain identity and so on.[25] However, so far as metaphysics goes Bradley insists that it is the concrete indefinitely multiform waking experiences enjoyed by the adult human agent in the complex activities, bodily and otherwise, that will go to make up his/her waking life in our historically real world that supplies the irreducible epistemological and ontological bedrock. No entity cognitively accessible in terms of concepts internal to an abstract theory, philosophical or scientific, could compare in the degree *of its reality* with *this* that I am enjoying *here* and *now*, in my immediate and thought-embedded waking experience, whatever its currently dominant mode, or complex of modes, might be: whether it be dominantly practical, cognitive, bodily, purely cerebral, self-reflective, solitary, communal, emotional, scientific, religious, aesthetic, athletic or whatever.

As Bradley puts it:

> What is the world which I am accustomed to call 'my real world'? It is (we must reply) the universe of those things which are continuous in space with my body, and in time with the states and actions of that body. My mental changes form no exception, for, if they are to take their place in time as 'real' events, they must, I think, be dated in connexion with the history of my body. Now if I make an ideal construction of this nature in space and time, I can arrange (more or less) in one ordered scheme both myself and other animates, together with the physical world. This arrangement is practical since I can act on it, and since I must act on it if I am to continue what I call my 'real' life. Again, this arrangement is true theoretically, so far as it serves to bring facts before my mind harmoniously and fully.[26]

Of course Bradley insists that there are many kinds of thing to which we assign some kind of reality (and which, therefore, a satisfactory metaphysics must give some account of) but which cannot be taken to exist at any time within the spatio-temporal framework of *this* our historically real world: for example, mathematical entities, counterfactual conditions, constructs identifiable in terms of concepts internal to the theories of fundamental physics, the intentional objects of peoples' dreams, literary fictions, religious beliefs, unfulfilled desires, and so on.[27] However, we can only have access to such entities through the *dateable* activities of human beings – through individuals' writings, theorising, recountings, behavioural expressions, and so on – and in that form at least such things must be able to make their appearance in the time series of our historically real world.[28]

The ideal construction in terms of which self-conscious human beings like ourselves can at waking moments think of the spatio-temporally extended universe in which we live will not by itself constitute a metaphysically adequate conception of reality. Given its internal incoherencies and disparate contents, which become patently obvious once we reflect on it, it 'could' only be allowed to yield a more or less adequate 'appearance' of reality. However, what Bradley will not allow is that a metaphysics – or an attempted coherent account of reality somehow 'as a whole' – could be coherent if it portrayed elements essential to our historically real world as merely illusory appearances, whilst distinguishing other elements accessible from within that world as independently real.

Here it is important to see that Bradley is not merely ruling out, e.g., a quasi-Lockean physicalism with its conception of consciousness as supervenient on an independently real brain stuff and in itself, within space and time, merely an impotent epiphenomenon. Human beings, and sentient individuals generally, on Bradley's view, essentially have bodies and thus of necessity there will be physical 'aspects' to the experiences, cognitive and practical, constitutive of their daily lives. So Bradley says, in regard to the Berkelian counter-move to Locke which was to posit the independent reality and real agency of a plurality of sentient individuals the essence of which was simply to perceive (individuals which, therefore, were not identical with perceptible three-dimensional human agents): 'To set up the subject as real independently of the whole, and to make the whole into experience in the sense of an adjective of that subject, seems to me indefensible. And when I contend that reality must be sentient, my conclusion almost consists in the denial of this fundamental error.'[29]

And distancing his metaphysics at one stroke from both scientific realism and an Hegelian idealism, Bradley famously says: 'That the glory of this world in the end is appearance leaves the world more glorious, if we feel it is a show of some fuller splendour; but the sensuous curtain is a deception and a cheat, if it hides some colourless movement of atoms, some spectral woof of impalpable abstractions, or unearthly ballet of bloodless categories.'[30]

The conception of mind that Bradley makes most use of within his philosophy is distinctively naturalistic and Aristotelian in tenor. According to it mind is construed as exhibited fundamentally in a complex of behavioural capacities that will normally develop during the early years of human beings' lives as they acquire an increasing mastery of their natural languages 'for social purposes'.[31] However, Bradley holds that such capacities in their paradigmatic human form are not to be construed as absolutely disparate in character from capacities possessed by other 'lower' species of animal and realised in the activities (the 'deeds and sufferings') constitutive of their waking lives. On Bradley's view, as for Leibniz's, no Cartesian break of a substantial kind is posited between rational and 'merely' sentient species of sentient animal.

The Bradleian conception of the human mind no doubt has similarities to Collingwood's own[32] and to that of Collingwood's successor in Oxford, as Wayneflete Professor of Metaphysical Philosophy, Gilbert Ryle.[33] But I must leave further discussion of this to another time.

NOTES

1 References in brackets within the text of this essay refer to the page numbers of Collingwood's manuscript.

2 For the most explicit statement of this view see F. H. Bradley, *Essays on Truth and Reality* (Oxford, Clarendon Press, 1962), chp III, 'On Floating Ideas and the Imaginary'.

3 F. H. Bradley, *Appearance and Reality* (Oxford, Clarendon Press, 1968) see e.g. Introduction, 1-6 for Bradley's own view of metaphysics.

4 John Locke, *An Essay Concerning Human Understanding* (London, William Tegg, 1880) cf. e.g. Bk 4 chp. 3 sect 6 p. 442.

5 J. J. C. Smart, 'Sensations and Brain Processes', *Philosophical Review*, LXVII (1959), 141-56. Jack Smart has a deep understanding of Bradley's philosophy obtained, I believe, when he was a pupil of C. A. Campbell at Glasgow.

6 Bradley, *Appearance and Reality*, chp I, 9.

7 W. V. O. Quine, *Theories and Things* (Cambridge, Mass: Harvard UP, 1981) chp. 11, pp. 97-8. For a discussion of some difficulties faced by Quine's physicalism see Dagfinn Follesdal 'In What Sense is Language Public?' in P. Leonardi and M. Santambrogio, *On Quine: New Essays* (Cambridge: Cambridge UP, 1995), 53-67.

8 Terence Horgan, 'From Supervenience to Superdupervenience', *Mind*, 102 (1993), 555-86.

9 Saul Kripke, 'Identity and Necessity' in Milton K. Munitz (ed.), *Identity and Individuation* (New York, New York UP, 1971), 135-64.

10 G. Frege, *Philosophical Writings*, P. Geach and M. Black (eds.) (Oxford, Basil Blackwell, 1960), 'On Sense and Reference', 56-78.

11 Cf Bradley, *Appearance and Reality*, chp. XXII where Bradley in effect acknowledges the brain-in-vat paradox; I use the term 'quasi-Lockean physicalism' to indicate that Locke himself should not be taken to be a committed physicalist.

12 For Bradley physics is one among other special sciences. It is concerned essentially with a *partial* aspect of reality and thus not – like metaphysics – concerned to give a coherent account of reality somehow as a whole.

13 David Hume, Treatise of Human Nature, A. D. Lindsay (ed.) (London, Dent, 1959) e.g. Bk. 1 pt. IV sect 6, 'Of Personal Identity'. On p. 245 Hume says: '. . . a question naturally arises concerning the relation of identity, whether it be something that really binds our several perceptions together, or only associates their ideas in imagination. This question we might easily decide, if we would recollect what has already been proved at large, that the understanding never observes any real connection among objects, and that even the union of cause and effect, when strictly examined resolves itself into a customary association of ideas.'

14 Hume, *Treatise on Human Nature*, see Sect V. On p. 232 Hume says: 'I have already proved, that we have no perfect idea of substance; but that taking it for *something that can exist by itself*, it is evident every perception is a substance, and every distinct perception a distinct substance.'

15 I. Kant, *Critique of Pure Reason*, trans N. Kemp-Smith (London, Macmillan, 1964) e.g. B, 129-131.

16 Kant, *Critique of Pure Reason*, B, 102ff 'The Clue to the Discovery of *All* Pure Concepts of the Understanding' (my emphasis).

17 Kant, *Critique of Pure Reason*, see e.g. B72.

18 Kant, *Critique of Pure Reason*, B, 311-12.

19 Cf. Guy Stock, 'Thought and Sensibility in Leibniz, Kant and Bradley' in G. Macdonald Ross and T. McWalter (eds.), *Kant and his Influence* (Bristol: Thoemmes, 1990), 104-25.

20 Bradley, *Appearance and Reality*, chp XIII, p. 120; and see Collingwood's manuscript p. 20.

21 Bradley, *Essays on Truth and Reality*, chp III. and *Appearance and Reality*, chp. XXIV.

22 Bradley, *Appearance and Reality*, chp. XXI, 218.

23 Bradley, *Appearance and Reality*, chp. XXVI, 439 and chp. XXII, 250-2.

24 F. H. Bradley, *Collected Essays*, vol. II (Oxford, Clarendon Press, 1935), chp, XXII, 364-86.

25 Bradley, *Appearance and Reality*, chp XXIII, 298; and chp. XXVI, 445 where he says: 'A future life is possible even on the ground of common crude Materialism. After an interval, no matter how long, another nervous system sufficiently like our own might be developed; and in this case memory and personal identity must arise. The event may be as improbable as you please, but I at least can find no reason for calling it impossible.'

26 Bradley, *Essays on Truth and Reality*, chp. XVI, 460-1.

27 Bradley, *Essays on Truth and Reality*, chp. III, esp. Sect I.

28 Bradley, *Appearance and Reality*, chp. XXIV, 336-7.

29 Bradley, *Appearance and Reality*, chp XIV, 128.

30 F. H. Bradley, *Principles of Logic* (Oxford, OUP, 1967) vol, II, BIII Pt. II chp. IV, p. 591.

31 Bradley, *Essays on Truth and Reality*, 356-7 and *Principles of Logic*, vol. I, chp. I, 30-38.

32 R. G. Collingwood *The Idea of History* (Oxford, OUP, 1973) e.g. 219 where Collingwood says: '. . . it is by historical thinking . . . that we discover the thought of a friend who writes us a letter, or a stranger who crosses the street. Nor is it necessary that the historian should be one person and the subject of his inquiry another.'

33 Gilbert Ryle, *The Concept of Mind* (London, Hutchinson's UP, 1949). It has always seemed to me that Ryle was insufficiently willing to acknowledge the similarity of some of the central doctrines of the *Concept of Mind* to things already said by Collingwood.

The Nature of Nature
in Collingwood and Hegel

G. K. BROWNING
Oxford Brookes University

The nature of nature in Collingwood and Hegel is a complex and controversial subject; the very phrase the nature of nature signals that the meaning of nature is not univocal and that the very characterisation of the natural world is likely to raise questions about the relationship between that world and the operations of reflective thought in characterising it. It is the argument of this article that the tracking of Collingwood's understanding of Hegel's philosophy of nature, exemplified in the published and unpublished material for *The Idea of Nature* and affiliated writings, shows how Collingwood developed his philosophical understanding of nature in terms of an engagement with Hegel.

Collingwood's conception of a philosophical understanding of nature will be shown to involve distinct elements, notably an appreciation of the historical conditionality of man's engagement with nature and an aspiration to provide a coherent logical basis to the processual character he attributed to nature. The published conclusion of *The Idea of Nature* confirms the impression of Collingwood's grasp of the historicity of conceptions of the natural world which is conveyed by the work as a whole. The recently discovered conclusions to *The Idea of Nature*, namely the 'cosmological conclusion' and the three pages of manuscript entitled 'B' by Price, and the unpublished 'Notes on Metaphysics' Collingwood composed in 1933 and 1934 furnish evidence of Collingwood's commitment to theorise the conditions of a first order conception of the nature of nature.[1] Both the historical and metaphysical perspectives, which are present with differing emphases in all these works and manuscripts, can be shown to derive inspiration from Collingwood's critical engagement with Hegel's conceptions of philosophy and nature. Indeed, Collingwood's reading of Hegel is multi-faceted in that it incorporates an appreciation of the historical and metaphysical dimensions of Hegel's conception of nature and, in so doing, admits the possibility of an emphasis upon one or the other of these dimensions. The differing emphases within Collingwood's conceptualisations of nature rehearse the tensions within Hegel's systematic conceptualisation of nature and so endorse the close links between their distinct projects to which this article testifies.

The preceding formulation of the argument of this article signals its opposition to the conclusions of Peters' recent article on Collingwood and Hegel entitled 'Collingwood on Hegel's Dialectic'. Peters imputes to Hegel a critique of the anthropomorphic character of Collingwood's thought, in observing, 'He (Hegel) would have criticised Collingwood for thinking that ideas can only exist in human mind'.[2] Peters is both plausible and enlightening in highlighting the distinctiveness of the Collingwoodian dialectic in terms of its development within the specifically human and historical process of questioning and answering. The putative Hegelian objection to a dialectic existing only in the human mind, however, depends on a metaphysical reading of Hegel, whereas a number of commentators in recent years have followed the lead of Hartman in construing the Hegelian dialectic in non-metaphysical terms.[3] According to this view, Hegel does not go beyond the bounds of experience in exhibiting the internal relations between human categories. Again, the identification of Collingwood's dialectic with the human mind runs counter to the concern within Collingwood's 'Notes Towards a Metaphysic' and in the lengthy cosmological conclusion to *The Idea of Nature* to theorise nature in terms of the nature of God.[4]

HEGEL ON NATURE

Collingwood's positive engagement in his published and unpublished writings, such as *The Idea of Nature* and 'Notes Towards a Metaphysic', with Hegel's philosophy of nature contrasts with the interpretative standpoint of many commentators on Hegel, whose distinct critical perspectives converge on the notion that Hegel's conception of nature is either unimportant or ill-conceived.[5] This disparagement of Hegel's philosophy of nature is promoted by the justifiable tendency amongst Hegel scholars to concentrate upon what has been taken to be the core of Hegelianism and its most plausible aspect, namely Hegel's account of the mind and human agency and activities. Hegel himself declared, 'The Absolute is Mind (Spirit) – This is the supreme definition of the Absolute.'[6] While the meaning of this Hegelian credo is not transparent, it certainly includes the notion that the achievement of harmonious forms of practical life and coherent cognitive perspectives depends on the positive activities of men and women. Nature, for Hegel, is not rational in itself; it is only rational for men who make and develop their own rational patterns of practical and theoretical activity. This explains why Hegel takes a philosophical understanding of nature to follow a process of historical development contingent upon the actual work of scientists and an on-going tradition of philosophical speculation.

Collingwood recognises in his unpublished 'Notes Towards a Metaphysics', the significance of Hegel's appreciation of man's subjectivity in his endorsement of Foster's comparative study of Plato and Hegel, in which Hegel is seen to supersede Plato precisely because his notion of reason includes the subjectivity of spirit.[7] Hegel's appreciation of the significance of human subjectivity and activity also inspires his subtle and masterly investigation of phenomenal forms of consciousness and self-consciousness, an influential and coherent political philosophy and a profound appreciation of the historical development of politics, culture and intellectual studies. Recognition of the significance and power of Hegel's philosophy of spiritual development has been matched in recent years by a tendency to play down the more controversial metaphysical claims about Hegel's system. According to these accounts, inspired by Hartman's avowedly non-metaphysical reading, Hegel is to be seen primarily as a philosopher tracing the interconnections between human categories of thought and action rather than a theorist making definitive claims about the nature of thought and reality.[8]

An alternative reading of Hegel is to see him as a theorist whose system does depend crucially on seeing human subjects within a framework established by a grander subject, either pure thought for Michael Rosen, or the Cosmic Spirit favoured by Taylor.[9] These readings invariably criticise Hegel for these purported presumptions about nature and thought. Collingwood, himself, at a moment when he had become unsympathetic to Hegel, disparaged Hegel for purportedly seeking to derive the concrete from the abstract. In *The New Leviathan* he notes, 'Hegel thought that a dialectical world is a world where everything *argued itself into existence.*'[10]

The foregoing synopsis of critical opinion on Hegel's conception of nature indicates a radical diversity of interpretative standpoints. On the one hand, Hegel's conception of nature is seen as implying its dependence upon the mediation of human thought and action, and on the other hand, nature, for Hegel, is seen as the concrete embodiment of the manoeuvres of an independently conceived abstract, logical subject. Adjudicating between these positions in appraising the character of Hegel's understanding of nature is a delicate undertaking. These interpretations both possess a plausibility evidenced in the distinct ways in which Collingwood engaged positively, in published and unpublished writings, with Hegel's conception of nature. Collingwood appreciates Hegel's 'historical' treatment of ideas of nature, while on occasion he derives inspiration from Hegel's metaphysical conception of nature. Any interpretation of the role of nature in Hegel's system, however, must contend with the Delphic nature of Hegel's specification of the crucial transition between the *Logic* and the *Philosophy of Nature* in his system. Hegel's system consists of three main elements; logic, nature and spirit. The *Logic* deals with the general categories of thought which in turn are shown to be exemplified and developed in nature and in the various human activities examined in *The Philosophy of Spirit*. Hegel's explicit derivation of nature from his dialectical examination of the inter-relations between general categories of thought is framed in metaphorical terms. The Absolute Idea or God is seen as '. . . freely releasing itself . . .' into the externality of space and time.[11]

Interpretative problems are multiplied by Hegel's observation that this derivation is not a real transition. In the face of a prospect of an interpretative impasse, the most plausible interpretative strategy is to take seriously the notion that the transition to nature is not to be seen as effected economically at the end point of the *Logic*, and to look to Hegel's repeated statements that his system should be seen as a circle. Thought for Hegel is infinite and a coherent notion of infinity is circular. Any particular thought for Hegel is a determination implying other determinations, which in turn return to the original determination in developing their and its meaning. Hegel's system expresses this infinity . It is a set of internally related thought determinations rather than the specification of an endless series of finite quasi-infinite thoughts, such as the notion of a purely quantitative determination of infinity.[12] Collingwood himself in his 'Notes Towards a Metaphysic' recognises the power of Hegel's conceptualisation of infinity. The three parts of Hegel's *Encyclopedia of the Philosophical Sciences* are not to be taken and comprehended as being outside one another. They are three interrelated aspects of a whole, and the project of understanding them and their relations presupposes this inter-dependence. Hence it makes no sense to demand an explanation of why there is a move to nature in Hegel's thought. In the project of thinking categorial thoughts conducted in the *Logic*, the process of becoming is implied in the act of thinking the most abstract general category, Being. This logical process of Becoming, central to much of Collingwood's thinking about nature, is taken by Hegel to imply objective thought about a real world.

White in his book, *Absolute Knowledge and the Problem of Metaphysics*, develops an interpretative standpoint which highlights the inter-dependence of elements in Hegel's system so that the concrete does not have to be seen as being produced by a mysterious process. He observes: 'At the end of the *Logic*, the extralogical has not been thematized as such, nevertheless, from the standpoint of the Absolute Idea, it is already clear that any extralogical realm would contain finite entities and finite subjects concerned with their determination. The *Logic* itself includes categories that would be applicable only within such a realm but it does not include the specific categories that would make determination within the extralogical realm possible.'[13]

The transition to nature effected at the end of the *Logic* is not to be seen as evidence of the magical, material power of pure thought, but as confirming the inter-dependence of thought, nature and human agency in any systematic attempt to theorise reality. Hegel, though, in inter-linking nature and human spiritual development with the general categories of universal thoughts outlined in the *Logic*, is not identifying nature and human beings with the pure universality of thought. The notion, the category of categorisation itself, is present only in an external way within the natural world where the essential inwardness of thought is outside itself in space and time. Likewise, human beings can express themselves and understand the world in terms of the universality of categorial notions but they are not identical with these notions. The notions of thought are to be presupposed in some sense as independent of natural and human articulation, but they are only to be known through human conception within natural and human contexts. The crucial but distinct role of human beings in developing conceptions which express and understand the thought patterns which condition reality explains why Hegel designates Spirit as the highest but not the sole definition of the Absolute. Notwithstanding the significance Hegel assigns human activity and understanding, the world of logical categories is conceptually distinct from human and natural experience. Findlay, whose critical work has done so much to establish the reputation of Hegel as a supreme philosopher of subjectivity, has observed in an article entitled, 'Hegelianism and Platonism', 'It is important to stress in the first place that while Hegel's Absolute Idea can be taken to be the Idea of Absolute Subjectivity, to have Absolute subjectivity for its content, it is itself an Idea, and unrealised form and in no sense an actual subject'.[14]

The natural world is involved in Hegel's project of thinking through the conditions of experience. Given the circle of thoughts described by Hegel's system, in which natural phenomena provide an external, opaque setting for thought as well as exhibiting its development, nature is conceptualised in two distinct ways. On the one hand, it provides an opposition to thought. It is the sphere of externality and otherness. While the hallmark of thought is internality and self-determination, nature appears as outside itself in space and time and resists attempts to mould it practically and to understand it theoretically. This very process of resistance is seen as positive by Hegel for it ensures that human activity must be resourceful. The Hegelian notion of the good incorporates resistance to as well as satisfaction in action. On the other hand, Hegel observes that nature does express thought, and in so doing registers the inwardly related self-determining aspect of thought which he takes to be its hallmark. 'The very stones cry out and raise themselves to spirit'.[15] Collingwood, in developing his conception of nature in his 'Notes Towards a Metaphysic' and in the cosmological conclusion to *The Idea of Nature* draws upon both of these Hegelianised ways of conceiving of nature.

In the introduction to *The Philosophy of Nature* Hegel emphasises the externality and otherness of nature. 'Nature is Spirit estranged from itself; in Nature Spirit lets itself go, a Bacchic God unrestrained and unmindful of itself, in Nature the unity of the Notion is concealed'.[16] The revelation of the rationality of nature and its determination by thought patterns is explained as being the concern of human beings who are conscious of their rationality. Hence, Hegel conceives of the rationality of nature as correlative to human understanding. The human understanding that is involved in recognising the rationality of nature is natural science and philosophy. In a remark, Hegel notes, 'not only must philosophy be in agreement with our empirical knowledge of Nature, but the origin and formation of the Philosophy of Nature presupposes and is conditioned by empirical physics'.[17] Hegel, like Collingwood in the published version of *The Idea of Nature*, takes the development of empirical science and the development of natural philosophy in the context of this science as historical conditions for the development of his own natural philosophy.

The circle of Hegel's thought is not completed, however, by observing the dependence of nature on human thought. Nature constitutes an ascending series of thought patterns which culminate in the achievement of Spirit. Hegel's *Philosophy of Nature*, as a whole, rests upon the teleology of the realised end, for Nature is conceived as a series of shapes of notional objectivity, the teleological end of which is the achievement of Spirit's free self-relation in thought. The stages by which that end is achieved are not external means to its accomplishment but objective stages which, in themselves, tend to that achievement. In the Introduction to the *Philosophy of Nature*, Hegel observed 'This notion of End was already recognised by Aristotle too, and he called this activity the nature of a thing: the teleological method – and this is the highest – consists therefore in the method of regarding Nature as free in her own peculiar vital activity'.[18] The Aristotelian language informing Hegel's philosophy of nature is noted and rehearsed in Errol Harris' thoughtful reading and defence of Hegelian natural philosophy. Harris observes, 'Not only is mind immersed in the petrified image, but it cannot rest in such petrifaction, it cannot remain strong and dead but is urged by its inherent nisus to develop – to come alive and conscious'.[19] The notion of the natural world exhibiting a nisus to develop new forms is taken up explicitly by Collingwood in the first order cosmology he undertakes in the cosmological conclusion to *The Idea of Nature*.[20]

COLLINGWOOD ON NATURE AND HEGEL

Collingwood's procedure for tracing and elaborating the idea of nature in *The Idea of Nature* edited by Knox, follows a trail which has been seen by Mink as Hegelian in terms of its explicitly historical standpoint. Mink urges that Collingwood's strategy of reviewing the idea of nature in relation to changing cultural presuppositions is a manoeuvre which testifies to the sense of historical perspective and intellectual change developed and elaborated by Hegel. Mink observes, 'The form which the latter (the dialectical analysis of the products of mind such as is conducted in *The Idea of Nature*) takes is a history of the development of fundamental concepts guided by the principle that in the history of thought such fundamental concepts develop in the mode of what Hegel called *Aufhebung*.'[21]

Mink is right to emphasise the impact of a particular kind of Hegelian influence upon *The Idea of Nature*, namely Hegel's appreciation of the historical development of spiritual activity and the historical character of conceptions of nature. The notion of nature in *The Idea of Nature* is explored historically, and Collingwood is enabled to highlight the specificity of a specific conception of nature such as the early modern or Renaissance view of nature by locating it contextually in a wider historical review of conceptions of nature which embraces the standpoints of ancient Greece and that implicit in more recent conceptions of physics and biology. In developing his historical account of conceptions of nature Collingwood draws upon his long-standing knowledge of Greek philosophical thought and his interest in contemporary scientific and cosmological thought. The brief published conclusion, which was substituted for the cosmological one, testifies to Collingwood's historical turn of mind and to an Hegelian influence in his invocation of Hegel's warning against predicting the future.[22] Collingwood emphasises the historical character of his account of the idea of nature. He allows himself, however, a brief prognostication of the future development of the idea of nature in which he highlights, and speculates about, an increasing recognition of the dependence of natural science upon history. Scientific observation and theory are held to turn upon historical action, and hence an understanding of nature should and, most likely, will recognise and assimilate an understanding of history.

The published conclusion to *The Idea of Nature* reinforces a reading of the work as essentially an historical project and testifies to a recognition that the idea of nature is an historical rather than a natural object. Within its account of historical conceptions of nature, Hegel's philosophy of nature is examined in an historical light. Hegel's cosmology is shown to have developed at a definite stage of historical development. His natural philosophy is taken as occurring at a time in which philosophers were ready and able once again to embrace ancient Greek notions, and it is related to contemporary achievements in the natural sciences. The account of Hegel's conception of nature is remarkable testimony to Collingwood's powers as an historian and philosopher. Against a background of critical neglect or dismissal, Collingwood reconstructs Hegel's natural philosophy with care and acumen. He points to its character as a response to the philosophical legacy of Kant and recognises its kinship with the objective idealism of Plato and Aristotle.[23]

Collingwood observes that nature for Hegel is real but incomplete when weighed in a dialectical scale including mind and spiritual activity. In so doing, Collingwood notes how Hegel reintroduces the ancient Greek notion of teleology into an understanding of nature; he refers approvingly to the nisus Hegel detects in nature for it to develop into the more authentic reality of mind.[24] Collingwood is sensitive to the roles of the various parts of Hegel's system. Logic, Nature and Spirit are seen as reciprocally inter-dependent but are not collapsed into one another. He plausibly notes that Hegel in reviving the objective idealism of Plato theorises the principle of rational order as dynamic, and in so doing, provides the logical form of the developmental character he ascribes to nature. In characterising Hegel's conception of man as a vehicle for God's mind or Spirit, however, Collingwood deploys a metaphor implying an externality between man and his universalising practical and theoretical activities in Hegel's thought which is controversial, and is not justified by substantial argument.

While Collingwood shows a sensitive appreciation of Hegel's deployment of teleology and the dialectical relations between mind, nature and logical process in Hegel's system, he does not develop these Hegelian ideas. Indeed, the ideas are implied to be superseded insofar as the narrative of *The Idea of Nature* extends beyond Hegel. Collingwood does not explicitly invoke their potential to construct a first order account of nature as he does, for instance, in the cosmological conclusion to *The Idea of Nature*.

Cosmology, speculation about nature, is presented by Collingwood as an historical subject conducted by human beings who build on preceding and contemporary achievements. Hegel, in *The Idea of Nature*, is presented as being unsympathetic to emerging notions of biological evolution and, of necessity, ignorant of theories of relativity in physics which highlight the processual nature of nature. Collingwood diagnoses the limits of Hegel's conception of nature. On the one hand, 'What is possible for Whitehead, however, is not possible for Hegel, because the physics of Hegel's day was still the physics of Galileo and Newton, a physics conceived in terms of things "simply located".'[25] On the other hand, Hegel is held not to take account of temporal notions of evolution which had been insufficiently developed scientifically. 'He insists that there cannot be a temporal transition, but only a logical transition, from the lower forms in nature to the higher.'[26]

This reading of Collingwood's *Idea of Nature*, then, highlights its historical character both in its formal procedure in reviewing the development of historical conceptions of nature and in its published conclusion that understandings of nature at whatever level of abstraction necessarily involve historical observations and theories. The importance of history for a study of nature, however, is depicted in a very different way in the additional brief conclusion for *The Idea of Nature,* entitled B, which has recently been discovered. In this short discussion organised around the topic of Alexander's 'The Historicity of Things', Collingwood points to the apposition between an historical conception of processes where identities are conceived as entirely involved in the continuous change which must be recognised as besetting natural phenomena. This standpoint does not merely rehearse the standpoint of the extant conclusion, in that the perceived commonality between nature and history is a positive contribution to the understanding of nature, in which the notion of history is not so much extended as is the notion of a process.[27]

The recently discovered lengthy cosmological conclusion to *The Idea of Nature* contains a substantive contribution to the formulation of the idea of nature and the relationship between nature and mind. In so doing it draws heavily upon Hegel's substantive understanding of nature as offering a substantial basis for a truthful perspective on the relationship between nature and mind, which Collingwood sees as central to a philosophical understanding of reality.

In the cosmological conclusion to *The Idea of Nature,* Collingwood is at pains to emphasise a reading of nature as one of development in which the impetus is to overcome the externality and outwardness of nature to achieve a perspective whereby outwardness and separateness is overcome. In developing this conception, Collingwood explicitly invokes the language of Hegel and Aristotle. 'The entire evolution of the world may therefore be conceived as a passage from outwardness to inwardness.' In developing this conception Collingwood refers to the necessity of imputing to nature the nisus or teleological purposiveness which he had deployed in his characterisation of Hegel's conception of nature in the body of *The Idea of Nature.* He refers to '. . . a nisus towards the production not exactly of life as we know it but of some form of existence in which the mutual externality of a thing and its environment should be overcome.'[29]

A particular concern of this newly discovered cosmological conclusion is Collingwood's commitment to elaborate the logic of what he takes to be the developing view of nature implicit in the processes assumed in contemporary science. He engages critically and correctively with Whitehead's cosmology, which is seen as undertaking to relate the thoroughly changing world of process to eternal objects. Collingwood invokes the concept of history assumed in the practice of historians to signal the notion of process as self-creating. A history of England, for instance, is shown to involve its creation and continuous change, though thoughts created in the process can stand outside the process of change and be rethought by historians.[30] Collingwood, however, does not see nature and mind as entirely self-composed. He urges that the cosmic process itself presupposes the notion of process as the logical basis of what it enacts. He notes, 'I am referring to certain fundamental conceptions like being, unity, necessity and so forth, which are logically presupposed by the very idea of process, or, in cosmological terms, to the fact that all process is essentially finite and must depend upon something other than itself.'[31]

The logical basis of process both in nature and human development Collingwood refers to as God, thereby invoking and re-working the language and system of Hegel, who had depicted the relationship between the three parts of his system as the relations between God and his creations.[32] The logical basis of God Collingwood sees as pure being, the starting point of Hegel's *Logic*. Collingwood rehearses the opening sections of the *Logic* which establish the rhythm of becoming underpinning its investigation of inter-relations between categories. Collingwood declares, 'God is infinite, creative in his relation to the world . . . He is pure and absolute being . . . the ocean or abyss of being which is indistinguishable from an abyss of nothingness'.[33] Collingwood continues by remarking, 'Pure Being is not a mere abstraction, an *ens rationis*, the empty form that is left in our minds when we have thought away everything particular; it is a real object of thought and (as Hegel points out) by no means difficult to think'.[34] The dialectic between Being and Nothing, according to Collingwood, and it must be said, Hegel, is 'thus a process from pure indeterminacy to determination'.[35] The logic of Being hereby constitutes the basis of a cosmology establishing the eternal independent objects of becoming which underlie cosmic processes.

Collingwood in elaborating the relationship between his logical iden-

tification of the nature of process and the natural world follows Hegel
in observing that in one way natural phenomena resist categorial determination. Their contingency and otherness thwart conceptualisation.
Nature, however, for Collingwood as it is for Hegel, is at the same time
intrinsically related to the categories of thought determination. The
processes of nature, therefore, are seen in themselves as creative of
eternal patterns, but these are grounded in the notion of being itself.
The evolutionary processes of nature are hereby understood by Collingwood as processes by which the shadows of externality and outwardness
cast by the cosmos are overcome by the development of inwardly
related thought patterns. Hence the perfect development of mind,
which constitutes the highest and limiting case of the achievement of
the creative process in developing such patterns and their understanding, Collingwood notes 'would seem to be a real elimination of the
process of nature.'[36] This language of Collingwood resonates with
Hegel's conception of Spirit as the opposite of the natural, and it is
unsurprising that Collingwood defines God, insofar as he can be defined
in terms of self-developing process, in a Hegelian way, as Spirit or
mind.

Collingwood's efforts in his original cosmological conclusion to *The
Idea of Nature* to think through the metaphysical conditions of nature
are not to be regarded as an isolated experiment. They reflect a considered engagement with both the questions posed by contemporary
science and an on-going concern to reconsider and rethink the terms in
which Hegel conceived of a systematic consideration of reality. In his
unpublished 'The Nature of Metaphysical Study' and his 'Notes
Towards a Metaphysics' which he worked on between 1933 and 1934,
Collingwood writes about nature and its ground in Being in ways
which reflect the longer unpublished conclusion to *The Idea of Nature*.
In these notes he explicitly invokes and develops his thinking in relation to a sympathetic reading of Hegel's system and natural philosophy.

In 'The Nature of Metaphysical Study' Collingwood contends that
contemporary discussion of idealism and realism is confused, observing
that the idealism of Plato and Hegel is not to be equated with a merely
subjective idealism. He also engages in a dialectical examination of
Being in a way that is evocative of the cosmological conclusion to *The*

Idea of Nature. Again, he sees the logic of Being as implying nothing and thence the process of determination between the two ideas.[37] In the initial notebook of 'Notes Towards a Metaphysic', he opens by re-marking upon the error of dismissing Hegel's natural philosophy. He emphasises that Hegel's natural philosophy contains, 'certain funda-mental ideas without which no cosmological theory can get along'.[38] To conceptualise the logic of the transition between nature and mind, Collingwood invokes his methodological doctrine of a scale of forms, itself derived from Hegel, by which mind is seen as a term which includes within itself lower forms of matter and life. The importance of understanding nature as exhibiting throughout a nisus, an immanent teleology, whereby what is virtual becomes actual, is emphasised.[39]

Collingwood's self-conscious reference to his metaphysical method as a recessive means of capturing progressive development harmonises with the Hegelian philosophical development of the more concrete from the more abstract. The core of Collingwood's speculation involves understanding the emergence of mind from what is not mind. This project involves the Hegelian concern to conceive of nature as virtual Spirit. For Hegel, Spirit is the highest definition of the absolute because men in spiritual thinking can recognise the thought determinations which are virtual in nature. Collingwood observes that 'the physical world is virtually mind'.[40] He confirms this developmental reading of Spirit by reflecting upon the trajectory of the human mind in achieving spiritual states from its basis in psyche. The mind in becoming actual is also seen as activating the real qualities in nature, which were in things but not appreciated before the onset of mind. For Collingwood, as for Hegel, the natural world is rational in itself, but not for itself. The human mind in realising, for instance, its perceptual capacities achieves a world of patterned relationships, which was already virtually rational. The human mind, then, for Collingwood, as for Hegel, acts as a focus-ing agent for the world of nature.[41]

This teleological reading of nature as a process whose overall concern is to achieve Spirit is identified by Collingwood as commencing with space and time. The patterns exhibited by space/time are considered to possess a nisus to achieve matter, and thereafter life and spirit. The overall pattern of evolutionary development which Collingwood is concerned to trace, rehearses the logical teleology which Hegel sees as at work within nature. For Hegel, this pattern of development is not a temporal process. What Collingwood is self-consciously concerned to achieve is a fusion of Hegel's notion of an ideal, logical pattern of development from space/time to the highest reaches of human awareness, with an actual temporal process of evolution. This objective is denoted explicitly by Collingwood. He observes, 'Hegel thought that all genuine concepts fell into a single unilear order. I do not know if he was right but I suppose it is probable. What I want to suggest is that history is the coincidence of logical with temporal order.'[42] The assignment of a logical and temporal order of development to nature entails, or so Collingwood infers, that nature must be seen as in some sense historical. Collingwood's concern to fuse the idea of temporal evolution with that of logical development is exemplified in his criticisms of Alexander's determination to see the provenance of creativity in nature within space/time itself. Collingwood notes that this ascription of developmental creativity to space/time runs counter to his own preferred Hegelian notion of the primordiality of categories. He observes, 'My conclusion is that a transcendental logic or theory of categories must precede a spatio-temporal world'.[43]

At the beginning of 'Notes Towards a Metaphysic 11' Collingwood revisits his thoughts on the nature of nature and mind. He observes, 'Mind is not the absolute though the absolute is thought'.[44] Collingwood, in this note, can be seen as rehearsing the Hegelian notion of how mind conceives of absolute thought but is not entirely coincidental with it. Collingwood registers the Hegelian provenance of his standpoint by observing that the remark is unintelligible to all those not conversant with objective idealism.[45] Furthermore, God, the fount of reality, is identified with the fundamental categories of logic, rather than the sum of all categories. Collingwood highlights the triad of Being, Nothing and Becoming as the essence of God and the inspiration of the world of space and time.[46] The power and creativity of God are identified with process itself, which logically is expressed in the category of becoming. If the category of becoming, here, is taken as a formula for the dialectical power of self-moving thought, then Collingwood is adopting a Hegelianised dialectical logic.

The world of space/time is taken by Collingwood to be a world of finitude in which externality and outwardness prevail. He runs through the Hegelian dialectic of finitude and infinity by rehearsing how the physical world throws up quasi-infinites of magnitude and quality in which the infinite is presented as another finite term outside an existing one.[47] The implicit suggestion is that true infinity, in parallel with Hegel, is taken as the circle of Being developing Being and thought thinking itself and its Being. In 'The Notes Towards a Metaphysic 11' Collingwood traces the development of the natural world in a Hegelian manner, whereby every complication of the physical world collapses into immediacy. He notes that the developmental patterns of nature trace a story of temporal development, which Hegel had reserved for the human world.

In the final fifth notebook 'Notes Towards a Metaphysic V' Collingwood attends in a substantial way to a prime inspiration of his reflections on metaphysics, namely Hegel's natural philosophy. His concern to take Hegel seriously is reflected in his consultation of different editions of Hegel's *Philosophy of Nature*.[48] Collingwood is critical about the details of Hegel's philosophy of nature. On the one hand, he is suspicious that Hegel's concern to reject Romantic notions, which see Nature as expressive of spiritual identity, leads to an underestimation of the prevalence of reason in natural phenomena in Hegelian philosophy. On the other hand, he is also suspicious of Hegel's apparent deduction of natural qualities as exhibiting a speciously precise logical order. He cites as an example of Hegel's specious logical approach, Hegel's 'logical' deduction of the five senses.

Collingwood, however, recognises an emphatic kinship between his own enterprise and Hegel's . He attends to the rationale of Hegel's rejection of physical evolution. He notes that Hegel is opposed to the notion that a low form of reality can explain, and in itself, produce a higher form. Hegel's invocation of the Idea or a teleological principle of rational development as the only satisfactory form of explanation is celebrated as methodologically sound. Collingwood endorses Hegel's standpoint, but is critical of Hegel's refusal to see natural development as developing over time as well as logically.

CONCLUSION

It is with some trepidation that I offer conclusions to what has been in part a discussion of a set of differing conclusions to *The Idea of Nature*. What can be concluded without reservation, however, is that a study of the unpublished and published writings on the idea of nature show Collingwood's close and thoughtful engagement with Hegel. The cosmological conclusion of *The Idea of Nature* and the 'Notes Towards a Metaphysic' to which it is closely affiliated, exhibit Collingwood's working out of a cosmology in relation to a metaphysical reading of Hegel's system in which nature is seen as virtual mind developing according to an independent logic of God or Being. The subsequent and published conclusion of *The Idea of Nature* again points directly to Hegel, but on this occasion suggests an historicised understanding of conceptions of nature. This conclusion, published by Knox in 1945, encourages a reading of *The Idea of Nature*, evidenced in its adoption by Mink, in which the idea of nature is to be seen as historical, depending crucially upon the developing ideas and assumptions of natural scientists and natural philosophers.

The radical change in Collingwood's conception of metaphysics expressed in the *Essay on Metaphysics* is certainly in line with the decision of Collingwood, as reported by Knox, to substitute what can be seen as a new and more historical conclusion for the original 'cosmological' conclusion to *The Idea of Nature*.[49] More speculatively, Collingwood's revision of his conception of metaphysics can be seen as rehearsing the tension in contemporary Hegelian studies where rival interpretations emphasise either absolute metaphysical claims or an historicised account of the inter-relations between developing human categories of thought at distinct levels. It might be thought that Collingwood's disavowal of metaphysics as a discipline concerned with substantive issues in favour of its conceptualisation as an historical study of absolute presuppositions involves a direct repudiation of Hegelian influences. The *Essay on Metaphysics* directly repudiates any metaphysical account of Being and *The New Leviathan*, as signalled earlier, lambasts the alleged Hegelian metaphysical deduction of Nature.[50] On the other hand, *The New Leviathan*'s account of mind and its account of a political association, draws heavily on Collingwood's dialectical and Hegelian accounts of a scale of forms and an historicised version of a social contract.[51] Moreover, in his repudiation of a metaphysical account of Being Collingwood refers positively to Hegel's linking of Being to Nothing. Again, the Collingwoodian turn to an historical rubric in formulating metaphysical presuppositions is compatible with interpretations of Hegel's enterprise which construe his accounts of logic and being as mapping the categories entertained in human experience.[52]

Notes

1 Throughout this paper the terms suggested by Boucher in characterising the 'conclusions' to *The Idea of Nature* have been used. The newly discovered conclusions which supplement the short one which was originally published by Knox are referred to as 'cosmological' and 'B'. See D. Boucher, 'The Principles of History and the Cosmology Conclusion to the *Idea of Nature*', *Collingwood Studies*, II, Perspectives, 1995.

2 R. Peters, 'Collingwood on Hegel's Dialectic', *Collingwood Studies*, II, *Perspectives*, (1995), 122.

3 See K. Hartmann, 'Hegel: A Non-Metaphysical View' in Alasdair Macintyre, ed., *Hegel: A Collection of Essays* (Garden City, N.J., Doubleday, 1971). For interesting commentaries on, and developments of, Hartmann's position see also, H. T. Engelhardt & T. Pinkard (eds.), *Hegel Reconsidered: Beyond Metaphysics and the Authoritarian State* (Dordrecht/Boston/London, Kluwer Academic Publishers, 1994).

4 R. G. Collingwood, 'Notes Towards a Metaphysic', Dep. Collingwood, 18. (A series of five red exercise books, containing notes on metaphysics and now on microfilm in the Bodleian Library, Oxford). Collingwood's cosmological conclusion, 'Sketch of a Cosmological Theory' was consulted by this author at Oxford University Press. It will soon be published, along with 'The Principles of History'.

5 The standing of Hegel's philosophy of nature amongst Hegel scholars is reflected in the lack of a critical paper upon it in the collection of essays, F. Beiser (ed.), *The Cambridge Companion to Hegel* (Cambridge, Cambridge University Press, 1993). Note also the brief coverage of Hegel's philosophy of nature in C. Taylor, *Hegel* (Cambridge, Cambridge University Press, 1975) and M. Inwood, *Hegel* (London, Routledge, Kegan and Paul, 1973), 6. G. W. F. Hegel, *The Philosophy of Mind* (Oxford, Oxford University Press, 1971), 18.

6 R. G.Collingwood, 'Notes Towards a Metaphysic', Dep. Collingwood 18/6, 65A.

7 For an interesting discussion of Hartmann's legacy see Beiser's review of Engelhardt and Pinkard's *Hegel Reconsidered*,'Hegel, A Non-Metaphysician? A Polemic' in the *Bulletin of the Hegel Society of Great Britain*, no. 32, (Autumn/Winter 1995).

8 Taylor, Hegel, and M. Rosen, *Hegel's Dialectic and Its Criticism* (Cambridge, Cambridge University Press, 1982).

9 R. G. Collingwood, *The New Leviathan* (Oxford,Clarendon Press, 1992), 278.

10 G. W. F. Hegel, *Hegel's Science of Logic*, trans. A. V. Miller (London and New York, Humanities Press), 843.

11 R. G. Collingwood, 'Notes Towards a Metaphysic', 18/4 76.

12 A. White, *Absolute Knowledge: Hegel and the Problem of Metaphysics* (Athens and London, Ohio University Press, 1983), 86.

13 J. Findlay, 'Hegelianism and Platonism', in J. J. O'Malley, K. Algozin and F. G. Weiss (eds.), *Hegel and the History of Philosophy* (The Hague, Martinus Nijhoff, 1974), 62.

14 J. Findlay, 'Hegelianism and Platonism', in J. J. O'Malley, K. Algozin and F. G. Weiss (eds.), *Hegel and the History of Philosophy* (The Hague, Martinus Nijhoff, 1974), 62.

15 G. W. F. Hegel, *Hegel's Philosophy of Nature* (Oxford, Oxford University Press, 1970) 15 (addition from student notes).

16 Hegel, *Hegel's Philosophy of Nature*, 14, (addition from student notes).

17 Hegel, *Hegel's Philosophy of Nature*, 6.

18 Hegel, *Hegel's Philosophy of Nature*, 6, (addition from student notes).

19 E. Harris, 'The Philosophy of Nature in Hegel's System', *Review of Metaphysics*, 111, September 1949, 226.

20 R. G. Collingwood, 'Sketch of a Cosmological Theory', 174.

21 L. O. Mink, *Mind, History and Dialectic* (Bloomington and London, University of Indiana Press, 1969), 17.

22 R. G. Collingwood, *The Idea of Nature*, 174.

23 Collingwood, *The Idea of Nature*, 122-126.

24 Collingwood, *The Idea of Nature*, 124.

25 Collingwood, *The Idea of Nature*, 128.

26 Collingwood, *The Idea of Nature*, 131.

27 R. G. Collingwood, 'Conclusion B 'discovered along with 'Sketch of a Cosmological Theory' at Oxford University Press.

28 Collingwood, 'Sketch of a Cosmological Theory', 172.

29 Collingwood, 'Sketch of a Cosmological Theory', 174

30 Collingwood, 'Sketch of a Cosmological Theory', 181.

31 Collingwood, 'Sketch of a Cosmological Theory', 183.

32 G. W. F. Hegel, *Hegel's Philosophy of Mind* (Oxford, Oxford University Press, 1971), 288.

33 Collingwood, 'Sketch of a Cosmological Theory', 184.

34 Collingwood, 'Sketch of a Cosmological Theory', 184.

35 Collingwood, 'Sketch of a Cosmological Theory', 184.

36 Collingwood, 'Sketch of a Cosmological Theory', 186.

37 R. G. Collingwood, 'The Nature of Metaphysical Study', Dep. Collingwood 18/2, 10. ('The Nature of Metaphysical Study', consists of two unpublished lectures Collingwood gave by way of introduction to a series of lectures on metaphysics by various speakers in January 1934). These lectures by Collingwood treat metaphysics in a similar way to that developed in the 'Notes Towards a Metaphysic'.

38 Collingwood, 'Notes Towards a Metaphysic', Dep. Collingwood, 18/3, 1.

39 Collingwood, 'Notes Towards a Metaphysic', 18/3, 4.

40 Collingwood, 'Notes Towards a Metaphysic', 18/3, 23.

41 Collingwood, 'Notes Towards a Metaphysic', 18/3, 40.

42 Collingwood, 'Notes Towards a Metaphysic', 18/3, 67.

43 Collingwood, 'Notes Towards a Metaphysic', 18/3, 78.

44 Collingwood, 'Notes Towards a Metaphysic', 18/4, 3.

45 Collingwood, 'Notes Towards a Metaphysic', 18/4, .3.

46 Collingwood, 'Notes Towards a Metaphysic', 18/4, 30.

47 Collingwood, 'Notes Towards a Metaphysic', 18/4, 76.

48 Collingwood, 'Notes Towards a Metaphysic', 18/6, 123.

49 T. M. Knox, 'Prefatory Note' in Collingwood, *The Idea of Nature*.

50 See R. G. Collingwood, *An Essay on Metaphysics* (Oxford, Oxford University Press, 1940), 11-15; and R. G. Collingwood, *The New Leviathan* (Oxford, Clarendon Press, 1992), 278.

51 See the following papers on *The New Leviathan* which emphasise its Hegelian character; – P. Nicholson, 'Collingwood's *New Leviathan*: Why Hobbes not Hegel', *Collingwood Studies* 1, (1994), and G. K. Browning, 'New Leviathans for Old', *Collingwood Studies*, II (1995).

52 For an account of Collingwood's later metaphysics which links it to Hegel's practice, see the relatively neglected, W. H. Walsh, *Metaphysics* (London, Hutchinson University Library, 1963). Walsh urges that while Hegel's metaphysics cannot be reduced to a self-conscious articulation of historical presuppositions, Hegel drew inspiration for his metaphysics from reflection on historical thought and practice.

From Illusion to Reality: R. G. Collingwood and the Fictional Art of Jane Austen

PHILIP SMALLWOOD
University of Central England

Does Collingwood matter to literary criticism – or rather should he? More perhaps than one might feel entitled to think; yet *why* he should matter will not be apparent from the corpus of either his published or his unpublished writings without some explanation. In the published *oeuvre*, one emphasis falls clearly on a general aesthetic theory of which the literary object is one part but by no means the whole. There are many references to poets, novelists and dramatists in Collingwood's writings, but they tend to be made in passing, as the tip of a vast pyramid of reading experience. Then, as a next step, if we turn to the unpublished pieces catalogued under 'Reviews and Criticism' in the Collingwood Papers in the Bodleian Library, we will see that they are mostly in the nature of jottings or personal notes. The strictly literary material of these papers (i.e. that on Shakespeare, Kyd, Racine and Greek tragedy) is of the somewhat preliminary or *ad hoc* kind, a record of *aperçus* which come together as a series of interim moments in a reflective process that for one or another reason did not develop into printable essays, argued through.[1] All the items tell us something about Collingwood's specifically literary interests and this is of value in assessing Collingwood's tastes, as it is in understanding the role that imaginative literature played in shaping his thought; but one could not say – for reasons I do not need to set out – that either the published references to creative writers, or the unpublished papers, serve to confirm without question Collingwood's strengths and capacities as a critic of literature in his own right. It seems possible to draw a line around Collingwood's many accomplishments that excludes literary criticism.

The exceptions to this rule, I would suggest, might be the two intact manuscript drafts of a lecture on the novels of Jane Austen. In these hand-written papers, as I shall seek to argue here, Collingwood is committing the resources of his humanity and intelligence to an act of literary 'judgement' which subordinates the larger framework of ideas to the particulars of the writer under discussion. The aesthetic philosophy is harnessed to the critical needs of a literary audience. One of the manuscripts is headed '*Jane Austen* – Johnson Society' and is dated 27 November 1921. The other – entitled simply 'Jane Austen' – carries no venue or date; but on internal evidence is possibly meant for the same or similar kind of occasion: the lecture's valedictory remarks suggest the paper was intended for a gathering in Oxford at University College.[2] Neither of these pieces seems generally known; but between them I believe they go further than any other specifically literary commentary in Collingwood's work in relaying a conception of criticism that is linked to, but not controlled by, the role of philosophical aesthetics. The significance of the Jane Austen lectures as critical practice forms the subject of the present essay.

First, though, since these manuscripts have not been widely discussed, I will need to say something about the relations between the drafts of the lecture, their structure, differences, common features, contents and style. Both versions are arranged according to a similar overall 'plan', so that while in some respects it would be fairer to speak of two lectures working within roughly the same limits of content and scope, we can also speak of 'a' lecture on Jane Austen that exists in two drafts standing chronologically an unknown distance apart. For the purposes of this paper I shall refer to the dated version (17/2 DEP in the Collingwood Papers in the Bodleian Library) as A and the undated version (17/3 DEP) as B. Both start with a survey of the general social, cultural and historical milieu of the later years of the eighteenth century, the early nineteenth century, and Jane Austen's place in her age. The latter half to two-thirds of each lecture is then set aside for the close analysis of particular novels in terms of character, situation and plot. Both allocate a substantial part of the available time to specific assessments of *Pride and Prejudice* and *Emma*; both culminate in the judgement that *Emma* is overall Jane Austen's best, most accomplished novel, 'the best novel ever written' as it is described in B (14). In A, Jane Austen's fiction is placed above that of the great pioneers in the form of the novel, Boccaccio, Cervantes and Fielding, and that of its later nineteenth-century practitioners and masters, Balzac, Dickens, Henry James and Dostoevski (A, 2). And in both drafts, Collingwood gives a broadly similar attention to Austen's childhood compositional habits and the influence on her writings of family background and 'world'. This has the advantage of allowing the lecturer to get in a dig at the academic world of the modern Oxford – as in the account of Mr. Austen's life as an eighteenth-century college fellow given in B:

> Genius is not produced *in vacuo*; on the contrary, it never arises except in social surroundings so exquisitely fitted to produce it that its voice seems almost the impersonal voice of these sur-roundings themselves. Jane Austen grew out of a soil now long ago exhausted, the deep and fertile soil of English middle-class country life. Her father was fellow of an Oxford college when fellows had time to improve their minds, if they wished to im-prove them, and country livings to support their bodies when, tired of improving their minds, they resolved to marry. The Oxford of Gibbon's undergraduate days & of the succeeding generation was not perfect; in some ways it was worse than the Oxford of today . . . (B, 4-5)

The value accorded to Jane Austen's novels, alongside other fiction, is extremely similar in A and B, and as we can see, extremely high; but one lecture is not a 'draft' of the other in the sense of being the same essay in a more obviously primitive 'state':[3] the differences in orien-tation and content are more thoroughgoing. Far more than A, for example, B sees Austen as important for solving the formal and tech-nical problems besetting the novel up to her time: '. . . the novel, which had hitherto been a mere succession of experiments towards a new literary form, reaches maturity and discovers a structure adequate to express the novelist's entire experience of life' (B, 3-4). B takes as a thematic and organisational axis a claim for the 'dramatic qualities' of Jane Austen's work, and to sharpen this point there is a discussion of the almost total collapse of 'modern' (post-Shakespearean) drama in the early pages which is missing from A. The discussion in B develops into a key distinction between the literary genres of the play and the novel, the form which Collingwood is arguing took over from drama in Jane Austen's time. Again, however, this material has no sustained parallel in A.

But despite these differences, and other variations I shall mention from time to time, the most useful approach will be to take the two lectures together. We need to experience their contents as the component parts of a single achievement or critical 'stroke'. This will yield the most rounded impression of Collingwood's critical engagement with Austen; it will also, I hope, suggest the relation between Collingwood's response to the novels and his 'thought' as a whole, and will indicate some areas of coherence between Collingwood's practice of literary criticism and the critical traditions of his time (and, as I hope to suggest, some aspects of ours). If, for example, Collingwood is at once a philosopher of history, and an historian of philosophy, he is also a critic who recognises that an estimate of an author's historical significance (how the author *once was* judged) is one of the ways that the author is *now* judged. The literary theorising of both the lectures is situated within an historical mode. This relationship is reciprocal: the literary judgement also provides the essential materials when drawing the map of literature's history. Thus, on the question of the transition between the drama and the novel, Collingwood can write that:

> One of the curious things about the modern or post-Napoleonic world is that it has no drama. It has a feeble and artificial reflexion of the drama that belonged to the previous period: Shakespeare and Racine,[4] whose spiritual progeny were active far into the eighteenth century, left no successors in the new age, and today the play is an extinct form of literature. Our few surviving playwrights are either tractarians or novelists, who have made use of the stage as an accidental medium of expression. If anyone doubts this, let him try to discover a single

great[5] play written in the nineteenth century. Instead, the nineteenth century wrote novels. The novel differs from the play by
being, as it were, less epigrammatic: less content to show a
single action in a vivid light and a simplified form, and more
anxious to delve into the secrets of personality. The play takes a
sample of a life and concentrates on that: it substitutes an
anecdote for a history. The novel protests against the formalism
of the play: a deepening interest in human character demands a
new and more flexible form, adequate to the new content: and
this is why the eighteenth century gradually turned from drama
to fiction. (B, 3)

This very general scope, and the large scale of the historical canvass on
which Collingwood is working in the lectures, exposes weaknesses and
strengths of critical approach. The common weaknesses reside in the
failure, in both versions, to resist an initial rhetorical flourish (excusable
as a speaker's ploy to gain the audience's attention perhaps). In A, for
example, Collingwood sets the scene for his audience by reminding us
of the world of the 1770s, and of Jane Austen's place at a moment of
triumph for all the arts:

Strange influences were abroad in the years 1770 to 1775. The
French Revolution was brewing, the Romantic movement was
unfolding itself, the whole world was coming to a new dawn:
and the spirit of the age produced a generation of geniuses that
has no parallel in the records of history. (A, 1)

The opening passage of B has more of this heroic gesture and historical
thunder and is even richer in its inter-disciplinary tributes to 'great'
minds, massive 'genius' and the like:

There are times in history when the powers that preside over
the birth of human beings seem bent upon squandering, in a
brief riot of prodigality, all the store of genius which in other
ages they would have frugally spread over centuries. At such
times the portents which we call great men, the brightest dynasts
that, shining in the ether of time, bring winter and summer to

mortals, appear, astronomically speaking, in conjunction; grouped in astonishing constellations, their radiance produces a cumulative effect, and the single notes sung by the spirits of their several spheres unite in a harmony whose unique character serves to define once for all the spirit of the time. (B, 1)

Jane Austen is 'the Napoleon of fiction' (B, 3), an artist alongside Turner in painting, Wordsworth in poetry, Hegel in philosophy and Beethoven in music. To the reader today, such comments may suggest why early twentieth-century critical writing can seem an age away from modern criticism and critical theory while ambiguously remaining its inspiration and source; and in one light, the authorial focus suggests a politically incorrect fixation with the status of genius and the importance of individual achievement now overturned by the 'death of the author'. For obvious reasons it is challenged by intolerance for a history of culture defined as a procession of 'great *men*'. In another light, such treatment is congenial to materialist critical ideals: it emphases the relations between the individual author and her cultural climate. Literary achievement is accorded its place in a cultural context, historically determined.

Their opening orations aside, however, the manner and 'address' of both the lectures is characterised throughout by an expressive economy and precision, a vertebrate clarity and edge of critical wit. In stylistic terms, both the lectures approach the standard of finished material that Collingwood elected to publish during his life. While they were assembled to be read *to* listeners rather than *by* readers, they are word-perfect as texts, fluent and precise on the page. At the same time, some of the best of Collingwood's writing on Austen can be found in the version of the lecture that structurally speaking is the less developed and 'finished' of the two (A). In this passage, Collingwood claims that with the possible exceptions of Mr. Knightley, Anne Elliott and Captain Wentworth, he could find no one in Jane Austen completely safe from her laughter:

> Any writer of ordinary talents . . . can give you a good description of a sensible man or of a striking character: but it takes a genius of no ordinary type to paint a fool who shall yet

be a solid human being – Shakespeare does it: his fools are unsurpassed in their sheer folly, yet Slender, Shallow, Aguecheek & the rest are as different from one another & as living as Richard III & Macbeth & Julius Caesar. And Jane Austen does it too: you could never mistake Miss Bates for Mrs. Allen, or Mrs. Norris for Mr. Collins, after reading a single sentence of their utterances. So far Archbishop Whately[6] and his judgment remains as true today as when it was written. Human silliness is a subject which tests to a quite extraordinary extent the powers of the dramatic writer: any failure either of intellect or of temper is at once revealed by the attempt to portray it. Shakespeare could draw a fool because not only did he know a fool when he saw one, but he could delight in his folly as a delicious and exquisite thing, as purely precious as the colour of a primrose or the song of a nightingale. (A, 3-4)

It is not the presence of fools, but the author's *delight* in folly which is the 'essential' quality of her work in Collingwood's account. The corollary of the Shakespearean parallel is that Collingwood can elevate Jane Austen above the Victorian novelist Meredith on the one hand, and above the fiction of Hardy and James on the other:

Meredith couldn't draw a fool really well, though he tried hard: his intellectualism deprives him of all delight in folly for its own sake, and he rages at the fool for being foolish – which is as if some fanatical follower of Peter Bell should tear up the primrose and stamp on it for being yellow. Even Henry James, for whom the human heart had no secrets, couldn't draw a fool, because the springs of pity were always, in his tender soul, ready to overflow and quench the dry light of reason for which alone folly is folly at all.[7] To Henry James, human folly is not a laughing matter but a crying matter: and the same is true of his great contemporary Thomas Hardy. Between these two extremes, the intellectualism of a Meredith and the emotionalism of a James, there is a mid-point of equilibrium, where the intellect is perfectly pitiless in its clear vision of truth, and the feelings are perfectly fresh in their ecstatic enjoyment of it. A step to one side or the other destroys this harmony: either the intellect dominates & the feelings become atrophied or embittered, or else the feelings dominate and the vision of life is blurred by tears or distorted by desire. The attainment of this perfect poise is the rarest thing in life.[8] (A, 4)

In order to locate this 'essential', Collingwood enumerates the various kinds and categories of human laughter in different modes. In so doing, he refines a criterion – a 'touchstone' (Collingwood adopts Arnold's famous term) – for isolating and judging Jane Austen's singularity as a fictional artist, and where 'artist' for Collingwood is the operative word. In the sentences I shall now quote, we can experience something of the trenchant muscularity and (Hobbesian?) directness of Collingwood's writing at its most wittily forceful:

> It is not enough, as Meredith's philosophy would have us believe, that a man should laugh. The comic spirit in itself has no special value over and above any other privilege of humanity, such as the possession of four incisors in each jaw. You must discriminate between laughter and laughter: the cracked laughter of the maniac, the boor's guffaw, the vacant giggle of the idiot, the snarl of the misanthrope, and so on. It is by this test that we begin to see the true greatness of Jane Austen. (A, 5)[9]

In writing of this kind, where the distinctions are drawn with an almost anthropological starkness, Collingwood is at once in tune with the critical thought of his age and apart from it – a critical 'personality' in his own right. Both the lectures mark an important stage in Collingwood's own development: they form part of the experience of thinking for oneself about art in the particular instance that an 'aesthetic' philosophy having any authority must at some time entail. If Collingwood can go on to distinguish Jane Austen's 'aesthetic vision of life' from that of the satirist, who is 'a flagellator, not an artist' and who 'lives at the very opposite pole of thought' (A, 6), he pointedly does not define her success in terms which condone the fashionable theory of 'art for art's sake'.[10] The aesthetic vision is not the vision of the aesthete. His praise leads on directly to an explicit contrast with the comedy of Molière, who 'uses a comic form half to conceal & half to express a very deep-lying melancholy and dissatisfaction' (A, 6), and whose plays 'are not of a piece with his life' but 'an escape from it'. At the same time, from our point of view, in admiring the capacity to see 'art and life as one', Collingwood may seem to endorse what has become since his day a discredited 'liberal-humanist' insistence on 'life' as a criterion or test of 'art' notorious in the writings of a Samuel Johnson, a Matthew Arnold, an Eliot or a Leavis. The practical bent, and the moral aware-ness, of all these critics leads them away from an abstract 'aesthetic', a universe of artistic value independently conceived; but Collingwood's thinking, while there is a sense in which it echoes or anticipates the teachings of these critics on the relations of art and life, also introduces a passage which gains from an aesthetic philosopher's reflective habit in defining difficult terms.[11] Collingwood here singles out the respect in which reality and artistry are related:

> . . . her novels are simply her actual world as she sees it. Her imagination illuminates her characters precisely as it illumi-nated, for her, the people she met in Hampshire or at Bath. The whole of life unrolled itself before her eyes in the form of one of her own books, or an infinite succession of them: and the novels she wrote are only a continuation and partial record of the novel in which she lived. (A, 7)

The perspectives of literary criticism and those of philosophy are not at odds in Collingwood's work. Here the distinctive quality of his stance is that while the 'world' that Collingwood refers to in A resembles the philosopher's 'world' in the sense that he uses the term in *The Idea of History*,[12] Collingwood seems also to be contributing to the literary context of his terms at the same point. Just as Jane Austen's work may seem to him inaccurately described as 'satire', so it is the 'realism' of literary theory – as his non-philosophical contemporaries might under-stand this term – that he seeks to re-define in the light of her fictional practice. Collingwood might be speaking to a community of literary criticism when he dissolves the false dichotomy between 'realism' and what T. S. Eliot called 'good writing for its own sake',[13] between art as the mirror or copy of nature, and art as a purely imagined, mentally generated reality:

I do not mean that her work was what is nowadays called realistic.[14] When an unimaginative person records the misunderstood facts which he half-sees, he calls it realism: what Jane Austen did was not to write down the way in which she saw her parents and friends behaving, but to see in their behaviour a whole world of subtle meanings and to make that world her home. (A, 7)

'Life' is what makes Jane Austen's novels 'great art', and Jane Austen herself, as F. R. Leavis was more famously to determine at a later date, 'the inaugurator of the great tradition of the English novel'.[15] To imagine for imagining's sake, however, is not to engage with 'life' in the special sense that Collingwood requires of art, and that is captured in the novels. Assuming the dating of manuscript A is correct, Collingwood (in 1921) anticipates at this point his own later definitions of 'art proper' in both his *Outlines of a Philosophy of Art* of 1925 and his *Principles of Art* of 1938, and the lectures on Austen have in this way a place in the body of Collingwood's work. In the *Outlines*, Collingwood was to distinguish between imaginative creation as mere dreaming and dreaming which 'in creating a work of art we are doing with critical care and labour'.[16] In the *Principles*, he identified 'a vulgar misconception, common in the nineteenth century, according to which the artist is a kind of dreamer or day-dreamer, constructing in fancy a make-believe world which if it existed would be, at least in his own opinion, a better or more pleasant one than that in which we live'.[17] In the lectures, the distinction between these different kinds of 'imagining out' (Collingwood's phrase in his *Outlines of a Philosophy of Art*) is conceived as the difference between 'great' and 'minor' art. The general theory is applied to – and arises out of – *the case in point*. There is a context of use for the aesthetic philosophy – a description of the categories in which the current and actual object of critical attention – the novels of Jane Austen – will need to be placed:

> Minor art is a dream, indulged because we cannot dominate it when we cannot dominate real life: great art is the domination of real life itself by our understanding of it. The minor novelist

invents imaginary old men by compensation because he cannot fathom the soul of his flesh & blood uncles: the great novelist invents them as a direct continuation of his insight into his uncles' characters. (A, 7)

Charlotte Brontë had complained about Jane Austen's work that 'it had no sentiment or poetry in it', but Collingwood quotes this comment to Austen's credit (A, 8).[18] The untemperamental essence of her art he sees drawn from the healthy quality of the practical daily life that surrounded the novelist as a young woman and as a girl: 'There is no sign that the great god Pan, in making an artist of her, found it necessary to cut the ties which bound her to the life of the world' (A, 9).[19] This again looks ahead to the *Principles of Art*, this time to the theme of 'that mysterious activity which occupies the waking and working lives of children',[20] and to the later account of how a '"corruption" of consciousness' creates artistic untruth.[21] The lecture explores the mesh between the creative psychology of the artist, and child psychology:

> . . . it is interesting in this age of infant prodigies to compare the childish notes of authentic genius with the knack, so often strangely developed in the very young, of turning out well-written stories – our nurseries are full of Daisy Ashfords: but there is all the difference between the light come & light go of an ordinary childish gift, which melts away at adolescence like the colours of the dawn, and a talent which weathers that crisis and rounds the cape of storms to reach the open sea of mature life. Jane Austen's early work consisted largely of parody or burlesque of the popular literary styles. This is very rare in children. A child does not objectify literary style as a thing by itself: when it writes, it may write imitatively but only because it is unconscious of imitating & because the style of a favourite author has tinged its outlook on life. A child with any literary gift will react to styles with pleasure or distaste: but it will not reflect on this reaction in the way that is implied by parodying a style. In Jane Austen's early burlesques one sees the premonition of a quite exceptional sense of language & literary form. (A, 10)

The essential distinction between Jane Austen's early practice (with its conscious detachment and control) and the common run of childish creative writing (in which so much is unconscious) Collingwood amplifies and illustrates more fully in B, where he conjures up the absurd types of fiction which Jane Austen parodies in her early writings. The wit of the passage, itself a response to Jane Austen's wit, requires a longer quotation to appreciate fully:

> Jane Austen was writing busily in the nursery. Plenty of children do that: it is common form in country nurseries where the children are at all intelligent. Do town-bred children do it? I have never known a case. But though these childish efforts are often surprisingly clever, they are almost always on the lower side of the line that divides nature from art. The child tells the story like that because that is how the story comes into its head: it is an immediate and unreflective reaction to stimulus, imitative very often of what the child has read, but imitating quite naïvely, without criticising what it imitates. Now the odd thing about Jane Austen's nursery output is that instead of imitating she parodies. Her heroines languish and faint not because she imagines real young ladies to do so, but because she regards the languishing and fainting heroine of the romantic novel as a delightfully funny figure, a figure to be treated ironically. And so we find in *Love and Friendship* the whole apparatus of the romantic novel – the innocent country-bred heroine, the interesting stranger arriving by night, the elopement, the accident to the coach, the swoon and all the rest of it, – treated as a joke whose point is that the author, for all her tender years, is making fun of the literary methods and conventions of eighteenth-century fiction. I have some curiosity in children's writings, and have seen many interesting and charming specimens; but I have never found any other case of a child indulging in sustained and deliberate parody.[22] This fact alone, if properly understood, would place Jane Austen by herself as a person who before she put her hair up had arrived instinctively at a conception of literary technique far in advance of the professional practice of her time. Even so might a Napoleon playing with tin soldiers have made fun of eighteenth-century tactics. (B, 7-8)

But if Collingwood places Jane Austen firmly on the anti-romantic, anti-mystical side of the moral and aesthetic divide, and if he also succeeds in impaling the literary follies of the eighteenth-century romance on the prongs of a mocking, satirical humour, we have seen that he does not exalt the nineteenth-century version of the same 'romantic' genre or type. There is no 'romantic revolution' in literary fiction for him to endorse in the lectures, and although, historically speaking, the times may have been right for Jane Austen's fiction, the times do not explain her achievement in full. Except in the sense that his own 'idea of history' comprehends the past from a point of view in the here and now, re-enacted in the mind of the historian, Collingwood does not adopt what would be nowadays called an 'historicist' position (or, for that matter, a 'New Historicist' one). What applies to history in general – that it is not a sequence or a series but rather 'a world' – also applies to *literary* history, to its own present in the past and its past in the present. To conceive Jane Austen's significance in the historical mode is to delve into the consciousness of this present. And in this, I should like to go on to suggest, we can find the more general importance of Collingwood's lectures on Austen, both for Collingwood and for us.

*   *   *

How, though, in the first instance, is Collingwood's judgement of the individual novels of Jane Austen actually pitched? The ideas developed in the 'general' sections of the lectures are carried through consistently to the practical assessments of particular works. Both versions of the lecture say something about all the major novels, very briefly in A and with critical attention more equitably distributed between them in B; both contain passages where whole novels are contrasted and compared. In A, for example, *Sense and Sensibility*, though 'merely a new version of an immature work', has 'vividness' and 'passion' (opposite 14). In B, it is 'less mature than *Pride and Prejudice*', though contains 'a great deal of brilliant writing' and would be 'hard to beat' for 'good rich pictures of thoroughly human vulgarity' (B, 12). In A, *Northanger Abbey* is notable for its 'rich detail and exuberance', but no more than 'a youthful frolic, a rag novel, raised to a higher power but still not serious work' (opposite 14). It is somewhat more amply (and sympathetically) treated in B,[23] where it is 'of all her books . . . the best fun', written in 'the author's happiest style' and where the 'handling of the whole thing is easier and more effortless than in *Pride and Prejudice*; the author is taking it more in her stride, setting herself a less ambitious task and performing it with far less trouble' (B, 12-13).

In the detailed commentary on particular novels, B offers the more connected and integrated analysis of the two, but the centrepiece of both lectures is the analysis of *Pride and Prejudice*, the novel to which Collingwood gives most of his time. In A, the attention falls on the portrait of Mr. Bennet, who is 'the real hero, the central figure, of the book. Nothing else in it comes quite up to the coherence & decision with which his subtle character is drawn . . . one of the most masterly things in fiction' (A, 11-12). In B, however, *Pride and Prejudice* matters not so much for its individual portraits, but for 'its solidity of structure and the absolute harmony between the story told and the method of telling it' (B, 8). It is also Collingwood's primary evidence to suggest how Jane Austen radically advanced the fictional art of the novel, and where the best examples of this form, judged by critical opinion to be the best, are what make its history. They constitute history's central 'events', just as the 'best poems', to adapt a remark by Yvor Winters, are 'the essential facts from which the historian must proceed':[24]

> When you travel through the history of the eighteenth-century novel, and give all the weight you can to the solidity of Fielding, the satire of Smollett, the humour of Sterne, and the delicacy of Richardson, to reach *Pride and Prejudice* is like coming out of a tunnel . . . (B, 8)

On one of the details (the sudden shift of the scene to Derbyshire) A and B are about equally critical; but the judgement on the novel's characterisation is decidedly less enthusiastic in B than in A. This goes with a stronger sense – on Collingwood's part – of the social significance of literary fiction in B. Despite the appearance in the novel of values rooted in mere surface politeness and drawing-room manners, Collingwood shows how *Pride and Prejudice* sheds light on what 'civility' means at the deeper levels of consciousness and conduct, and suggests a standard for the relations of duty within a society. In these respects, the critical occasion of Collingwood's response to Jane Austen's fiction anticipates interests that were to develop into a political-philosophical analysis of human 'civilisation' (as antidote to human barbarity) in his *New Leviathan*. In reading Austen, Collingwood had found a fictional form for portrayals of human conduct viable as insights into different kinds of 'demeanour' – in character, action, re-action and speech.[25] This is not to say that Jane Austen always gets the portraits themselves exactly right, nor sufficiently respects her characters' sensitivity to each other, and for all her delicacy, she can write with too heavy a hand:

> . . . in the depiction of character there is genuine exaggeration: the vulgarity of the Bennets, the pride of Darcy, the selfishness of the Bingley sisters, and the arrogance of Lady Catherine, are all a little overdrawn, and I cannot acquit Mr. Collins of improbability. The author is getting her whole picture a shade out of key in an uneasy anxiety to make each colour tell . . . in order to disgust Mr. Darcy it was not necessary for Mrs. Bennet to misbehave nearly so grossly as she did. (B, 8-9)

And again a few pages later:

> The author is too eager to give Elizabeth an annihilating moral victory over Lady Catherine: the old Lady is too rude, too stupid, too conceited; the younger one too firm, too spirited, too devastatingly ready in repartee. (B, 11)

One further sense in which lecture B might seem to develop beyond a position adopted in A is in the treatment of Mr. Bennet ('clever and sensitive . . . a little too clever'). This portrait is now at the service of the larger point:[26] that, while Jane Austen exaggerates, she is still 'subtle' in her exaggeration; and the stress now falls on 'the texture of the plot' (B, 10). This proceeds along 'two different lines that are bound to meet again' (B, 11). In the interview between Elizabeth and Lady Catherine which Collingwood (in B) calls 'hardly short of sublime' (11), and in A 'that consummate scene' (14), there is the exquisite irony of Elizabeth's refusal to promise never to marry Darcy: 'the first thing that gives him the idea of renewing his addresses to Elizabeth' (B, 11). But it is in A – the lecture that seems overall the less 'developed' of the two – that Collingwood can show how Jane Austen links the units of plot by a chain of cause and effect that almost recalls the course of a Greek tragedy. The purity, economy and compactness of Jane Austen amounts to a vision of fictional art unusually free from distracting 'literary' frills (on the one hand), and from the irrelevancies of an *explicit* social and political comment on the other:

> To this scene all the elements of the book contribute. It is the direct effect of Mr. Collins's servile garrulity, fed by a chain of gossip as inevitable as the law of gravitation: and it is the direct cause, when reported by Lady Catherine to Darcy, of his seeing that the moment was favourable for renewing his suit to Elizabeth, his coming hastily from London, & his being accepted. The whole thing makes a denouement of quite exceptional brilliance, where nothing is wasted and nothing is accidental. (A, 14)

As for the novels in the later group, Collingwood draws attention in manuscript A only to the 'descriptions of festivities' in the 'laboured' and otherwise unspontaneous *Mansfield Park* (opposite 14); but in B, after explaining the 'gap' in Jane Austen's output between 1798 and 1811 (not in his opinion a case of disappointed literary ambitions[27]), he outlines at greater length, and with more attention to detail, why in his estimation this novel is not nearly as good as most people think. According to the standards of judgement that Collingwood had established in the course of his lectures, there is too little comedy and an absence of drama; too much telling and too little showing. Jane Austen is misguidedly denying her nature as a novelist, and those who think too well of *Mansfield Park* will fail to comprehend the bases of Jane Austen's achievement:

> The first of this batch, *Mansfield Park*, is regarded by many as her best. To me, such a judgment can only indicate a blindness to all her highest merits. The narrative is brilliantly and firmly-

drawn, but the plot and characters are not at her highest level. The characters of Fanny Price and Edmund Bertram are praiseworthy but dull; both have admirable principles, warm hearts, and all the domestic virtues, but I cannot help thinking that Miss Austen has depicted them under the quite mistaken idea that, being no longer young, she must now be serious and choose characters whom she will not be forced to laugh at. The result is unfortunate; and the best parts of the book are the most comic, for instance the descriptions of the theatrical rehearsals at Mansfield and of the sordid but jolly Price household at Portsmouth. If anybody seriously thinks *Mansfield Park* up to Jane Austen's standard, let me remind him that all the latter part of the main plot develops off the stage & is merely reported in letters, a clear sign that the author has not a firm enough grasp on the development to place it before our eyes. A Richardson can be forgiven for such weakness; not a Jane Austen. (B, 13-14)

Emma of course, as mentioned at the start of the present discussion, is the novel that defines Jane Austen's powers as a writer at their artistic and fictional height: '*Emma* is one of the prime treasures of literature', Collingwood writes in A: 'for a story so convincing and inevitable has seldom been told' (A, opposite 14). The whole remainder of lecture A is given over to a commentary based on a lively re-telling of the plot of *Emma*, and a favourable comparison with *Pride and Prejudice*. The contrast between these novels comes down to the scene where Mr. Elton proposes marriage to Emma, a scene whose superior realisation as fiction Collingwood memorably fixes thus: 'Where *Pride and Prejudice* is modelled in relief, this is modelling in the round' (A, 17). Comparing *Emma* with *Pride and Prejudice* in B, Collingwood concludes that:

> . . . it has gained immensely in solidity, in balance, in justice; the parts are played without the least exaggeration; the author never raises her voice to make her effects . . . In *Emma*, as in *Pride and Prejudice*, the rarest & most brilliant merit is the construction of the plot, which unfolds itself with unerring logic and, here as in the earlier work, culminates in a motive of Sophoclean irony. But here the irony is subtler. (B, 16)

This detailed appreciation (with some brief remarks on *Persuasion*) follows a passage in B on the current (1920s) estimate of all of the novels. There are some scathing comments on 'the average English reader' who 'goes to fiction only for sympathetic characters, and finds that he is not quite sure whether he likes Emma Woodhouse' (B, 14). From here, Collingwood is carried forward to challenge the 'highbrows' who attack Jane Austen for her 'narrow middle-class provincial outlook' and compare her on these grounds unfavourably with Dickens or Wells 'with his profound insight into social and philosophical problems' (a judgement palpably mistaken from Collingwood's point of view). To this Collingwood's reply is that Jane Austen is first and last a 'test case of pure literary genius': 'anyone who admires her must admire her on literary grounds' (B, 15):

> . . . for with the austerity of the highest genius she makes no other appeal: she had no meretricious arts, she asks nothing from anyone except the appreciation of her purely literary qualities; and if on irrelevant grounds someone chooses to deny these qualities, one can only say in the immortal words of Thomas Ingoldsby: 'No doubt he's a very respectable man, but I can't say much for his taste'. (B, 15)

*   *   *

At a time when the boundaries of 'literature' have been called into question by doctrines of 'anti-elitism', by radical theory and priorities determined by an explicitly political criticism, the reception of literary work for its 'purely literary qualities' might be one of the general motives for drawing attention to both of Collingwood's lectures here. Taken together, Collingwood's writings on Austen enter the academic debate by reminding us that literary criticism is dealing with 'art' and that 'literature' is one of the departments of it; but it is also clear that Collingwood does not see literary values and the matters of life, death and ethical conduct – as a moralist would regard them – as unconnected. The classes overlap.[28] He defines the distinctive literary quality in terms of a moral problem that writers such as Dickens and Arnold Bennett ('snobs and sentimentalists') are not able to face (B, 18). It is the problem which from first to last runs through Collingwood's own philosophy, as it does through the whole history of philosophy as Collingwood conceives it:

> The problem in all her books is the problem of knowing one's own mind. Every one of her heroines is placed in a situation where a resolute and fearless facing of her own motives is demanded of her.[29] The catastrophes are one and all caused by failure to distinguish one's real thoughts and desires from those which one idly supposes oneself to have;[30] and the happy endings take place invariably by a moral crisis in which these illusions are swept away and the heroine is left face to face with her real self. This crisis, tragic as in *Emma*, or comic as in *Northanger Abbey*, is the turning-point of all the books, whose common theme is thus the conversion of the soul, as Plato would call it, from illusion to reality. (B, 18)

Firstly, and most specifically, the lectures are documents in the history of Austen's earlier twentieth-century reception. Though the date of B is unknown, lecture A was prepared at a time of accelerating interest in Jane Austen's work. A. C. Bradley had lectured on Jane Austen in 1911, and a Centenary Memorial to her had been unveiled at Chawton in Hampshire in 1917. In 1913, William Austen-Leigh and Richard Arthur Austen-Leigh published their *Jane Austen: Her Life and Letters, A Family Record*,[31] and in 1920 Mary Augusta Austen-Leigh had published her *Personal Aspects of Jane Austen*.[32] Both these works were widely reviewed,[33] and Collingwood's lectures join the chorus of praise that was to inspire a flowering of twentieth-century attention to her novels and her world that dates from this time. Collingwood, in his lectures, challenges the apologist's view of Austen that the world of her novels is shuttered and 'narrow', that it lacks reference to the Napoleonic wars, the poor, society at large and so forth – an issue that remains a topic of discussion in Jane Austen scholarship to this day.[34] The lectures look forward to the later claims for Jane Austen's novels made by such writers as Q. D. Leavis (in *Scrutiny*) or F. R. Leavis in the opening essay of his *Great Tradition*. Whether Collingwood was right in the matter of Austen is a question for critical debate: his judgements will need to be placed in the scales; but the reaction of a major philosopher to the novels of a major novelist is a rare event, as frequent as the passing of a comet.

Next in order is the role these lectures have in the study of Collingwood's 'thought', and their contribution to his 'intellectual project', as David Boucher has called it.[35] While in no sense 'political criticism' as the term is nowadays understood, they include within literary criticism aspects of Collingwood's work as a moralist, a classicist, an aesthetician, and as a political and social thinker concerned to explore what 'civilisation' is. In this Collingwood's thinking on Austen is linked to other aspects of an early twentieth-century 'classical' renaissance promoted in different ways by T. S. Eliot (in his defences of the poetry of Dryden and Johnson for example) and Ezra Pound (in *Make It New* and his translations from Greek).[36] Such an historical affinity goes some way to qualify the perception that the literary 'field' of Collingwood's thought belongs to a loosely Coleridgean, romantic, aesthetic (or aestheticist) point of view, as it does the conclusion that Collingwood was committed to an idea of the artist as a kind of pseudo-divine, expressivist, 'fount'.[37] The romantic legacy is under fire in the lectures. To the question 'What is Man?' that sets the scene for the *The New Leviathan*, Jane Austen's fiction had provided the literary and fictional beginnings of an answer. The play of comic yet 'pitiless' irony in Jane Austen's works had prepared the ground for the more abrasively sardonic vision of a latter-day Hobbes, and the content of the lectures on Austen is wedded inextricably to Collingwood's 'intellectual project' in this way. We have seen how the lectures are a milestone on the mental and aesthetic journey leading both to the *Outlines* and to the *Principles of Art*.

Within this larger context – Collingwood's thought about art as a whole and the relation of this 'whole' to contemporary changes of taste – the Jane Austen lectures have a role to play. Collingwood's 'literary criticism' is not a product of the archaically 'belletristic' pose rightly repudiated by modern theorists in their response to the literary attitudes of his time. The lectures on Austen reveal Collingwood's intellectualist vigour on the very problems that criticism still finds difficult to solve for itself – 'what is comedy?' 'how do satire and comedy differ?' 'how is literature real?' 'what kinds of experience sustain art?' 'what are the special characteristics of the novel as opposed to the play?' Issues of this kind are addressed at other points in Collingwood's writings. Here the analysis is applied. The question is not 'What is the truth about art?'; it is 'What is the truth about Austen?'[38] Like little else in Collingwood's writings as far as I am able to tell, the lectures reveal Collingwood in the guise of a literary critic in one indispensable respect – exercising judgement over the critic's only relevant object: the work.

I have suggested that aside from the lectures on Austen, Collingwood does not on the whole submit examples of literary works and authors to evaluation, but uses them as illustration; and if we confine our attention to the Collingwoodian *oeuvre* currently in print, we find that the figure of the *literary* critic, when the critical function is defined in this way, never really rises clear of the surface.[39] But this does not discount the sense in which literary criticism is equipped to draw from philosophical and historical aspects of Collingwood's thought, or eliminate his unusually close historical affinities with literary critical tradition. It is for example a fact that F. R. Leavis placed *The Idea of Nature* on his shortlist of essential reading in philosophy for his undergraduate students of English at York.[40] Writing as a philosopher and historian, Collingwood perfected an accomplished 'literary' style (the wit, pungency and immediacy of which I have commended here). His *Autobiography* of 1939 is a type of literary practice in its own right, and Collingwood thought of philosophy as a 'literary' form (different from the 'literatures' of history and science and open to that special kind of 'literary' criticism that philosophers perform on each other).[41] Moreover Collingwood insists on the sense in which art is a 'language';[42] and this seems to make literary examination his paradigm-situation for looking at art. But it is the work that Collingwood has done *on behalf of* literary criticism – in thinking through the problems of method from points of view that are most often outside it – that gives a context of critical significance to the two lectures on Austen, as to much else that he wrote, and this is the context of immediate interest here.

A final example (concerned with criticism's own essential nature) will suffice to make this point. Collingwood's conceptions of the historian's commitment to 're-enacting' the past, and the philosopher's commitment, when reading philosophers, to 'reconstruct in ourselves'[43] their processes of thought while 'living through the same experience [as the author]',[44] belong (respectively) to history and to philosophy. But historical and philosophical thinking may also take literary form and the criticism of this form may often have an historical or philosophical aspect, as – from a reciprocal point of view – Collingwood's history is ideally a 'critical history': it is brought alive by the historian's contemplation of self, by evaluating sources, by selecting evidence, by thinking, or by an act of imaginative sense-making usually found in novels.[45] Collingwood's historical and philosophical thought can therefore run in the same channels as literary criticism. This may include the critical channels that found expression in Collingwood's judgement and enjoyment of literature in the Jane Austen lectures; but it is also apparent in the 'historical' and 'philosophical' aspects of the work of Collingwood's leading contemporary literary critics – not in some subordinate branch of this work, but in their work as critics as such, and in the 'thought' (itself part of their criticism) which justifies and explains their judgements. The theory of history as a 'world' in which the various elements bear on each other and criticise each other is the parallel of Eliot's theory of the past and present of a literary tradition:

> It involves, in the first place, the historical sense . . . and the historical sense involves a perception, not only of the pastness of the past, but of its presence; the historical sense compels a man to write not merely with his own generation in his bones, but with a feeling that the whole of the literature of Europe from Homer and within it the whole of the literature of his own country has a simultaneous existence and composes a simultaneous order.[46]

Collingwood accordingly defines 'criticism' in *An Essay on Philosophical Method* as the reader's requirement to 'share' the experience of the author. This experience is always a part of the past because literature, being a record of experience past, is always a part of history. To be present to the reader it must therefore be re-lived: 'Criticism does not begin until the reader has . . . submitted to the discipline of following the author's thought and reconstructing in himself the point of view from which it proceeds'.[47] The context for this remark is the philosopher's criticism of other philosophers. However the liveliness and expressive concision I have said we have found in the Austen lectures, and Collingwood's direct appreciation and judgement of the novels' permanent presence in the here and now (not in the past 'as such',[48] not purely aesthetically), suggests how little different was the conception of criticism that supports Collingwood's practice as a literary critic where we have evidence for it. It is in fact little different from that of his colleagues in the central stream of literary criticism – from Pound's commitment to the concept of 'making it new' (by creative translation), to Leavis's belief in criticism's 're-creative' functions. The reader (as critic) works in each case from inside the experience of his author, and from the experience of the author in him. For Collingwood, the critic must think along with his author; he must re-trace his steps:

> . . . criticism has two sides, a positive and a negative, neither of which can be altogether absent if it is to be genuine or intelligent. The critic is a reader raising the question whether what he reads is true. In order to answer this question he must disentangle the true elements in the work he is criticizing from the false. If he thinks it contains no true elements, or that it contains no false, that is as much as to say he finds in it no work for a critic to do. The critic is a reader who agrees with his author's views up to a certain point, and on that limited agreement builds his case for refusing a completer agreement.
> The critic must therefore work from within.[49]

For Leavis, writing out of an 'idea of criticism' that differs from Collingwood's in seeing the critic as 'anti-philosopher', the same 'idealist' requirement nevertheless applied:

> By the critic of poetry I understand the complete reader: the ideal critic is the ideal reader . . . His first concern is to enter into possession of the given poem (let us say) in its concrete fullness, and his constant concern is never to lose his completeness of possession, but rather to increase it. In making value-judgments (and judgments as to significance), implicitly or explicitly, he does so out of that completeness of possession and with that fullness of response.[50]

If Collingwood matters to literary criticism, this demand for sympathetic inwardness with the object of critical attention, as this object is re-constructed by the critic in time present, and the inwardness he reveals in practice in his own work, makes the concept of Collingwood's 'aesthetic philosophy' a far less Olympian, abstracted and impalpable thing than it might otherwise seem – far less like the 'system' that Leavis repudiates in the name of criticism and far more like the 'organization of similarly "placed" things . . . that have found their bearings with regard to one another'[51] that he requires. Collingwood's and Leavis's valuations of 'thought' contain similar resonances. As a focus for the critical intersection of a number of disciplines, Collingwood's conception thus engages his historical and philosophical analyses in common cause with the 'mission of criticism' but without blunting its edge, and Collingwood's part in the history of aesthetics has therefore a simultaneous role in criticism's history as that history is defined in Collingwood's terms. Collingwood may never have planned a '*rapprochement*'[52] of this particular form, but it is a connecting thread within the interdisciplinary web of his work. From the viewpoint of the literary critic, it enables us to 'make use' of what he has done. I will conclude with a point that is so general it is bound to seem lame. For Collingwood's lectures on Austen perform a further secondary function in addition to their primary one of distinguishing the quick from the dead. This is to enable us to re-live within critical practice and critical theory alike some of the values of the common reader that are now on the brink of extinction – clarity, evaluative conviction, coherence, the unity of the ethical and aesthetic; but also to include within the language of critical commerce values of good sense and politeness that are not without their relation to Austen, to 'manners' as much as to matter. In all of these aspects, Collingwood's writing deserves to be held in tension with the extreme anti-essentialist, occult and obscurantist trends in Anglo-American criticism of more recent years. Its qualities highlight vividly and tragically the terrible collapse in human intelligibility that that particular development has brought in its wake and the logical wreckage that lies scattered behind it.

NOTES

1 Aside from the pieces of philosophical reviewing, there are extant 'Notes on various works by Racine' (1938), an 'Analysis of Aeschylus's *Agamemnon*, lines 1343-69', a set of 'Notes on Euripides' with 'Brief notes on "The Electra-Story"' (in the versions of Aeschylus, Sophocles and Euripides) and an 'Analysis of "Hieronimo and Hamlet"', all undated.

2 University, Collingwood's undergraduate College, did not have a 'Johnson Society' (so called) in the 1920s, but it is clear from the concluding comments in the undated draft that University College is one of the venues that Collingwood had in mind. He mentions having 'repaid a debt, for many years ago it was in this college that, as an undergraduate, I listened to a paper on Jane Austen by Warde Fowler . . .' But these comments are deleted in the same draft, and while the replacement text pencilled in above the original in the undated version still suggests an Oxford venue attended by Austen enthusiasts, it is no longer clear from internal evidence where the meeting was held. The University College literary society which was active at the time was called the 'Martlets' and it is apparent from the minute books of this society that Collingwood addressed them twice in the 1920s, once as an undergraduate and again as a young fellow of Pembroke College – on both occasions on Sir Thomas Browne (See Bodleian MS Top. Oxon. d.95/3), returning in June 1936 to give a paper on King Arthur. There is no evidence that he offered a paper on Jane Austen in 1921 or at any later date. Perhaps the deletions indicate a lecture adapted for delivery on different occasions and in different places of which only one was a 'Johnson Society'. The McGowin Library at Pembroke College holds no records of their Johnson Society meetings between 1913 and May 1923. However the minute books of the Pembroke Beaumont Society, active at the time, do record Collingwood as having read 'a most entertaining paper on Jane Austen' to this Society on 11th February 1923, and it is clear from the contents of the minute (taken by T. A Good) that Collingwood was reading from his dated (1921) draft on this occasion. When records of the Pembroke Johnson Society resume in 1923, the minute books of the Society show that he spoke at least twice on Austen. He was a guest of the Society on 16th November 1924 and at that time, as the contents of the minute suggest, his dated (1921) version of the Jane Austen lecture was before him. A further report of Collingwood's having lectured to the Pembroke Johnson Society on Austen appears nearly ten years later in the minutes for 4th February 1934. Then, however, it is clear that the meeting heard a revised version of the lecture whose details seem to correspond with the undated version. All three reports praise Collingwood's reading of quotations from Austen. In 1934 the Secretary notes that: 'Mr. Collingwood read extracts from her works, enjoying himself so much that the society could not help but be charmed. The paper met with an enthusiastic reception'. I am indebted to Naomi van Loo, Deputy Librarian of Pembroke College, and to Dr. Robin Darwall-Smith, Archivist at University, for their invaluable advice on the activities of their respective Oxford college societies in the 1920s. I owe the references to reports of the Austen lectures to Dr. James Connelly, to whom I am most grateful.

3 I am inclined to disagree with Donald S. Taylor's judgment that '[t]he undated manuscript [on Austen] seems to be a source for the more polished 1921 manuscript'. See *R. G. Collingwood, A Bibliography* (London and New York, Garland, 1988), 53. From the three reports of the lectures' delivery contained in the minute books of the Pembroke Beaumont and Johnson Societies, the 'more polished 1921 manuscript' (A) was given

in 1923 and 1924, the 'undated' one (B) ten years later in 1934. (See note 2 above). In terms of transitional continuities the 'undated' manuscript (B) seems to me the smoother and more 'polished' of the two. In A Collingwood wrongly refers to Jane Austen's mother as a 'daughter of the then Master of Balliol' (A, 8); in B, she is correctly referred to as his 'niece' (B, 5). He gives different ages at point of death for Jane Austen's admiral brothers – 73 and 92 in A (9), 75 and 90 in B (6). The correct ages are 73 (Charles) and 91 (Francis).

4 Collingwood has struck out 'Corneille' and substituted 'Racine'.

5 Originally 'good'.

6 Richard Whately (1787-1863), archbishop of Dublin, author of *Historic Doubts relative to Napoleon Buonaparte* (1819). Collingwood called Whately 'a very competent man' and is referring to 'an article upon her [Jane Austen's] work some three years after her death in which he maintained that her power of characterization could only be compared to Shakespeare's' (A, 2-3). The article in question is in the *Quarterly Review*, 24 (1821), 352-76. It was reprinted as 'Modern Novels' in Whately's *Miscellaneous Lectures and Reviews* (London, Parker and Son, 1861), 282-313, and is cited by Mary Augusta Austen-Leigh in her *Personal Aspects of Jane Austen* (London, John Murray, 1920), 97. Whately had written of Jane Austen as having 'a regard to character hardly exceeded even by Shakespeare himself. Like him, she shows as admirable a discrimination in the characters of fools as of people of sense; a merit which is far from common . . . it is no fool that can describe fools well; and many who have succeeded pretty well in painting superior characters, have failed in giving individuality to those weaker ones which it is necessary to introduce in order to give a faithful representation of real life . . . Slender, and Shallow, and Aguecheek, as Shakespeare has painted them, though equally fools, resemble one another no more than Richard, and Macbeth, and Julius Caesar; and Miss Austin's [sic] Mrs. Bennet, Mr. Rushworth, and Miss Bates, are no more alike than her Darcy, Knightley, and Edmund Bertram' (362).

7 See the Preface to *The Princess Casamassima*, in *Henry James, The Critical Muse, Selected Literary Criticism*, ed. Roger Gard (London, Penguin Books, 1987), 501-02, 'Verily even, I think, no "story" is possible without its fools – as most of the fine painters of life, Shakespeare, Cervantes and Balzac, Fielding, Scott, Thackeray, Dickens, George Meredith, George Eliot, Jane Austen, have abundantly felt'.

8 The latter part of this passage applies to the novelist's treatment of folly what Matthew Arnold had said about the perfect balance necessary to the critic of poetry: 'To handle these matters properly there is needed a poise so perfect that the least overweight in any direction tends to destroy the balance'. See 'Last Words' (1861), 'On Translating Homer IV', *The Complete Prose Works of Matthew Arnold*, I, *On the Classical Tradition*, ed. R. H. Super (Ann Arbor, University of Michigan Press, 1960), 174.

9 Collingwood is apparently referring to Meredith's essay 'On the Idea of Comedy and of the Uses of the Comic Spirit', first printed in the *New Quarterly Magazine*, 8 (June-July 1877), 1-40. Meredith had said that 'Emma and Mr. Elton might walk straight into a comedy, were the plot arranged for them' (29), and 'the test of true Comedy is that it shall awaken thoughtful laughter' (33).

10 Or, for example, A. C. Bradley's 'Poetry for Poetry's Sake' (1901), where the poem has 'intrinsic value', and the experience of it is 'an end in itself'. See *Oxford Lectures on Poetry* (London, Macmillan, 1909), 4. The suggestion that Collingwood 'closely follows' Bradley in his early aesthetic theory is made by Peter Jones, 'A Critical Outline of Collingwood's Philosophy of Art', in Michael Krauz (ed.), *Critical Essays on the*

Philosophy of R. G. Collingwood (Oxford, Clarendon Press, 1972), 45-46. I would argue that the Austen lectures show Collingwood's theory of literature as part of his theory of art in a less abstracted light, and as the *product* of literary experience.

11 Compare F. R. Leavis, 'James as Critic', *Henry James, Selected Literary Criticism*, ed. Morris Shapira (London, Heineman, 1957), rpt. in G. Singh (ed.), *The Critic as Anti-Philosopher, Essays and Papers by F. R. Leavis* (London, Chatto and Windus, 1982), 114: 'It doesn't take a great deal of reflection to establish that "life" is a large word and doesn't admit of definition. But some of the most important words we have to use don't admit of definition. And this truth holds of literary criticism. Not only can we not, for instance, do without the word "life"; any attempt to think out a major critical issue entails using positively the shifts in force the word is bound to be incurring as it feels its way on and out and in towards its fulfilment'.

12 See, in particular, the passages in the chapter on 'Scientific History' in England where Collingwood is summarising (in approving terms) Oakeshott's theory of history, *The Idea of History*, revised ed., by Jan van der Dussen (Oxford, Oxford University Press, 1994), 153: 'History is not a series but a world: which means its various parts bear upon one another, criticize one another, make one another intelligible'.

13 T. S. Eliot, 'Johnson as Critic and Poet' (1944), in *On Poetry and Poets* (London, Faber and Faber, 1957), 191.

14 Collingwood took up the general question in *Speculum Mentis or The Map of Knowledge* (Oxford, Clarendon Press, 1924), 63: 'The artist as such does not know what the word reality means; that is to say, he does not perform the act which we call assertion or judgement. His apparent statements are not statements, for they state nothing; they are not expressions, for they express no thought. They do not express his imaginations, for they are his imaginations. What he imagines is simply those fantasies which compose the work of art'.

15 F. R. Leavis, *The Great Tradition* (London, Chatto and Windus, 1948), 16.

16 *Outlines of a Philosophy of Art* (1925; rpt. Bristol, Thoemmes Press, 1997), 22.

17 *The Principles of Art* (Oxford, Oxford University Press, 1938), 138. Cf. also the discussion in *Speculum Mentis*, 91-92: 'Pure imagination, devoid of any trace of assertion, would be a mere chaotic riot of fantasies in which every image, by its mere transitoriness, would be wholly indeterminate . . . Not this condition, but something approximating to it by reason of the random and disconnected character, is found in the vague day-dreaming and night-dreaming of the mind whose control over itself is relaxed'.

18 Letter 341 (264) To G. H. Lewes, Jan 18th, 1848: 'What a strange lecture comes next in your letter! You say I must familiarise my mind with the fact that "Miss Austen is not a poetess, has no 'sentiment'" (you scornfully enclose the word in inverted commas), "no eloquence, none of the ravishing enthusiasm of poetry"; and then you add, I *must* "learn to acknowledge her as one of the greatest artists, of the greatest painters of human character, and one of the writers with the nicest sense of means to an end that ever lived."

The last point only will I ever acknowledge.

Can there be a great artist without poetry?'

See *The Shakespeare Head Bronte*, ed. T. J Wise and J. A. Symington, *The Brontës, Their Lives and Friendships & Correspondence in Four Volumes, Vol. II, 1844-1849* (Oxford, Blackwell, 1932), 180.

19 Perhaps an allusion to Arthur Machen's horror story, *The Great God Pan*, published in 1894.

20 *Principles of Art*, 80.

21 *Principles of Art*, 215-221.

22 In *An Autobiography* (Oxford, Clarendon Press, 1939), Collingwood recalls that 'from an early age I wrote incessantly, in verse and prose, lyrics and fragments of epics, stories of adventure and romance, descriptions of imaginary countries and bogus scientific and archaeological treatises' (3). See also Collingwood's linking of the child's imaginative productions to his theory of the primitive status of art in *Outlines of a Philosophy of Art*, 17.

23 This needs qualifying to some extent. On a deleted but legible page and a half of A (15-16), Collingwood had begun a more detailed treatment of *Northanger Abbey* and had planned to read out a plot summary and passages from the book to his lecture audience, but had then obviously changed his mind, doubtless through shortage of time. Catherine Morland is referred to as 'a Don Quixote in petticoats' in the deleted section, and Mrs. Allen 'one of Jane Austen's best silly old women', 'The plot is slender: it has none of the solid construction of *Pride and Prejudice*, but the richness & felicity of the rambling detail is unequalled, & the comparatively bald patches which one sees here & there in the earlier work are quite absent'.

24 Yvor Winters, *The Function of Criticism* (London, Routledge and Kegan Paul, 1962), 197.

25 See *The New Leviathan or Man, Society, Civilisation and Barbarism*, revised edition, ed. David Boucher (Oxford, Clarendon Press, 1992), esp. Ch. XXXVII, 'Civilisation as Education', 308:

> '37.14. To recognize the freedom of others is to respect them.
>
> 37.15. The civility about which I have said so much is respect for others as shown in demeanour towards them.
>
> 37.16. Civility towards others is, therefore, inseparably bound up with self-respect.
>
> 37.17. This enables us to distinguish two different kinds of demeanour which are often confused, *civility*, or the demeanour of the self-respecting man towards one whom he respects, and *servility*, or the demeanour of a man lacking self-respect towards one whom he fears'.

The latter definition precisely recalls Mr. Collins's grovelling demeanour in the presence of Lady Catherine. Apropos Jane Austen's 'themes' in the novels, see also Collingwood's thoughts on 'Duty' in *Essays in Political Philosophy*, ed. David Boucher (Oxford, Clarendon Press, 1989), 150-159.

26 This is consistent with the view that B is the later manuscript. See also notes 2 and 3 above.

27 Collingwood attributes the 'gap' in output to domestic causes, looking after her parents etc. (B, 13). Writing in *Scrutiny*, X (1941), Q. D. Leavis could find no gap. The process of drafting and copying peculiar to Jane Austen's compositional methods was continuous throughout these years. See 'A Critical Theory of Jane Austen's Writings', Part 1, *A Selection from Scrutiny* (Cambridge, Cambridge University Press, 1968), II, 4.

28 See *An Essay on Philosophical Method* (1933; rpt. Bristol, Thoemmes Press, 1995), 31: 'The specific classes of a philosophical genus do not exclude one another, they overlap one another. This overlap is not exceptional, it is normal; and it is not negligible in extent, it may reach formidable dimensions'. For F. R. Leavis, *The Great Tradition* (London, Chatto and Windus, 1948), 15, Jane Austen 'does not offer an "aesthetic" value that is separable from moral significance'.

29 Philosophical analysis and critical definition are both users of the fictional form. In the

Life of Dryden (1779), Samuel Johnson had written critically of Dryden on the importance of literary self-knowledge: 'We do not always know our own motives. I am not certain whether it was not rather the difficulty which he found in exhibiting the genuine operations of the heart than a servile submission to an injudicious audience that filled his plays with false magnificence'. See *The Works of Samuel Johnson, LL.D.*, ed. Robert Lynam (London, 1825), III, 468.

30 Cf. D. H. Lawrence's distinction between 'real feelings' and 'mental feelings' in *Apropos of Lady Chatterley's Lover* (1930; Harmondsworth, Penguin, 1961), 93.

31 William Austen-Leigh and Richard Arthur Austen-Leigh, *Jane Austen, Her Life and Letters, A Family Record* (London, Smith, Elder and Co., 1913).

32 Mary Augusta Austen-Leigh, *Personal Aspects of Jane Austen* (London, John Murray, 1920).

33 The latter by Katherine Mansfield in *The Athenaeum* and by Virginia Woolf in the *TLS*. See David Gilson, *A Bibliography of Jane Austen* (Oxford, Clarendon Press, 1982).

34 See, for example, Tony Tanner, Introduction, *Jane Austen* (London, Macmillan, 1986), 2-42.

35 See 'The Life, Times and Legacy of R. G. Collingwood' in David Boucher, James Connelly and Tariq Modood (eds.), *Philosophy, History and Civilisation, Interdisciplinary Perspectives on R. G. Collingwood* (Cardiff, University of Wales Press, 1995), 11.

36 Collingwood's pencilled amendment to B, 18 claims that: 'there is no English writer more purely representative of the classical spirit in literature than Jane Austen'.

37 Louis O. Mink, *Mind, History and Dialectic, The Philosophy of R. G. Collingwood* (Bloomington, Indiana University Press, 1969), 236, notes that: 'Collingwood's theory of art is, like every expression theory, in an important sense "romantic," but it is also the exact opposite of those romantic theories which have claimed for the artist the capacity to soar on the wings of imagination and bring back supernal truths and exalted emotion from the top of the mountain which ordinary men cannot climb'.

38 Collingwood is using an instance from Austen – but only *as* an instance – when in *Speculum Mentis* he explores the sense in which art is 'true' (60): 'It is not true that Catherine Morland's father was called Richard, for Catherine Morland never existed . . .' The point is analogous to the one made in the literary critical context of the famous pamphlet 'How Many Children Had Lady Macbeth?' See L. C. Knights, *Explorations, Essays in Criticism Mainly on the Literature of the Seventeenth Century* (London, Chatto and Windus, 1946), 13-50.

39 By this I mean that there is little sustained discussion of any work of any poet, novelist or dramatist considered in their wholeness or at length: most of the allusions that Collingwood makes to ordinarily designated literary artists (mainly in *The Principles of Art*) are introduced briefly and in passing. We *hear* of Rupert Brooke, Catullus, Cervantes, Coleridge, Dante, Donne, Dryden, Eliot, Euripides, Galsworthy, Graves, Homer, Henry James, Jerome K. Jerome, Ben Jonson, Kipling, Kyd, Marlowe, A. A. Milne, Molière, Morris, Poe, Pope, Anne Radcliffe, Sappho, Shakespeare, Shaw, Shelley, Sitwell, Spenser, Wilde, and Yeats. However with the possible exception of Eliot's poetry, praised by Collingwood in the closing pages of *The Principles of Art*, we do not hear of them for more than a sentence or two.

40 See Ian MacKillop, *F. R. Leavis, A Life in Criticism* (London and New York, Allen Lane, 1995), 392. The other three books on this very short list, according to MacKillop, were Marjorie Grene's *The Knower and the Known*, Michael Polanyi's *Knowing and Being* and J. Andreski's *Social Sciences as Sorcery*. MacKillop claims that Leavis was particularly

impressed by the conclusion to the Collingwood volume, with its attack on White-head, known to him through a 1934 article in *Scrutiny* by James Smith.

41 See Ch. X, 'Philosophy as a Branch of Literature', *An Essay on Philosophical Method*, 199-220.

42 See Ch. XI of *The Principles of Art*.

43 *An Essay on Philosophical Method*, 211.

44 *An Essay on Philosophical Method*, 212.

45 See, for example, *The Idea of History*, 245-46 on '[T]he resemblance between the historian and the novelist': 'Each of them makes it his business to construct a picture which is partly a narrative of events, partly a description of situations, exhibition of motives, analysis of characters. Each aims at making his picture a coherent whole, where every character and every situation is so bound up with the rest that this character in this situation cannot but act in this way, and we cannot imagine him as acting otherwise. The novel and the history must both of them make sense; nothing is admissible in either except what is necessary, and the judge of this necessity is in both cases the imagination. Both the novel and the history are self-explanatory, self-justifying, the product of an autonomous or self-authorizing activity; and in both cases this activity is the *a priori* imagination'.

46 T. S. Eliot, 'Tradition and the Individual Talent' (1919), *Selected Essays* (London, Faber and Faber, 1932), 14. Writing in his essay on 'Metaphysical Poetry' in 1921, Eliot had claimed (famously) that while Tennyson and Browning do not 'feel their thought', 'A thought to Donne was an experience; it modified his sensibility'. See *Selected Essays*, 287. Both philosophically and historically, Collingwood prized the experience of thought.

47 *An Essay on Philosophical Method*, 218-219.

48 Cf. *The Idea of History*, 154.

49 *An Essay on Philosophical Method*, 219. Cf. *The Idea of History*, 252, '. . . a critic is a person able and willing to go over somebody else's thoughts for himself to see if they have been well done'.

50 F. R. Leavis, 'Criticism and Philosophy', *The Common Pursuit* (London, Chatto and Windus, 1952), 212-213. MacKillop, *F. R. Leavis, A Life in Criticism*, 392, finds it 'evident from Leavis's chapter on "Burnt Norton" in *The Living Principle* that he had known *The Idea of Nature* for some years'; but it also needs saying that Leavis not only 'knows' Collingwood, but is able to apply his thinking to the practice of criticism, Leavis invokes Collingwood's *Idea of Nature* against Eliot's 'reality' in the line '. . . human kind/Cannot bear very much reality'. See *The Living Principle*, *'English' as a Discipline of Thought* (London, Chatto and Windus, 1975), 166. For an articulation of re-creative thought in literary criticism, see Leavis's fellow *Scrutiny* editor, H. A. Mason, *Humanism and Poetry in the Early Tudor Period* (London, Routledge and Kegan Paul, 1959), 3, where he writes with respect to the responsibilities of critical scholarship that: 'Literature . . . cannot be thought of as something *totally* outside us . . .' Peter Jones, 'A Critical Outline of Collingwood's Philosophy of Art', *Critical Essays on the Philosophy of R. G. Collingwood*, links Collingwood with I. A. Richards in 'the view that we "imaginatively construct" works of art, which are thus not to be identified with physical objects' (42).

51 F. R. Leavis, 'Criticism' and Philosophy', *The Common Pursuit*, 213.

52 The term that Collingwood used to characterise his lifetime's wish to bring philosophy and history together.

Natural Science, History and Christianity: the Origins of Collingwood's Later Metaphysics

JAMES CONNELLY
Southampton Institute

INTRODUCTION

In this paper I explore certain aspects of the intellectual background to Collingwood's propounding of the conception of metaphysics as the disclosure of absolute presuppositions. I suggest that in response to the rise of logical positivism, and under the influence of his critical interest in anthropology, he laid aside the attempt to develop a speculative cosmology and embraced instead a view of metaphysics which displayed an affinity with the work of Michael Foster and A. N. Whitehead. I shall conclude by suggesting that the differences between Collingwood's different conceptions of metaphysics are in many ways less pronounced than they appear on the surface.

The Collingwood of the early 1920s was heavily influenced by the Italian idealists and in particular Gentile and de Ruggiero. This fact meant that he tended to devalue nature and natural science. For Gentile there could be no philosophy of nature and its presence in Hegel's system was intolerable. However, by 1928 Collingwood was moving towards a different view which asked the Kantian question 'what makes science possible?' and the answer he gave was the existence of a rational faith in the order of things. By 1933 Collingwood had moved (post Whitehead's *Process and Reality* of 1929) to a view which encompassed the possibility of a full scale philosophy of nature or cosmology. However, this enterprise was later abandoned and he reverted in *An Essay on Metaphysics* to a position resembling that of *Faith and Reason*, 'Reason is Faith Cultivating Itself' and 'The Nature of Metaphysical Study', that metaphysics articulates the presuppositions on which natural science at a particular stage in its development rests.[1]

This later position is similar in many ways to that found in Foster and some aspects of Whitehead. But it should be remembered that Collingwood pursues two distinct but related lines of thought in *An Essay on Metaphysics*. First, he develops a general argument concerning the nature and existence of absolute presuppositions, an argument explicitly related to the logic of question and answer. This is a doctrinal hardening (as it were) of similar positions he had previously advocated and it goes together with a new description of the activity of discovering and codifying these presuppositions as 'metaphysics'. Secondly, he gave examples of metaphysics as he now understands the term, and argues that historically particular constellations of absolute presuppositions, for example, those associated with Christianity, have a particular role to play in the development of natural science and civilization. The second argument presupposes some version of the first, that is, it presupposes the existence of a certain type of fundamental presupposition; but it does not presuppose the precise argument that Collingwood provides in terms of the logic of question and answer. Foster and Whitehead, for example, argue for the existence of unprovable first principles or presuppositions, but do so without the encumbrance of the logic of question and answer. There are many examples in *An Essay on Metaphysics* where Collingwood does the same. Neither Foster nor Whitehead dwell on the matter; neither identifies the search for such presuppositions with metaphysics; and both concentrate on the historical articulation of absolute presuppositions.

FOSTER, WHITEHEAD, SCIENCE AND CHRISTIAN THEOLOGY

From 1912 until the mid-1930s Collingwood met regularly with 'the Group' or the 'Cumnor Circle' a discussion circle of theologians and philosophers who shared a modernist approach to theology. Members included A. E. J. Rawlinson, F. A. Cockin, B. H. Streeter and Lily Dougall. Later, during the late 1920s through to 1939 Collingwood did a lot of work more specifically on the relation between science and religion and faith and reason. These researches bore fruit at various times in 'Reason is Faith Cultivating Itself', *Faith and Reason*, *The Idea of Nature* and *An Essay on Metaphysics*, together with related series of lectures, including two on the nature of metaphysical study. Foster and Whitehead were both at this time working on similar themes and topics, with, in many respects, strikingly similar conclusions. For example, Whitehead in *Science and the Modern World* (1926), *Process and Reality* (1929), *Adventures of Ideas* (1933) and *Modes of Thought* (1938) has a lot to say both about the task of philosophy as the search for presuppositions and also about the relationship between the presuppositions of modern science and the Christian Faith.[2] Foster in his articles 'The Christian Doctrine of Creation' (1934) and 'Christian Theology and Modern Science of Nature' (1935-6) was writing exclusively on the presuppositions of science and their relation to Christian theology; Collingwood (in the early 1930s) and Whitehead went further into trying to develop a contemporary metaphysics or cosmology adequate, as they saw it, to present day scientific thought.

In a number of his post-war papers and broadcasts Foster[3] refers approvingly to Collingwood's work, in particular *An Essay on Metaphysics* and *The Idea of Nature*. He clearly sees Collingwood's work as having affinities with his own. Here I wish to reverse the equation by asking whether Foster's work influenced Collingwood. Foster's account of the presuppositions of natural science and their relationship with Christianity, published in 1934, clearly finds later echoes in Part IIIa of *An Essay on Metaphysics*. In reading this and the preceding sections, it is hard not to think that Collingwood had taken careful notice of Foster's articles of the mid 1930s, even though he does not mention Foster by name; and I think that such a view is merited. However, Collingwood clearly also had other sources and influences, and he had already been working on this theme at the same time as Foster published his papers. For example, in early 1934 he lectured on 'The Nature of Metaphysical Study', (in which he explicitly discussed the presuppositions of modern science), and was already working at and lecturing on the themes which later emerged as *The Idea of Nature*; earlier in 1927 and 1928 he had published pieces on 'Reason is Faith Cultivating Itself' and *Faith and*

Reason in both of which he discussed, both philosophically and historically, the linkages between science, faith and presuppositions. It is likely, therefore, that the relationship between Foster and Collingwood was in this respect one of mutual reinforcement rather than clearcut indebtedness one way or the other. There is, however, one other connection worth mentioning: in 1935 Foster published his book *The Political Philosophies of Plato and Hegel*. Collingwood read this for the Clarendon Press, and the book as eventually published owed a great deal to his critical comments. His report for the press ran to a great many pages and was extremely detailed; Foster acknowledges Collingwood's help in his preface.

Foster's central contention was that a science of nature must rest on a philosophy of nature, and a philosophy of nature must in turn rest on a theological point of view. Foster's articles on 'The Christian Doctrine of Creation and the Rise of Modern Natural Science' and 'Christian Theology and Modern Science of Nature', which appeared in *Mind* between 1934 and 1936 have long been regarded as seminal works in the historical and philosophical re-examination of the relationship between science and religion. His fundamental thesis that the two were not antithetical but, on the contrary, that modern science of nature could only arise on presuppositions supplied by a Christianity purged of alien Greek influences, has been influential in work in the history and philosophy of science. Gradually, they have been given the attention that was their due.

Foster argues that if natural objects are conceived as unreal (because only forms or universals are considered real) modern natural science cannot develop because nature can at most be an appearance. Reality is to be found in the study of the forms which are eternal and known only by the intellect, not the senses. Nature might therefore at most be used to illustrate a truth known by the intellect, but it cannot be the source of evidence within scientific inquiry. Such inquiry, for Plato and Aristotle, consists in knowledge of a form through a definition of its essence, and this knowledge does not require empirical evidence. However, the emergence of the Christian religion, because it posited a God who created the world out of nothing, reversed matters. It led to a new conception of knowledge in which we come to understand and know nature through examination of objects in the natural world. We cannot know the form of things independently of this because there is no eternal form or blueprint which guided God in his creation of the natural world precisely because it was a creation ex nihilo and not the act of a demiurge. Thus modern natural science, characterised by its empirical seeking of evidence in (and experimentation upon) the natural world is made possible. In his articles Foster argues that not only is it possible to work back from an existing science of nature to its presuppositions, as Kant's critical method requires, but also that prior to the firm establishment of the modern sciences of nature philosophers ascribed to the world of nature those very characteristics which the modern science of nature must presuppose in it as the condition of its own possibility. Thus Descartes, for example, denied that final causes are operative in nature; and modern physics was based upon the presupposition that final causes are not operative in nature. Locke declared that the real essence of natural objects was unknowable; and the modern empirical sciences of nature presupposed that the real essence of their objects was unknowable. In a word: 'the early modern philosophers ascribed to nature the character which constituted it a possible object of modern natural science in advance of the actual establishment of that science.' (Foster, 1992, p. 66)

This was possible not because Locke or Descartes had proof of it, but because they were reliant on the Christian revelation of nature as created *ex nihilo* by God (Foster, 1992, p. 71). Experimental natural science, then, was historically contingent and could only come into being under certain historical circumstances. It rests upon presuppositions which are necessary to its being and which cannot be proved true by science itself:

> Every science of nature must depend upon presuppositions about nature which cannot be established by the methods of the science itself . . . the uniformity of nature is incapable of being established by the methods of inductive science . . . the possibility of . . . extending the method of mathematics to the science of nature depends upon a presupposition about nature which cannot itself be demonstrated, namely that nature is a homogeneous material substance, determined throughout by

subjection to universal and necessary laws. To assert the truth of what natural science presupposes is not science of nature but philosophy of nature. . . . Philosophy of nature is dependent in its turn upon theology . . .

The methods of modern science, precisely in so far as they differ from those of Greek science, must presuppose a philosophy of nature correspondingly different. But a different philosophy of nature in its turn presupposes a different theology. The transformation of theology by the introduction of elements from the Christian revelation involved as a necessary consequence a corresponding modification in the philosophy of nature . . . the modification of the philosophy of nature necessitated by the peculiarities of Christian theology is precisely that presupposed by the peculiarities of modern natural science.

(Foster, 1992, pp. 89-93)

There are two fundamental presuppositions of modern scientific method: 'the first [is] the assumption that the scientist has to look nowhere beyond the world of material nature itself in order to find the proper objects of his science, the second . . . that the intelligible laws which he discovers there admit of no exception.' (Foster, 1992, p. 133).

Both are consequences of the doctrine that the material world is the work, not of a Demiurge, but of an omnipotent creator. It is because a demiurge has to work in an alien material that he never wholly realises in it the idea which his reason conceives, so that the observer of the product, the object of whose search is to discover the idea of the producer, can never discover in the material product the object of his search, but only such an approximation as may enable him to conceive it as it is in that intelligible perfection in which it is present to the mind of the producer, but in none of his products. But a divine creator who is not limited by a recalcitrant material can embody his ideas in nature with the same perfection in which they are present to his intellect, so that the scientist can find in nature itself the intelligible objects of which he is in search, and not merely imperfect ectypes of them. Similarly, the laws of an omnipotent lawgiver cannot be related to the objects of his creation as ideals to which they more or less conform, but as rules to which their submission is absolute, both extensively, in the sense that there can be no exceptions to them, and intensively, in the sense that there can be in no given case a degree of submission which is less than perfect.

(Foster, 1992, pp. 133-4)

Nature is not divine, but other than God, hence a science of nature is possible without blasphemy or idolatry; and nature is not in principle mysterious – there is no mystery in nature which human intelligence cannot penetrate and dispel. This passage is very similar to a passage of Collingwood's which Foster later quotes with approval in one of his more popular pieces:

> The Platonic revival in natural science was possible . . . only because the revived Platonism was Platonism with a difference. Genuine Platonism holds out no hope of a scientific applied mathematics. It teaches that nothing in nature admits, strictly speaking, of mathematical description, for in nature there are no straight lines, no true curves, no equalities, but only approximations to these things . . . Genuine Platonism does not believe in a science of nature at all. It believes that nature is the realm of imprecision, no possible object of scientific knowledge. [But] Christianity, by maintaining that God is omnipotent and that the world of nature is a world of God's creating, completely altered this situation. It became a matter of faith that the world of nature should be regarded no longer as the realm of imprecision, but as the realm of precision. To say that a line in nature is not quite straight means for a Platonist that it is an approximation to a straight line, the result of a praiseworthy but not altogether successful attempt on the part of some natural thing to construct a straight line or to travel in one. For a Christian it cannot mean that. The line was drawn or constructed by God, and if God had wanted it to be straight it would have been straight. To say that it is not quite straight means therefore that it is exactly something else. The natural scientist therefore must find out what it exactly is.   (Collingwood, 1940, pp. 252-4)

According to Foster both presuppositions are consequences of the doctrine that the material world is the work not of a Demiurge, but of an omnipotent creator. The congruence is obvious. Later I shall say something about Foster and the genesis of *An Essay on Metaphysics*. But first I shall quote Whitehead to indicate a parallel line of thought:

> the greatest contribution of medievalism to the formation of the scientific movement . . . [was] the inexpugnable belief that every detailed occurrence can be correlated with its antecedents in a perfectly definite manner, exemplifying general principles. Without this belief the incredible labours of scientists would be without hope. It is this instinctive conviction . . . which is the motive power of research: that there is a secret, a secret which can be unveiled. How has this conviction been so vividly implanted in the European mind?
>
> When we compare this tone of thought in Europe with the attitude of other civilisations when left to themselves, there seems but one source for its origin. It must come from the medieval insistence on the rationality of God, conceived as with the personal energy of Jehovah and with the rationality of a Greek philosopher. Every detail was supervised and ordered: the search into nature could only result in the vindication of the faith in rationality. Remember that I am not talking of the explicit beliefs of a few individuals. What I mean is the impress on the European mind arising from the unquestioned faith of centuries. By this I mean the instinctive tone of thought and not a mere creed of words.
>
> In Asia, the conceptions of God were of a being who was either too arbitrary or too impersonal, inscrutable origin of things. There was not the same confidence as in the intelligible rationality of a personal being. I am not arguing that the European trust in the scrutability of nature was logically justified even by its own theology. My only point is to understand how it arose. My explanation is that the faith is the possibility of science, generated antecedently to the development of modern scientific theory, is an unconscious derivative from medieval theology.
>
> (Whitehead, 1932, pp. 15-16)

Whitehead, while being in broad agreement with Foster here, is nonetheless emphasising different aspects of the relationship between Christianity and natural science. Perhaps, as E. L. Mascall argues, it is best to take the views of Whitehead and Foster together and construe them as complementary:

> While Foster and Whitehead both derive the rise of modern natural science from the Christian conception of a God who is both free and rational, with the natural consequence of a world which is both contingent and regular, they tend to place their emphasis in different places. For Foster it is the *freedom* of God and the consequent *contingency* of the world in Christian thought that is the main stimulus provided by Christianity for modern science, in contrast with the logicism and necessitarianism of the Greeks; for Whitehead it is the *rationality* of God and the regularity of the world that is the main stimulus, in contrast with the views of God as either impersonal or altogether arbitrary in Asiatic thought. Foster explains why modern science did not arise in ancient Greece, Whitehead why it did not arise in India; but this difference only serves to bring out more clearly the point at issue, which is that it is precisely the *combination* of the two notions, and not either of them in isolation, which is presupposed by the application of the modern scientific method. For empirical science to arrive at all, there must be the belief – or at least the presumption – that the world is both contingent and regular. There must be regularities in the world, otherwise there will be nothing for science to discover; but they must be contigent regularities otherwise they would not need to be looked for, they could, at any rate if we were clever enough, be thought out *a priori*.
>
> (Mascall, 1956, pp.95-6)

COLLINGWOOD ON THE PRESUPPOSITIONS OF NATURAL SCIENCE

Let us return to Collingwood, starting with 'Reason is Faith Cultivating Itself' (1927), *Faith and Reason* (1928) moving on to his lectures on 'The Nature of Metaphysical Study' (1934) and concluding with *An Essay on Metaphysics* (1940). In the first two pieces Collingwood argues the general case that science as knowledge of the parts presupposes faith as knowledge of the whole; in the third he gives examples of particular presuppositions held by seventeenth century science; and in the fourth this is supplemented by an explicit statement of these presuppositions as derived from belief in the Christian God.

In 'Reason is Faith Cultivating itself' and *Faith and Reason* Collingwood argues that reason and faith are inseparable elements in knowledge:

> The details of the world are the proper theme of scientific thought; but its characteristics as a whole, its unity and the implications of that unity, are not matters for scientific inquiry. They are, rather, a foundation on which all scientific enquiry rests. . . .The scientist may be unconscious that the experiment which he is making rests upon his certainty that the universe as a whole is rational; but his unconsciousness of the fact does not alter the fact. Without an absolute confidence in the 'uniformity of nature', or whatever name he gives to the rationality of the universe, he would never try any experiments at all.
>
> (Collingwood, 1968, pp. 138 & 141)

> Faith cannot be the product of reason. . . .you cannot produce faith by arguing. Faith is presupposed in the argument itself. People do not, and never can, come to believe in God, or in anything else as a result of ratiocination. The function of ratiocination is not this, but the development or reasoned statement of what faith finds within itself.
>
> (1968, p. 118)

Seven years later, in 'The Nature of Metaphysical Study' (1934), Collingwood argues that in the seventeenth century metaphysics and natural science worked together in harmony and that the natural sciences at that time were based on two principles:

> (1) Nature works according to fixed and definite laws, which are exemplified in all that really exists and happens; and that we know in advance of experiment what the general nature of these laws is . . . Independently and in advance of experiment because unless we did know this, we should not know that experiment could teach us what we wanted to find out.
>
> (Collingwood, 1934a, p. 17)

(2) Things in nature are really measurable and whatever is not measurable is not real:

> This means that things in nature really are extended in space and moving in time, really possess shape and weight and number, but only seem to be, and in reality are not, coloured and scented and sonorous, hot and cold and the like. Whereas Aristotelian and medieval physics had tried in vain to produce a successful science of nature on the assumption that all these qualities were equally real, Galileo found it possible to advance and achieve solid results by substantially ignoring secondary qualities as mere appearances, and concentrating on primary qualities as alone real.
>
> (Collingwood, 1934a., p. 18)

He then goes on to discuss the relationship between these principles and the respective tasks of science and metaphysics:

> These two principles are the assumptions on which seventeenth-century science rested, and if that science was to be regarded as real knowledge of the real world these two assumptions must be true. But obviously physical science could not prove their truth; it could only begin to use its own methods when they had been assumed. Their truth was a matter for investigation by metaphysics. Consequently seventeenth-century metaphysics from Descartes to Locke, took this as one of its main tasks, to prove the truth of these two assumptions.
>
> (Collingwood, 1934a., p.18)

It will be noticed here that Collingwood writes of proving 'the truth of these two assumptions', just as Foster had written that 'to assert the truth of what natural science presupposes is not science of nature but philosophy of nature'. However, in *An Essay on Metaphysics* Collingwood converted talk of 'assumptions' into talk of 'absolute presuppositions' and went on to argue that these cannot be proved true or false. This appears to be a radically different doctrine from that shared by Collingwood and Foster in 1934. I will return to this issue later and for the present focus on the content of Collingwood's assertions in the

Essay, where he characterises the metaphysical implications of the Christian faith as a belief that:

> There is a world of nature; that this world of nature is a world of events; that throughout this world there is one set of laws according to which all movements or events, in spite of all differences, agree in happening; that nevertheless there are in this world many different realms. . . . This new analysis they called the 'Catholic Faith' . . . By believing in the Father they meant . . . absolutely presupposing that there is a world of nature which is always and indivisibly one world. By believing in the Son they meant absolutely presupposing that this one natural world is nevertheless a multiplicity of natural realms. By believing in the Holy Ghost they meant absolutely presupposing that the world of nature, throughout its entire fabric, is a world not merely of things but of events or movements . . . The presuppositions that go to make up this 'Catholic Faith' . . . have as a matter of historical fact been the main or fundamental presuppositions of natural science ever since.'
>
> (Collingwood, 1940, pp. 222-7)

These claims are in all essentials identical with Foster's assertions of five years earlier. There may be a difference in their respective understanding of the truth status of the claims made, but there is no difference in content.

CONTRAST BETWEEN COLLINGWOOD AND FOSTER

We have seen that there is obviously a marked similarity between Collingwood's claims in *An Essay on Metaphysics* and Foster's argument in his *Mind* essays. Neither offers a philosophy of nature as such. Rather they suggest that a science of nature presupposes an idea of nature which in turn rests on theology. They differ in that Foster does not go on to make any claim akin to Collingwood's view that absolute presuppositions are neither true nor false and neither does he make a general claim about the nature of metaphysics. Unlike Foster, Collingwood is fighting on a number of fronts. He is engaged in making specific historical claims about certain fundamental presuppositions and their relationship with Christianity and natural science at the same time as arguing for a characterisation of metaphysics as exclusively concerned with the uncovering of a particular type of presupposition. This difference arises from his desire to rescue metaphysics from recent attacks made on it.

It is perhaps only a coincidence that Foster's first paper came out in the issue of *Mind* which included Ayer's article on 'The Elimination of Metaphysics'; but it would seem that Collingwood learned from Foster while at the same time seeking to mount a defence of the possibility of metaphysical enquiry as such against the positivist attack. I will fill out this adumbration later. There are also, of course, significant differences between Foster and Collingwood. I will merely indicate one of them here. Collingwood argues that a necessary presupposition for a science of nature is that there is a natural world and that the existence of a natural world is not revealed by inspection. The article of faith that God created the world means that the idea of a world of nature is an absolute presupposition of natural science (Collingwood, 1940, p.219). In other words, Greek science, which was already a going concern prior to the rise of Christianity, was labouring under the misapprehension that the existence of a world of nature was revealed by the evidence of the senses. This misapprehension, which was part of Aristotle's metaphysical analysis, was corrected by Christianity. It is clear that Collingwood is here arguing in a slightly different manner to Foster. Foster's argument is that modern natural science was *impossible* on the Greek view. Collingwood's view, by contrast, was that science was already a going concern, and therefore necessarily making the presuppositions essential to its existence, but that Aristotle made a metaphysical mistake by misdescribing the presuppositions of the science of his day and falsely claiming that the existence of a world of nature is an observed fact rather than a fundamental presupposition of any natural science. It will immediately be noticed that Collingwood's argument here is not simply one to the effect that Aristotle failed to note down correctly the presuppositions that scientists were actually making. He is arguing that the belief in the existence of a natural world is *necessarily a presupposition,* and cannot be derived from inspection: 'the existence of natural things is not a fact discovered by experience but a presupposition without which we could never convert the data of experience into a science of nature' (Collingwood, 1940, p.217).

PRESUPPOSITIONS AND SCIENCE: TRUTH, FALSITY AND RELEVANCE

Talk of presuppositions in the context of natural science is often objected to in a number of ways. For example, Arthur Pap (1953), simply denies that science makes metaphysical presuppositions in any relevant or interesting sense. Others argue that 'revisionist' claims such as those made by Collingwood or Foster (and in the history of science by Hooykaas) assert a spurious causal connection between religion and science or that, even where the claims are true they are irrelevant to the work of the practising scientist. A. J. Ayer responded rather bluntly in this way; Rolf Gruner presents a subtle and historically informed argument which takes issue with, and offers a serious challenge to, the 'revisionist' claim that Christianity was somehow necessary for the emergence of natural science. Gruner is highly critical of 'revisionist' approaches to the relationship between science and Christianity. He does not deny everything that the 'revisionists' (including Foster) assert, but he takes issue with many matters of substance, and denies the necessary connection that writers such as Foster claimed to find between the two. Gruner accuses Foster and the others of asserting a necessary connection between Christianity and modern natural science such that the latter was bound to follow the former. He finds it easy to pour cold water on this contention and argues that the weaker argument, i.e. that the former made the latter possible, is too weak a thesis to be worth a great deal. It is wrong, I think, to assert that Foster claimed a necessary historical connection such that one was logically bound to follow the other. Foster was occupying a middle ground in which theological developments not only made modern natural science possible but actively nourished its possibility. Gruner makes no allowance for such a middle ground; rather he states the matter in terms of a rather harsh dilemma: either b) follows a) by necessary logical/historical inevitability (strong) or a paves the way for b) but b) might not have happened and therefore the success of b) cannot be credited to a). But this is to ignore the extent to which the occurrence of significant theological (or more broadly) intellectual developments not only make something possible, but by clearing impediments in its path actively encourage its flourishing.

In 'The Nature of Metaphysical Study' Collingwood explicitly states that metaphysics is concerned not only with uncovering assumptions (and thereby revealing the general conception of reality within which the special sciences operate) but also has the task of demonstrating the *truth* of those assumptions. Thus, although there is considerable similarity between this statement of the task of metaphysics and that later propounded in *An Essay on Metaphysics*, on this point there appears to be a very sharp difference indeed as in that book he states that absolute presuppositions are neither true nor false and cannot be justified or proved by metaphysics. Further, this conception of metaphysics is set up in open competition with others such as its characterisation as the science of pure being.

Foster would be unwilling to call absolute presuppositions neither true nor false. On the contrary, as a Christian he presumably believed presuppositions derived from the Christian faith to be true. He agrees, as we have seen, that presuppositions presupposed by a science cannot be proved true by that science itself; but he doesn't take Collingwood's view that their truth cannot be established. Here there is a clear difference, at least on the surface, between the two.[4] Again, the views of Whitehead and Collingwood converge, but in *Science and the Modern World* Whitehead makes a claim which Collingwood would be unlikely to accept:

> The faith in the order of nature which has made possible the growth of science is a particular example of a deeper faith. This faith cannot be justified by any inductive generalisation. It springs from direct inspection of the nature of things as disclosed in our own immediate present experience. There is no parting from your own shadow.
>
> (Whitehead, 1932, p. 23)

This is surely akin to the mistake Collingwood attributed to Samuel Alexander which, in his view amounted to claiming that 'empirical things are as it were visibly stamped with the categories' (Collingwood,

1945, p.162); and it is directly related to the mistake we saw Colling-wood convict Aristotle of. For Collingwood, absolute presuppositions are certain, but their certainty cannot derive from anything like perception or simple inspection. However, despite this, the similarities between many of Whitehead's statements and Collingwood's own are striking. For example, in *Adventures of Ideas*, Whitehead argues that 'All argument must rest on premises more fundamental than the con-clusions. Discussion of fundamental notions is merely for the purpose of disclosing their coherence, their compatibility, and the specialisa-tion's which can be derived from their conjunction', (Whitehead, 1933, p. 379). From which it follows that the task of the philosopher is one of 'assemblage' and 'disclosure' (Whitehead, 1938, pp. 267). Whitehead's formulation in *Process and Reality* is, in part, more ambitious, but fundamentally the same:

> the true method of philosophical construction is to frame a scheme of ideas, the best that one can, and unflinchingly to explore the interpretation of experience in terms of that scheme. . . . all constructive thought, on the various special topics of scientific interest, is dominated by some such scheme, unack-nowledged, but no less influential in guiding the imagination. The importance of philosophy lies in its sustained effort to make such schemes explicit, and thereby capable of criticism and improvement.
>
> (Whitehead, 1929, p. x)

Whitehead's conception of the task of philosophy is here very close to Collingwood's characterisation of the task of metaphysics. And both philosophers are clearly aware that the ideas which the metaphysician assembles and discloses have a peculiar character deriving from their status in systems of thought. From this follows both the issue of the sense (if any) in which they can be said to be true or false, and the sense (if any) which it makes to talk of constructing a metaphysical system or criticising or improving a system independently of the work of scientists themselves. In what sense can the metaphysician anticipate the results of presuppositions of the natural sciences? This is a point on which Collingwood for one was always ambiguous.[5]

I will not rehearse here the well known arguments which Colling-wood puts forward for the existence of absolute presuppositions, but press on by asking some important questions about their status, the development of Collingwood's philosophy and the relation between presuppositions and natural science. Suffice it to say here that absolute presuppositions exist as framework or boundary propositions to which the categories 'true' and 'false' do not and can not apply in the way in which they apply to normal propositions. Let us look at this a little more closely.

Two things strike me about Collingwood's claims concerning the truth status of absolute presuppositions. First, that he is right to claim that absolute presuppositions are not like normal propositions whose truth can be verified or demonstrated in a straightforward way. This is because they do not stand, as it were, within our everyday thought but rather constitute the boundary of that thought; as such, the methods for determining truth and falsehood which apply to everyday propositions do not apply to them.[6] Secondly, Collingwood is quite clearly restrict-ing the reference of the term 'true' to 'what can be verified'. This is because he has accepted Ayer's verification principle for the sake of argument (Collingwood, 1940, p.165). Thus, in the *Essay on Meta-physics* the terms 'truth' and 'falsity' mean no more than 'what can or cannot be verified', and this is a concession to Ayer's verification prin-ciple. But his agreement with Ayer is only on the surface: his concern is to show that, even granted Ayer's verification principle, metaphysics is still both possible and necessary and that if we deny the existence of absolute presuppositions we deny the very grounds of our own think-ing. He is arguing that a class of meaningful statements exists which are neither analytically true nor empirically verifiable. Thus, if the term 'true statement' *means* one that is empirically verifiable, the conclusion must follow that absolute presuppositions are neither true nor false. Ayer, of course, regards them as meaningless; Collingwood does not. However, given that he adopts this approach for the sake of argument in the course of his polemic against Ayer and others, and that what he is essentially drawing attention to is the different roles that absolute presuppositions and empirically verifiable propositions play in our thought, we should not go on to conclude that there is *no* possible sense in which absolute presuppositions can be true. The only conclusion we can validly draw is that if the term 'true' is artificially restricted they cannot be true, but that if the restrictions are removed they can be true or false. In the argument as he presents it Collingwood restricts the methodological possibilities to verification alone, but if there are other methods of ascertaining truth or falsity the impossibility of empirical verification does not preclude the possibility of another sense in which metaphysical presuppositions might be considered true or false.

On the assumption that this re-interpretation is permissible, how might absolute presuppositions be justified or rejected? How, in other words, is critical metaphysics possible? The answer is that absolute presuppositions do not occur singly, but as constellations of presuppositions which must be consupponible in that it must be logically possible for a person to suppose the entire constellation concurrently (Collingwood, 1940, p.66). They are bound up with historically developing systems of thought and inquiry and part of the task of the metaphysician is to trace how one set of absolute presuppositions turns into another.[7] This approach can be clearly seen in the comment from *The Idea of History* (dating from 1936):

> What Kant . . . wanted to do when he set out to justify our use of a category like causation, can in a sense be done; but it cannot be done on Kant's method, which yields a merely circular argument, proving that such a category can be used, and must be used if we are to have Newtonian science; it can be done by research into the history of scientific thought. All Kant could show was that eighteenth century scientists did think in terms of that category; the question why they so thought can be answered by investigating the history of the idea of causation. If more than this is required; if a proof is needed that the idea is true, that people are right to think in that way; then a demand is being made which in the nature of things can never be satisfied. How can we ever satisfy ourselves that the principles on which we think are true, except by going on thinking according to those principles, and seeing whether unanswerable criticisms of them emerge as we work?
>
> (Collingwood, 1946, pp. 229-230)

It would seem to follow from some of the foregoing that Collingwood's later position is far less radically different from his earlier position than it would at first glance appear. It is true that Collingwood denies that absolute presuppositions are true or false: but we have already seen that this is because he identifies truth and falsity with the possibility of verification or otherwise in the positivist sense. This still leaves open the possibility that there are other senses (which Collingwood for rhetorical purposes did not want to discuss in *An Essay on Metaphysics*) in which the philosopher can show absolute presuppositions to be 'true' as part of a coherent world of ideas. The quotation above shows that whatever view one takes it can be no simple matter to 'prove' either the truth or falsity of the basic presuppositions of a form of inquiry. There is no archimedean standpoint from which the claim can be validated and perhaps all we are left with is an argument flowing from coherence (or its absence). In this Collingwood in his later work is no great distance from his predecessors such as Bradley.[8]

We have seen above that Collingwood has strong reasons for denying that absolute presuppositions are true or false, at least in any everyday sense of those terms. And we have seen that one of the ways in which we can appraise their 'truth' or 'falsity' is by appreciating their role within systems of thought as they develop historically. However, there are other ways in which, it is sometimes suggested, we can apprehend the truth or falsity of our fundamental presuppositions. One of these arguments rests on the claim that the success of natural science proves the truth (or at least the relative superiority) of the fundamental presuppositions on which it rests. For example Mascall argues that:

> It might furthermore be suggested that the spectacular success which has attended the application of the scientific method supplies strong grounds for asserting that the presumption upon which modern science has proceeded is in fact true. There are, I know, people who say that, since all that the scientific method is made for is to discover regularities, there is no particular significance in the fact that it discovers them, just as, to adapt an example of Sir Arthur Eddington's, there is no particular significance in the fact that, if a fishing net has a two-inch mesh, it only catches fish that are more than two inches long. If

it did not discover regularities, what could the scientific method do? It is perhaps sufficient to answer 'Nothing'; the impressive fact is that, whereas the pre-empirical attempts to investigate the universe did discover nothing, or almost nothing, about it, the empirical method of modern science has discovered so much. To return to Eddington's illustration, there must as least be considerable significance in the fact that the ocean contained the fish which were caught, whatever smaller specimens may have eluded capture; and I should maintain that there is considerable significance in the fact that modern science has managed to find out so much about the universe and how to control its forces, which ancient Greece and Asia failed to discover. An advertisement of Imperial Chemical Industries some years ago characterised the difference between the old-fashioned alchemist and the modern organic chemist by saying that the latter practitioner, in contrast with his predecessor, is everywhere welcome because the changes which he renders possible are always for the better. It would, I think, be more realistic and less naive to say that the main difference is that the modern scientist usually succeeds in doing what he set out to do, whereas his predecessors usually failed. It is the success of the modern scientific method that is the really impressive thing about it. The scientific method may have originated in an act of blind faith, but, like some other acts of faith, it may claim to have been verified by its results.

(Mascall, 1956, p. 96)[9]

This sort of argument did not convince Collingwood. He does not deny the success of modern natural science; but he does deny that this proves the truth of its presuppositions. Thus in his manuscript on 'The Function of Metaphysics in Civilisation' he argues that:

But the propositions of metaphysics are not conclusions drawn, whether certainly or probably, from what we know of the world. What we know of the world is what we have found out about the world by thinking: this thinking implies certain presuppositions; and the function of metaphysical propositions is to serve as these presuppositions. They come at the beginning of our researches into the nature of the world, not at their end. If we work from one set of presuppositions we get one set of results which we call our knowledge of the world; if we work from another set of presuppositions, we get another set of results. In neither case do the results make the presuppositions probable. On the contrary, it is our acceptance of the presuppositions that makes the results certain.

(Collingwood, 1937-8, p. 39)

This of course is very close to *An Essay on Metaphysics*. It is interesting, therefore, to note that he argues in an identical manner in *An Essay on Philosophical Method*. The significance of this is that the *Essay* was written directly before 'The Nature of Metaphysical Study' and it therefore shows that whatever test Collingwood had in mind for proving true the assumptions of natural science it cannot have been the pragmatic test of the success of the science built upon them.

> The principles of induction, like those of exact science, are of two kinds. Some of them are purely logical principles, which begin by being certain and can never become either more or less so as induction proceeds. Others, when we come to consider them, prove to be not only assumptions but assumptions having little or no inherent plausibility; the most we can say for them is that they are not known to be untrue, and that it is expedient to assume them. Of these two kinds of principles, the first are logically presupposed by all induction whatever; they therefore cannot be established by inductive reasoning. Nor, in any case, could an inductive argument suffice to establish them; for being logical principles they must be categorically affirmed, and, as we have seen, the conclusions of induction are never more than probable.
>
> The second kind of principles (for instance, that the future will probably resemble the past, or the known the unknown) are necessary assumptions if we are going to argue, as in inductive thinking we always do, that because some S is P therefore probably all S is P. But these principles are in no sense confirmed by the successful conduct of the arguments based on them. Unless we assumed them, we could never conduct argu-

ments of this kind at all; but however long and however successfully we go on conducting arguments of this kind, we always know that these assumptions are assumptions and nothing more. What is increased by the success of our inductive inquiries is not the probability of such principles as that the future will resemble the past, but the probability of such hypotheses as that fermentation is due to micro-organisms. The principles never appear as conclusions, even in the modified sense in which conclusions exist in inductive thinking . . . The principles on which induction rests receive in return no support from the inductive process itself. Either they are certain from . . . beginning to end, or from beginning to end they are mere assumptions.

(Collingwood, 1933, pp. 166-7)

METAPHYSICS AS CATEGORY DISCLOSURE OR AS COSMOLOGY?

The answer to the question posed above is, then, that despite Collingwood's desire to produce a fully developed philosophy of nature or cosmology, he had the greatest difficulty in constructing a 'meta-metaphysics' able to justify such a strong metaphysical urge. But nonetheless Collingwood may have been committed to something not far removed from it. In so far as the rather strict conditions laid down upon metaphysical inquiry by *An Essay on Metaphysics* can be relaxed by the considerations adduced above, then so far it may be possible to envisage a form of metaphysics which not only articulated the absolute presuppositions of the science of the age, but also was critical in respect of them. What I have tried to show is that this is possible: however, whether Collingwood's or Whitehead's cosmology satisfies the relevant criteria is another matter. Collingwood, in seeking to justify the role of metaphysics in his later work, was certainly squeamish about making extravagant claims on its behalf. His purpose was to show the possibility of a form of metaphysics, not to offer a substantive metaphysical system.

In what sense is it possible to write a cosmology? Surely on Collingwood's own later account absolute presuppositions are neither true nor false; besides, they are either presupposed by science or they are not. If they are it is the task of the metaphysician to report them; if they are not it is his task not to report them. Given this, what space can possibly be left for creative metaphysics? The answer lies in the task of propounding a categorial scheme adequate to the activity of actually existing science. This would consist in drawing out the implications of the science of the present day, reporting its presuppositions, and showing how the whole becomes a system. In his cosmology and the related notebooks Collingwood is clearly trying to achieve a good characterisation of the idea of nature into which our thinking can fit. It is here that Collingwood's two conceptions of metaphysics come into play.[10] On the one hand, as we see in the lectures of 1934 and *The Idea of Nature* there is a need to understand the history of our engagement with the natural world and to understand the presuppositions fundamental to our prevalent conception at a given time; on the other, it is to delineate a framework adequate to present needs. In this latter case Collingwood is striving for a contemporary metaphysics which will do justice to, and unify, what is presupposed in present day scientific inquiry.

THE ORIGINS OF *AN ESSAY ON METAPHYSICS*

One thing is clear from the argument presented above, and that is that Collingwood in *An Essay on Metaphysics* only gave us half of the story. Certainly that book construes and exemplifies metaphysics in the weaker sense of category disclosure. But I have already argued that there were particular reasons for Collingwood's reluctance to offer a full-blooded metaphysics, and hinted that these reasons are to be found in part in his acceptance of Ayer's verification principle and also in Collingwood's response to some of his influences in the work of Whitehead and Foster. Let me now try to make good some of these claims and to offer further suggestions concerning the genesis of the *Essay on Metaphysics*.

The themes Collingwood addresses in the *Essay* and the answers he gave were not entirely new to his thinking in the late 1930s, but can be traced back to his earliest writings. What *was* new, however, was the identification of the activity he describes with *metaphysics* and also the particular form the argument took. The explanation for this lies in the genesis of the work – in the stimuli which prompted Collingwood to offer the *Essay* to the Clarendon Press. In my view the genesis of *An Essay on Metaphysics* owes much to the influence on Collingwood of two factors: a) his work in anthropology and b) the work of Ayer and Foster together with his election as Waynflete Professor of Metaphysical Philosophy in 1935.

Anthropology
It is now well known that in the mid-1930s Collingwood took a great interest in anthropological writing and forms of explanation, and that he wrote a book length manuscript on the subject. It is also clear that a particular influence was E. Evans-Pritchard's *Witchcraft, Oracles and Magic Among the Azande*. This book undoubtedly influenced Collingwood's thinking concerning absolute presuppositions and their historical and cultural relativity, and the nature of science, religion and civilisation (see James, 1997). I shall try to make good this claim.

Collingwood was probably the first person to quote *Witchcraft, Oracles and Magic* in print and it is fairly certain that he read the book prior to publication. The passage he quotes runs as follows: 'Let the reader consider any argument that would utterly demolish all Zande claims for the power of the oracle. If it were translated into Zande modes of thought it would serve to support their entire structure of belief.' (Evans-Pritchard, 1937, pp. 319-20). This is quoted on page 8 of *The Principles of Art*, a book which contains, in its chapter on art as magic, a summary account of Collingwood's more extensive writing on magic and anthropology. So far so interesting: but I want to make a further and stronger claim about the influence of Evans-Pritchard. My suggestion is that Collingwood's reading of *Witchcraft, Oracles and Magic* materially influenced the formulation of his doctrine of metaphysics as presented in the 1940 *Essay* and its immediate predecessor, the unpublished manuscript 'The Function of Metaphysics in Civilisation'. I am not suggesting that it was the only influence, nor that Collingwood could not have formulated his views independently of this work; I am merely suggesting that the form it took, and some of its content, would have been otherwise in the absence of his reading of Evans-Pritchard.

The influence of Evans-Pritchard is most noticeable, not surprisingly, in the chapter 'Religion and Natural Science in Primitive Society'. In that chapter we find the following passage:

> Anthropologists tell us of peoples who believe that there is no such thing as natural death. They think, we are assured, that every instance of death is due to magic. If that is so there might be peoples who hold the same belief about everything whatever . . . It might be fancied that the mere course of experience would suffice to destroy it . . . An absolute presupposition cannot be undermined by the verdict of 'experience', because it is the yard-stick by which 'experience' is judged. To suggest that 'experience' might teach my hypothetical savages that some events are not due to magic is like suggesting that experience might teach a civilised people that there are not twelve inches in a foot and thus cause them to adopt the metric system. As long as you measure in feet and inches, everything you measure has dimensions composed of those units. As long as you believe in a world of magic, that is the kind of world in which you live. If any group or community of human beings ever held a pan-magical belief about the world, it is certainly not 'experience' that could shake it. Yet certainly it might be shaken. It might be shaken through the influence of a very powerful tribesman who found himself taking a different view; or by the prestige of some other community, accepted and revered in the first instance as extremely powerful magicians, and later found to reject and despise it.
>
> (Collingwood, 1940, pp. 193-4)

This is very clearly a reference to *Witchcraft, Oracles and Magic* both in respect of the denial of natural death and also in respect of the way in which experience does not undermine the belief. In 'The Function of Metaphysics in Civilisation' Collingwood presents a slightly more developed account of the idea of a 'catalogue raisonée' than that found in the *Essay*. This account argues the case that within a living system of thought, the appearance of contradictions is frequently false because in practice principles or beliefs are employed depending on case and context.

> [in] a *catalogue raisonée* . . . each principle is not merely stated but expanded and commented on in detail, showing how it is used in being applied to this or that kind of case. By a system of principles I mean a treatment in which the relations between these principles form an integral part of the exposition; so that if two principles A and B are inconsistent, an inquiry is instituted into the whole method by which this inconsistency is overcome in the actual application of them . . . The presence of a given item in a metaphysical system is a question of fact . . . the metaphysician . . . has to settle it . . . by studying the actual way in which the people whose thought he is analysing treat their presuppositions. It is theoretically possible that these people should habitually think in such a way that they react to certain types of situation by applying principles which in other types of case they would not dream of applying, though they could give no reason why these principles should apply in one type of case and not in the other. In such circumstances it is not the metaphysician's business to invent a reason. His subject matter presents itself to him simply as a series of juxtaposed facts, and that is how he must report it. When he tries to present it systematically, the nearest approach he can make to a system is to point out that although abstractly considered the principles he enumerates might conflict with one another, in fact they do not conflict because they apply to different groups of cases. The *status* of a case in one or other group determines what principle it shall fall under.
>
> (Collingwood, 1937-8, pp. 31-2)

This passage clearly bears the imprint of Part III, Chapter IV of *Witchcraft, Oracles and Magic* – the chapter quoted in *The Principles of Art*. The title of this chapter is 'Problems that arise from consultation of the poison oracle', and Collingwood was clearly impressed by the way in which the Azande system of belief was flexible enough to resolve apparent contradictions in its actual application. To appreciate the full flavour of the comparison, it is necessary to quote Evans-Pritchard at some length.

Azande are dominated by an overwhelming faith which prevents them from making experiments, from generalising contradictions between tests, between verdicts of different oracles, and between all the oracles and experience. To understand why it is that Azande do not draw from their observations the conclusions we would draw from the same evidence, we must realise that their attention is fixed on the mystical properties of the poison oracle and that its natural properties are of so little interest to them that they simply do not bother to consider them . . . If a Zande's mind were not fixed on the mystical qualities of *benge* and entirely absorbed by them he would perceive the significance of the knowledge he already possesses. As it is the contradiction between his beliefs and his observations only become a generalised and glaring contradiction when they are recorded side by side in the pages of an ethnographic treatise.

I have collected every fact I could discover about the poison oracle . . . and built all these jottings into a chapter on Zande oracles. The contradictions in Zande thought are then readily seen. But in real life these bits of knowledge do not form part of an indivisible concept, so that when a man thinks of *benge* he must think of all the details I have recorded here. They are functions of different situations and are uncoordinated. Hence the contradictions so apparent to us do not strike a Zande. If he is conscious of a contradiction it is a particular one which he can easily explain in terms of his own beliefs.

. . . Azande observe the action of the poison oracle as we observe it, but their observations are always subordinated to their beliefs and are incorporated into their beliefs and made to explain them and justify them. Let the reader consider any argument that would utterly demolish all Zande claims for the power of the oracle. If it were translated into Zande modes of thought it would serve to support their entire structure of belief. For their mystical notions are eminently coherent, being interrelated by a network of logical ties, and are so ordered that they never too crudely contradict sensory experience but, instead, experience seems to justify them.

(Evans-Pritchard, 1937, pp. 318-320)

And a later passage makes very clear the misrepresentation that Evans-Pritchard thought inevitable when real practices were rendered abstract and placed coldly side by side within the pages of an academic treatise:

> I am aware that my account of Zande magic suffers from lack of co-ordination. So does Zande magic. Magical rites do not form an interrelated system, and there is no nexus between one rite and another. Each is an isolated activity, so that they cannot all be described in an ordered account. Any description of them must appear somewhat haphazard. Indeed, by treating them all together . . . I have given them a unity by abstraction that they do not possess in reality. This lack of co-ordination between magical rites contrasts with the general coherence and inter-dependence of Zande beliefs in other fields . . . Throughout I have emphasised the coherency of Zande beliefs when they are considered together and are interpreted in terms of situations and social relationships. I have tried to show also the plasticity of beliefs as functions of situations. They are not indivisible ideational structures but are loose associations of notions. When a writer brings them together in a book and presents them as a conceptual system their insufficiencies and contradictions are at once apparent. In real life they do not function as a whole but in bits. A man in one situation utilises what in the beliefs are convenient to him and pays no attention to other elements which he might use in different situations. Hence a single event may evoke a number of different and contradictory beliefs among different persons. I hope that I have persuaded the reader of one thing, namely, the intellectual consistency of Zande notions. They only appear inconsistent when ranged like lifeless museum objects.
>
> (Evans-Pritchard, 1937, pp. 540-1)

I hope that this is sufficient to show that Evans-Pritchard's work[11] was at least one of the factors uppermost in Collingwood's mind when he was composing *An Essay on Metaphysics*; but what of the others?

Foster and Ayer
For the effect that the work of Foster and Ayer had on Collingwood we only need to look at the dates. Foster was publishing the seminal articles

already discussed in 1934-6; Ayer published an article on 'The Elimination of Metaphysics' in *Mind* 1934 (in the same volume as Foster) and *Language Truth and Logic*, which was devoted to the same enterprise, was published in 1936. Meanwhile in 1935 Collingwood was elected to the Waynflete Chair of Metaphysical Philosophy.

It is evident that Collingwood took Ayer's challenge to metaphysics and the challenge to his own professing of metaphysics in Magdalen College seriously and wished to rebut it. But how best to achieve a successful rebuttal? It is perhaps fanciful, but surely not far from the truth, to imagine him re-reading the volume of *Mind* in which Foster's first paper and Ayer's article were published and asking the question how is metaphysics possible in the face of Ayer's challenge? His answer was to accept (as we have seen) much of what Ayer says, but to argue that this still leaves something standing after Ayer's demolition. What was left standing? – Absolute presuppositions as a subject matter suitable for the attention of the philosopher. The next step was simply to christen the activity of elucidating and articulating these absolute presuppositions 'metaphysics'. And if this seemed a little thin, the best way to bolster the argument was by historical example and some strong claims for the importance within natural science of the sorts of presupposition that logical positivism denied the existence of. And this is exactly what he found in Foster's articles: there he finds an example of metaphysics (in his newly redefined sense of the term) in the historical analysis of presuppositions together with the claim that experimental natural science of the sort of which Ayer and logical positivist approve, is possible only on the basis of certain absolute presuppositions which it cannot justify itself and which emerged historically out of belief in the Christian religion. Thus, from the conjunction of Ayer's negative criticism, (together with Collingwood's determination to show that something can be salvaged for metaphysics), and the example of Foster's article, emerges *An Essay on Metaphysics* Parts I and III. In other words Collingwood christens the articulation of what he now comes to call absolute presuppositions 'metaphysics': it is a minimalist metaphysics which escapes Ayer's philosophical scorched earth policy.

It is important to note also that Collingwood wanted to mount his argument independently of the help of his idealist contemporaries and forebears. He saw clearly that if he simply invoked the shades of the idealist great and good he would not succeed in overwhelming the young whippersnapper Ayer and his supporters. On the contrary, the only way to succeed was to restate the case afresh, to assert by new argument a form of metaphysics which could survive even the greatest logical positivist onslaught. He showed that, even under the handicap of conceding the terms of debate to positivism, a minimalist metaphysics could survive. He then reinterpreted the work of philosophers accordingly and showed that despite the sweeping scepticism of positivism they were nonetheless engaged in something real and valuable. Aristotle and Kant are thus rescued from philosophical oblivion when judged against his new criterion of metaphysical respectability and contemporaries such as Foster, Alexander and Whitehead are similarly fig-leafed as reformed metaphysicians. But there clearly still remains a residual problem. Take Whitehead, for instance. It is easy to show (as we have above) that in some of his moods he can be construed as a metaphysician in Collingwood's sense. But it is far less clear that the speculative aspects of, for example, *Process and Reality* could possibly satisfy the stringent criterion erected in *An Essay on Metaphysics*. That criterion, at least in appearance, is scarcely less stringent than the verification principle it was designed to supplant. However, I have already argued that the form of Collingwood's argument was in large measure shaped by the agenda of those he was opposing. Given this, it is perhaps reasonable to suggest that in practice he would in the end have been happy to apply a less stringent criterion. His target in the *Essay* was quite specific and his response was designed merely to show that metaphysics could not be eliminated. To do this all Collingwood had to show was that at least a minimal metaphysics could survive, even on the terms set by logical positivism itself. This left open the question of whether something more would also be possible and permissible. This he never went on to address explicitly; but now the threat of logical positivism is long gone, perhaps we should expect more abundant and exotic metaphysical blooms to grow in the soil Collingwood saved from Ayer's scorched earth policy.

References

Ayer, A. J. (1984) *Philosophy in the Twentieth Century.* London: Unwin Paperbacks.

Collingwood, R. G. (1924) *Speculum Mentis.* Oxford: Clarendon Press.

Collingwood, R. G. (1933a) *An Essay on Philosophical Method.* Oxford: Clarendon Press.

Collingwood, R. G. (1933b) 'Notes towards a Metaphysic'. Bodleian Library.

Collingwood, R. G. (1934a) 'The Nature of Metaphysical Study'. Bodleian Library.

Collingwood, R. G. (1934b) 'Sketch of a Cosmological Theory'. Bodleian Library.

Collingwood, R. G. (1939) *An Autobiography.* Oxford: Clarendon Press.

Collingwood, R. G. (1940) *An Essay on Metaphysics.* Oxford: Clarendon Press.

Collingwood, R. G. (1945) *The Idea of Nature.* Oxford: Clarendon Press.

Collingwood, R. G. (1946) *The Idea of History.* Oxford: Clarendon Press.

Collingwood, R. G. (1968) *Faith and Reason*, edited by L. Rubinoff. Chicago: Quadrangle.

Douglas, M. (1980) *Edward Evans-Pritchard.* New York: Viking Press.

Evans-Pritchards, E. E. (1937) *Witchcraft, Oracles and Magic Among the Azande.* Oxford: Clarendon Press.

Foster, M. B. (1957) ' "We" in Modern Philosophy', in Mitchell, B. (ed.), *Faith and Logic*, London: Allen & Unwin.

Foster, M. B. (1992) *Creation, Nature, and Political Order in the Philosophy of Michael Foster.* Edited by C. Wybrow. Lewiston: Edwin Mellen Press.

Hooykaas, R. (1972) *Religion and the Rise of Modern Science.* Edinburgh: Scottish Academic Press.

James, W. (1997) 'Collingwood, Evans-Pritchards and Anthropology', paper presented to Collingwood Conference, st. Catherine's College, Oxford, July 1997.

Mascall, E.L. (1956) *Christian Theology and Natural Science.* London: Longmans.

Mays, W. (1977) *Whitehead's Philosophy of Science and Metaphysics.* The Hague: Nijhoff.

Pap, A. (1953) 'Does Science Have Metaphysical Presuppositions?', in *Readings in Philosophy of Science*, ed. P .P. Wiener. New York: Scribner's.

Peacocke, A. R. (1979) *Creation and the World of Science.* Oxford: Clarendon Press.

Whitehead, A. N. (1929) *Process and Reality.* Cambridge University Press.

Whitehead, A. N. (1932) *Science and the Modern World.* Cambridge University Press.

Whitehead, A. N. (1933) *Adventures of Ideas.* Cambridge University Press

Whitehead, A. N. (1938) *Modes of Thought.* Cambridge University Press.

Wolpert, L. (1994) *The Unnatural Nature of Science*, London: Faber.

Notes

1   Of course Collingwood did not limit metaphysics to the articulation of the pre-suppositions of natural science alone, but as this paper is concerned primarily with the philosophy of science I shall, for convenience, write as though he did.

2   Whitehead's work includes both aspects of Collingwood's in that he addresses the role of presuppositions in the history of science as well as attempting to develop his own speculative cosmological metaphysics in *Process and Reality*.

3   Michael Foster was a Student of Christ Church who had studied at the University of Tubingen in the late 1920s. He was a commentator on Hegel, and published papers and a book on Hegel. He was apparently a rather austere character; after the war he

became a Buchmanite, committed to the doctrines of Moral Re-armament. His last book, *Philosophy and Mystery* was published in 1957. In 1959 he committed suicide.

4 In addition, he accuses Collingwood of historical relativism, see Foster, 1957, p. 202.

5 See, for example, the comments on Hegel in *An Essay on Metaphysics,* pp. 271-2 and *The Idea of Nature*, pp.127-132.

6 For a strikingly similar line of thought see Wittgenstein in *On Certainty*. For example, he writes that 'It may be . . . that *all enquiry on our part* is set so as to exempt certain propositions from doubt, if they are ever formulated. They lie apart from the route travelled by enquiry' (§88).' A few remarks later he says that 'I did not get my picture of the world by satisfying myself of its correctness; nor do I have it because I am satisfied of its correctness. No: it is the inherited background against which I distinguish between true and false (§94). In a later passage he makes it clear that there is something peculiar about referring to certain propositions as either *true* or false: 'If the true is what is grounded, then the ground is not true, nor yet false' (§205); and this is because these propositions occupy a unique position in our inquiries, 'the *questions* that we raise and our *doubts* depend on the fact that some propositions are exempt from doubt, are as it were like hinges on which those turn' (§341).

7 Collingwood is not necessarily committed to the view that all absolute presuppositions change. Some, contingently, might be made *semper, ubique, ab omnibus* (Collingwood, 1940, p.47); some are necessary to the very existence of natural science (Ibid., p.215, and 1945, p.30); there is no reason to suppose that Collingwood regards transcendental and basic logical terms as subject to historical change. In *An Essay on Metaphysics* he is silent on this, but he is certainly not necessarily committed to denying that certain basic categories are universal and necessary.

8 On the relation between Bradley and Collingwood see my 'Bradley, Collingwood and the "Other" Metaphysics', in *Bradley Studies*, Vol. 3, No. 2, 1997.

9 More recently practising scientists such as Lewis Wolpert have also argued this way. See Wolpert (1994).

10 On Collingwood's two conceptions of metaphysics in its relation to Bradley, see my 'Bradley, Collingwood and the "Other" Metaphysics'.

11 For an account of Evans-Pritchard's work in relation to these themes, see Douglas (1980), chapter nine on 'Contradiction'.

Tales of Enchantment
Collingwood, Anthropology, and the 'Fairy Tales' Manuscripts*

WENDY JAMES

Institute of Cultural and Social Anthropology, Oxford

After half-a-century and more, the experience of reading R. G. Colling-wood's writings can prompt a surprising sense of recognition in the reader. This is true in some quite particular ways for the anthropologist, who today finds a prophetic quality in Collingwood's vision of a 'historical method' exploring reflexively the ways in which human beings have thought and lived. The kind of questions being posed today in social, cultural, and general anthropology closely echo many of those outlined by Collingwood in relation to the 'historical' understanding of human reason, feeling, and action. Anthropology had been oriented more to varieties of scientific positivism in the early part of the century, but it was at a turning point in Britain in the 1930s. It is possible to argue that Collingwood himself had some influence on the way it then developed, and is still developing, as I shall seek to explain in detail elsewhere. There can be no doubt that the subject of anthropology has drawn closer to what Collingwood saw as the essentially philosophical enquiries of historical practice. These focus not only upon the way human beings have thought, at different times and places, as individuals; but also and inextricably as participants in shared forms of life, linked with others in a mutually defining choreography of action and experience.

In the growth of Collingwood's own work, I believe it is worth considering how he responded critically to the orthodox anthropology of his day and associated himself rather with the newer attitudes and methods developing in the 1930s. He was often dismissive of the mistaken naturalism of well-known mainstream anthropological writings; several references can be found for example in *The Idea of History*, where anthropology is opposed, as 'a kind of natural history of man', to history.[1] 'Herder is thus the father of anthropology', he writes, in distinguishing the variation of human physical types and the associated range of manners and customs, but Herder's conception was not a genuinely historical one. 'There is still no conception of a people's character as having been made what it is by that people's historical experience', and against the racism of Herder he suggests that following the work of modern anthropologists 'We know that physical anthropology and cultural anthropology are different studies'.[2] He makes a dismissive reference to historical positivism 'as practised by the naturalistic anthropologists and their chief, Sir James Frazer',[3] and of course argues throughout *The Idea of History* and elsewhere that there cannot be a generally valid conception of human nature, that 'there can never be a non-historical science of mind.'[4] Although the label 'social anthropology' was established at Oxford as early as 1910 with the title of R. R. Marett's Readership, Collingwood did not often use it, possibly feeling uncomfortable with the hint of scientism it carried.[5] Indeed A. R. Radcliffe-Brown, following Marett as the first Professor of Social Anthropology at Oxford from 1937, later campaigned for his discipline to be recognized as 'the theoretical natural science of human society'.[6] Collingwood had clearly been more comfortable with 'cultural' anthropology, a broad category already associated with the world of museum archaeology and ethnology. T. K. Penniman, the Curator of the Pitt Rivers Museum, had classed 'social' anthropology as a subdivision of the 'cultural' variety.[7]

Whatever the changing terminology, there is plenty of evidence in Collingwood's writings from the mid-1930s of a growing interest in the newer, linguistically sensitive and humanistic anthropology based on personal enquiries in the field. This tradition was represented especially well in the key figures of Bronislaw Malinowski based at the LSE and of E. E. (later Sir Edward) Evans-Pritchard. There is a particular sympathy, I believe, between the work of Evans-Pritchard and that of Collingwood. Evans-Pritchard was trained originally in Modern History at Oxford in the early 1920s, and then attended Malinowski's anthropology seminars in London. He proceeded to carry out research in Africa intermittently from the late 1920s to 1940 while maintaining links with Oxford, later succeeding to the Chair of Social Anthropology in 1946. Collingwood draws directly and indirectly on the newer humanistic anthropology in, for example, *The Principles of Art* (1938), *An Essay on Metaphysics* (1940), and *The New Leviathan* (1942).[8] But beyond the published evidence of his interest in anthropology, there is the little-known set of fascinating manuscripts known as the 'Fairy Tales' of 1936-7.[9] Anthropology at the time was supposed to be, roughly speaking, the comparative study of peoples remote in time or place from 'ourselves' comfortably ensconced in European civilization, and mainly important for the light the evidence of their customs might throw on the origins of our own civilization. Collingwood's manuscripts go far beyond his published work in indicating the depth of his interest in and familiarity with the subject matter of anthropology and its internal debates. They also demonstrate eloquently how he saw this field of study as a 'branch of historical science'.

Interestingly for us in anthropology, later commentaries from American and continental philosophers have recognized, at least from the 1960s, the 'anthropological' qualities even of Collingwood's published work (judged by post-war criteria).[10] This has become quite an orthodoxy among philosophers. Thus for example Stephen Toulmin used an 'anthropological' perspective from which to criticize, by implication, the Oxford which still did not recognize the 'justice of Collingwood's analysis' (he can only have meant the Sub-Faculty of Philosophy, rather than the anthropologists). He invokes Collingwood in attacking Peter Strawson's unimaginative starting point of 'our everyday conceptual framework': 'Just *whose* "everyday conceptual framework" are we to take seriously? Consider a community of animists living in a nomadic forest culture. Is it entirely clear that they must necessarily share, e.g., Euclidean ideas about spatial relations, or our own industrial, citified notions of causality? People who grow up in circular huts . . . even experience different optical illusions from those of us who live in square houses . . .'[11] But this imagined Collingwoodian response goes almost too far, in its anthropological relativism, for the real Collingwood. His speculations on variation in the thought systems of other places and other times were always directed to concrete, not purely imagined difference. They were bound by the discipline of careful evidence, and by the assumptions of inter-translatability, the fragility of systematic thought as such, and the interpenetration of archaic with new forms. These assumptions, traceable also in the work of Evans-Pritchard, have become absorbed into today's anthropology and could be said to mark our discipline today as distinctly one of the humanities.

Among philosophers, Sir Isaiah Berlin has helped maintain a particular 'Collingwoodian' link with anthropology. In his writings and lectures (including at least one I remember well in the early 1970s when he was invited by Evans-Pritchard to the Institute of Social Anthropology in Oxford) he alerted students to the world of Vico. Berlin represented Vico as the inventor of a new field of social knowledge, including social anthropology, with Collingwood among his 'progeny'.[12] It was Collingwood personally who had alerted Berlin to the translation he had done of Croce's book on Vico, and had urged him to read it. 'This opened my eyes to something new. Vico seemed to be concerned with the succession of human cultures – every society had, for him, its own vision of reality, of the world in which it lived . . .'[13]

It was in 1932 that the first indication of Evans-Pritchard's interest in Collingwood appeared, with his very appreciative review in *Man* (published by the Royal Anthropological Institute) of the second edition of *Roman Britain*.[14] At this time, anthropology in Oxford (outside the Pitt Rivers Museum) was still effectively the domain of R. R. Marett, who drew a wide range of practitioners and students to his seminars at Exeter College. The intellectual agenda of Marett's circle was still however dominantly that of the naturalistic evolutionary anthropology which had developed from the late nineteenth century on. Within the next few years, both Evans-Pritchard and Collingwood were to write significant critiques of this agenda, and to bring anthropological studies more convincingly into the fold of the humanities. Evans-Pritchard was the first to do this, with his 1932-3 lectures in Cairo on Tylor, Frazer, Lévy-Bruhl and Pareto.[15] He had already finished his Azande research in the Sudan and his first period of fieldwork among the Nuer, had been publishing ethnographic articles about these and other Sudanese peoples since 1928, and was now bringing his field experience to bear on theoretical questions. The first Cairo lecture for example on 'The Intellectualist (English) Interpretation of Magic' contained criticisms of Tylor and Frazer while deploying some of his own Zande field data in his arguments for the intelligibility of 'witchcraft' beliefs, the general human capacity for clever argument, and the historically enduring character of cultural axioms. This first paper, and the second which dealt in a subtle and appreciative way, if a critical one, with Lévy-Bruhl's theory of primitive mentality, were written while Evans-Pritchard was already drafting his first major book, *Witchcraft, Oracles and Magic among the Azande* (Oxford, 1937). It is clear from some of Evans-Pritchard's later commentaries and elaborations of his views on Lévy-Bruhl that the book was designed in part as an answer, from the field, to the theories of the latter. Having dealt with the leading approaches of the time in the preliminary papers and having secured their publication, the book itself did not need to refer to them and could stand on its own merits.

The point I wish to make here is that these early critical papers, together with a series of fairly straightforward, descriptive articles on the Azande, were part of Evans-Pritchard's preparing the ground for the writing of what was to become a classic text, combining fieldwork with sophisticated theoretical analysis and a philosophical ambition not yet seen in anthropology. In a manner which remains striking, the account itself highlights the inner dialectics of debate among the Azande about the moral nature of human beings, about life, and death, reponsibility and political regulation (as well as the questions of 'causation' and 'rationality' for which it has been most often remembered). Moreover, these are not explored as a closed cultural system, as some commentators have suggested, but are historically situated within the changing patterns of political and judicial control resulting from the incorporation of parts of the old Zande empire into the Anglo-Egyptian Sudan in the early years of this century. Evans-Pritchard also wrote extensively on Zande history, folklore, and a range of other domains of practical and artistic life among these people. This further work, much of it published many years later, is less well known than his sparkling monograph, but testifies to his temperament and gifts as a historian as well as a field anthropologist.[16] In particular, Evans-Pritchard re-invigorated the study of what had long been dubbed 'folklore'. Together with his younger colleague Godfrey Lienhardt, he fostered after the war a new generation of research in this field, re-shaping and dignifying its subject-matter as 'oral literature' and claiming for the arts of spoken language a new respect from sociologists, historians and literary critics alike, an effort which Collingwood would surely have applauded. Among the achievements of Evans-Pritchard and Lienhardt in this field was their founding, together with the linguist Wilfred Whiteley, of the important series *The Oxford Library of African Literature*, published by the Clarendon Press at Oxford from 1964 over the subsequent two decades or so. An early volume in the series was devoted to a selection from Evans-Pritchard's own collection of Zande folk tales.[17]

It was in the early to mid-1930s that Collingwood's work began to encompass questions parallel to those which were concerning Evans-Pritchard and to pursue very similar lines of enquiry, though from the perspective of a philosopher whose 'fieldwork' was concerned with evidence from remote times, rather than from the living societies of remote places. As far as I am aware, Collingwood had not drawn on any anthropological writings or evidence in his publications or in his teaching before this time. Even the short manuscript of 1933 'Outline of a Theory of Primitive Mind' is concerned with general psychological themes and not with ethnographic evidence or the concepts of anthropology.[18] But there seems to have been a change at about this time. I think it is reasonable to ask the question as to what might have stimulated this interest, and I would like to suggest that one factor was an increasing exposure to ethnographic monographs and anthropological debate as a result of his work with the Oxford University Press. As a Delegate of the OUP (from 1928-41), he was likely by the 1930s to be reading quite a number of anthropology manuscripts submitted. He is almost certain to have seen Evans-Pritchard's manuscript text of 'Witchcraft, Oracles and Magic among the Azande', the major bulk of which was submitted in early 1935. It was offered to the Press with a letter of recommendation from Marett, who was encouraging Evans-Pritchard to return to Oxford at this time. Although they recognized that the book was a valuable anthropological study and that its publication was desirable, the Delegates were concerned that it was 'narrowly specialized, and previous experience shows that the public ready to buy books of this kind is not large, and that a new loss on the whole enterprise must be expected.'[19] The book was said to need a subsidy; in the event this was forthcoming from the Sudan Government by the end of 1935. It seems likely that copies of Evans-Pritchard's earlier relevant papers, possibly including his Cairo lectures, might also have been made available to the Delegates, or at least their existence mentioned in accompanying correspondence or discussion, though I have not been able to find definite evidence of this. It is possible that Collingwood also saw the manuscript of Evans-Pritchard's second classic, *The Nuer* (1940); though this was accepted by the Delegates in February 1938 on the basis of Radcliffe-Brown's reading of only the first part of the manuscript and the assurance of a further subsidy from the Sudan Government.[20]

Evans-Pritchard had come back to Oxford to join Marett, as a Research Lecturer in African Sociology, in 1935. Collingwood's election to the Waynflete Chair of Metaphysical Philosophy was also in 1935. From this position he continued to develop his ambitious argument that philosophy, in its pursuit of human life and thought, should leave aside that model of objective understanding offered by the natural sciences since the Enlightenment. It should endeavour rather to build upon the alternative model of understanding offered by history, accepting the inter-subjective aspects of its methods of enquiry. The lecture 'Method and Metaphysics' which Collingwood gave to the Jowett Society in 1935 does include explanation and discussion of the 'scale of forms' and other ideas from the *Essay on Philosophical Method* (1933), arguing for example the need to go beyond the existence of classificatory forms as such, to their historical context. The lecture also indicates as a major question the long term fact that 'mind' has come into existence in a world which was once a world of mere body.[21] In my reading this has the feel of an 'anthropological' or 'prehistorical' question, one of a longer term and more philosophical kind about the nature of consciousness than one can pursue through normal historical sources or even through the discipline of field archaeology. Had it become a part of Collingwood's intention at this time to apply the philosophical methods of his 1933 book, and in particular the notion of the 'scale of forms', to human history in the widest sense, and to turn to what the folklorists and anthropologists had been investigating as a part of this project?

This at any rate is the context in which Collingwood took on the task of going down to the Bodleian and checking systematically through the volumes of the journal *Folklore* and related anthropological works; the notes he made (a couple of hundred pages) are not dated but seem to come from the mid-1930s.[22] Authors to whom he refers in these notes, concerning 'primitive man' in the broadest sense, include Hartland, Freud, Hocart, Frazer, Maret on Wundt, Jung, Lévy-Bruhl, Durkheim (briefly), Brenda Seligman, Tylor, Grimm, Malinowski, Cox (on Cinderella). The notes (frequently giving Bodleian shelf marks for works referred to, as though he were ordering them up on the spot for consultation) clearly preceded the main set of manuscript texts which has become known as the 'Fairy Tales' or 'Folk Tales', also a couple of hundred pages and undated, though van der Dussen's list suggests 1936-37.[23] In this set of essays and chapters, clearly intended as a book, Collingwood interrogates the earlier literature and develops an approach to the study of long term continuities in human consciousness through the evidence of oral narratives. He develops a view of living language, and the traditional arts and rituals associated with it, as a fresh kind of source for the historian, extending the horizons of enquiry beyond those of conventional written history. The scholarly study of such evidence to date has, he argued, been hampered by the rationalism and scientism of anthropology; and by the way that modern scholars distance themselves from the supposed 'objects' of their study, the 'primitives' or 'savages' who are assumed to be swayed by an irrationalism and emotion which we have left behind. In fact, he suggests, our utilitarian civilization has denied the place of emotion in our own lives; we should rather try to recognize its role, and to admit even a 'magical' element in our own lives. The 're-creation in the historian's mind of the past experience he is trying to study'[24] can then contribute to the basis on which we attempt to interpret those civilizations which are remote from us in time and space, and which seem even more so because of their apparent irrationalism and susceptibility to emotion.

The 'Fairy Tales' manuscripts

Some accounts have already been published of the handwritten texts known as the 'Fairy Tales', in particular by van der Dussen, who has summed them up as 'really a prolegomenon to anthropology',[25] David Boucher,[26] and Sonia Giusti.[27] A doctoral thesis has also been completed by Maureen E. Rudzik on this material, offering a very interesting commentary, making connections with the history of folklore studies and pointing to links with archaeology, including Collingwood's own archaeological practice.[28] In order to give a slightly fuller impression of the significance of the manuscripts than has hitherto appeared in print, I offer a descriptive outline of the scope of these writings here, indicating how far they go beyond the bounds of what might conventionally, even today, be regarded as the specific field of 'folklore' studies or even 'anthropology'. One could perhaps evoke their range of reference, and theoretical ambition, by giving them a broad new title such as 'Essays in the archaeology of reason, poetry, and magic'. It can be argued that they contribute significantly to a full appreciation of Collingwood's notion of the 'historical method', for in these chapters we are led to periods of history beyond the reach of orthodox historical evidence; to materials of human culture, knowledge and experience embodied in living language, and transmitted through oral communication down to the present day. Collingwood speaks in this regard of the mixed historical sources of 'English culture'.[29] The pattern of transmission had many breaks, discontinuities, and reformulations, especially with the advent of literacy and the divergence between the study of folk tales and modern literary criticism. Partly because of this divide, many modern scholars, including the major anthropologists of his day, were so blinded by the distancing strategies of modern utilitarian modes of thought that they could not fully enter into the world of 'primitives' or those from whom we had received so much through the transmission of spoken language. It was necessary to recognize the neglected, emotional side of our own lives, and consciously re-engage with it, in order to understand better, from within, the significance of evidence bearing on human history in the remoter times or places. This evidence included, for Collingwood, the 'Fairy Tales' of European culture, which though made to appear archaic and fossilized in much scholarly industry, were nevertheless a vital source of our greatest literature and art. In the course of these arguments, Collingwood refers to quite a range of poets and artists, including for example Yeats, Shakespeare, Wordsworth, Tennyson, Homer, Eliot, Marlow, Spenser, Herrick, Gray, Landor, as well as to Walter Scott, to the Bach family, Mozart, Handel and Beethoven, and to Michaelangelo. It is quite clear that he is enquiring into the folk arts not simply for their own sake, but because of the continuity with high civilization.

The most important manuscripts consist of six closely related texts. 'Fairy Tales "A"'[30] surveys the kinds of evidence available to the historian for the era before written materials were produced. These have included the artefacts of the archaeologist, but an important extension could be made to include 'fairy tales' – or what scholars of today would call 'oral literature'. They are 'handed down by oral transmission from the past', and while they are 'not necessarily about fairies', they are about 'faëry . . . fays' work or enchantment'.[31] Such tales may be transmitted over very long periods of time, and spread from place to place, undergoing modifications and reconstruction in the process but retaining some elements of consciousness from the past. They belonged to past 'forms of social life' to which they were organically connected, as much as were tools and implements,[32] but have continually been transformed and recreated in a way that artefacts are not. We can attempt to 'excavate' their history, and that of the people who produced and transmitted them; here Collingwood proposes a 'new kind of archaeology'.[33] This is to be more than simply placing stories in the context of the past, for they are with us today, and yet have a history. Collingwood's use of the idea of 'archaeology' as a model for uncovering something of the past which lies behind the living present prefigures Foucault's very fertile use of the same image.[34] Collingwood notes how our literary heritage has depended on the reworking of older themes transmitted by word of mouth, for example, how much Shakespeare drew for his plots upon English and European examples of folk tales. He identifies what he calls a 'magical' element in such tales, which he suggests we find difficult to accept easily because of our modern, rationalistic way of thinking. 'The laws of the fairy-tale country, in so far as they are based on what we call magic, are certainly very different from the laws of natural science'.[35] Ethnologists have however often exaggerated the difference between ourselves and those peoples who live with magic in their daily lives.

In 'II: Three Methods of Approach – Philological, Functional, Psychological'[36] Collingwood argues that the ethnological data used by leading theorists from the mid-nineteenth century on was being misunderstood for this main reason, through a lack of proper historical sympathy with the peoples concerned. Their customs were distanced from the present by assumptions of a clear evolutionary divide between the primitive and the civilized. He develops specific and very detailed cases against Grimm and Max Müller; Tylor and Frazer; and Freud and Jung. With reference to the main founding figures of anthropology, Collingwood makes many criticisms of what he castigates as the 'functional' or naturalistic school of anthropology, which he dates to the period 1870-1910, starting with the writings of Tylor on the intellectual sources of animism. I should make the point that he has adopted the term 'functional' here in an idiosyncratic way: it was certainly current in the 1930s, but had been promoted, mainly by Malinowski at the LSE, to mark a distinction between the community-based field studies he recommended and the older evolutionary and comparative library-based studies of Tylor, Frazer and Marett. In responding to such library-based efforts of one kind or another towards the inductive comparison and 'explanation' of strange customs, Collingwood begins to recommend his own alternative lines of interpretation and understanding: here we find many of the characteristic themes which run through his writings on history in general. For example, 'In anthropological science man is trying to understand man; and to man his fellow-man is never a mere external object, something to be observed and described, but something to be sympathised with, to be studied by penetrating into his thoughts and re-enacting those thoughts for oneself. Anthropology – I refer to cultural, not physical, anthropology – is an historical science'. He uses the example of mathematics; Greek or Egyptian geometry may be a crude and primitive thing, but if we are to study historically we must think again for ourselves the thoughts of those early geometers. 'There is no difference of principle between this and any other case in which an attempt is made to study the early history of human ideas. The universal rule in every such case is to reconstruct for oneself and in oneself the ideas whose history one is trying to study. If one cannot do this, one may speak with the tongues of men and of angels, but the result is not anthropology'.[37] This effort required a reorientation of the anthropologist in relation to his materials, a kind of Copernican revolution.[38]

It is to this end that Collingwood devoted his efforts in preparing his arguments, explicitly at book length, dealing nimbly and effectively with a large range of existing literature, and with the tangled technical terminology of debates over exogamy, endogamy, incest, totemism, taboo and magic. To an average reader, questions in this area may not look like 'history', but of course Collingwood is not limiting himself to the orthodox notion of what history might be. By using 'fairy tales' or oral literature as a source of evidence about the human past, he is in fact extending the conventional scope of historical investigation beyond the material factuality of relics or written texts to the more intangible realm of spoken language as a vehicle for the transmission of social forms of experience.

His third chapter 'The Historical Method'[39] might well surprise an orthodox historian. Despite its praise for the much improved methods of modern anthropological fieldwork, its arguments for the possibility of understanding ethnographic reports on such matters as belief in 'magic' rest primarily upon the inner capacity of the historian for feelings of recognition. Despite the emotional aridity of modern, utility-obsessed life and scholarship, this capacity is present in people and should be allowed its place in the study of remote times and places. This is a very engagingly written chapter, evoking the fragility of what we may take to be European civilization in the broadest sense, the 'waste-land' of its modern collapse (a purposeful reference to T. S. Eliot's co-option of Frazer[40]) and a highly personal appeal to the reader's own sense of a feeling self. This sense is what Collingwood invokes in his discourse on 'our' experiences of the everyday rituals of dress or cleanliness; of the satisfaction of using powerful machines like vacuum cleaners, or even controlling other people; of the joy of shaping and controlling fine instruments like sailing boats; of being linked intimately with the works of art we have created, and so on. Modern utilitarianism, which he condemns as permeating the anthropology of his time, cannot give an account of such feelings, nor their effectiveness in the world.

The discussion includes explicit reference to art, and it is in this section of the manuscripts that the closest relation can be traced with the published arguments in *The Principles of Art*. The opening chapter of the book makes explicit reference to the Azande, and in the chapter 'Art as Magic' Collingwood writes that he is trying to rescue the word 'magic' from its degradation by earlier anthropologists of 'two generations ago', who sought the explanation of magical acts in the terms of a prevailing positivistic philosophy, labelling them as false science, and thus bringing into contempt civilizations different from our own.[41] However, he then points out, in spite of the 'inexhaustible scrap-heap of good reading' people still enjoyed in *The Golden Bough*, 'anthropologists of the present day have very little use for the Tylor-Frazer theory, or for Lévy-Bruhl's psychological embroidery of it. They are far more intimately acquainted with the facts of 'savage' life than the men who invented and elaborated that theory; far more intimately, indeed, than the best-informed of the field-workers on whom these theorists depended for their data'.[42]

These published arguments had already been developed at length in the fourth manuscript chapter of the 'Fairy Tales' entitled 'Magic'.[43] Collingwood points out that anthropologists do not always recognize that personal experience, including its emotional side, may be a surer route to understanding of some savage practice than pure reason. He states that we must understand 'the nature of magic', not by defining the term, which is merely a convenient label, the investigation of which would only tell us about 'minds of anthropologists'. What we should rather do is to understand the beliefs and customs to which the label has been applied, and this requires becoming aware of the emotional side of our own experiences.

In some ways, and probably to most readers, Collingwood's championing of the 'magical' element in life reads in a slightly uncomfortable way today. However, we could come to his defence, remembering how such terms of the English language have shifted their shades of meaning over the centuries, how they have always had a tremendous amount of intrinsic ambiguity in popular colloquial usage, and how they have escaped most attempts of scholars to classify, define and pin them down. By suggesting that there is 'magic' in our lives too, Collingwood was of course intending to shock his readers a little, though the effect today is often a sense of puzzlement rather than of revelation. The idea of 'magic' has a kind of quirky appeal in popular usage today (as in the magic of fashion or films), but as a scholarly category it has lost its seriousness and just looks antiquarian. Within anthropology, people have on the whole dropped the term, partly because (as Collingwood saw) it seems to imply a distinctly alien mind-set. Of course one of the main reasons why it carries this implication is that many scholars in the past have castigated it as a phenomenon counter to religion and enlightened civilization. One scholarly approach to magic in the West has been the story of its marginalization by the growth of the Church.[44] From the mid-nineteenth century on, there has been a series of attempts by humanists and anthropologists to place it within the broad evolutionary frame of one theory or another of the growth of reason. 'Magic' in scholarly interpretations, if not even in social life itself, has thus often been cast in opposition to orthodoxy and authority. Marcel Mauss and Henri Hubert characterized it in a classic essay of 1904 as essentially anti-social, as something pursued by individuals against the dominant collective interests of society.[45]

Arguments about 'magic' became highly technical among anthropologists of the early twentieth century. The effect of competing professional efforts to define it, and to specify its locus within the 'primitive' world, was to make it even more of a specialist antiquarian topic. Even Evans-Pritchard, in a sense, found himself arguing on his opponents' grounds when he shaped his book on Azande beliefs into a justification of their intellectual rationality, even about witchcraft and magic. Intent on undermining the stereotype of the primitive as lacking reason and always swayed by emotion, he failed perhaps to give the affective aspects of witchcraft and magic, or even of the motivations of jealousy, vengeance and punishment, their due. He based his argument on very specific definitions of his key terms, keeping close to the way that the Zande language differentiates technical concepts within a field of connected notions about substances, practices, and the moral context in which they are applied. He restricted the English word 'magic' to the application of a specific range of medicines and technical practices supposed to counter sorcery and witchcraft (themselves emanating from the moral evil embodied in certain persons). Collingwood, similarly motivated in defence of the intelligibility of 'primitive' thought, used the English 'magic' in a much more diffuse and general way, drawing on some of its older layers of use in European history and literature to evoke a sense of what we might call 'felt power'.

We should remember that many of the over-technical terms of early twentieth century anthropology have since been dropped. 'Totem' for example, or 'taboo' and 'fetish', are no longer used as plain or technical descriptions of anything. But then they were all co-opted into scholarly use from the indigenous languages of remote areas, and the only echoes they retain are with the anthropology of the period and its own stereotypes of the world outside Europe.[46] We have become more aware of the implications of the English-language terms we ourselves use; we approach 'gods' or even 'spirits' in a gingerly way, and terms like 'ritual' have been themselves historicized and critically localized in our discussions.[47] Colleagues would agree that 'magic', which like 'ritual' is an old part of religious discourse in Europe, is no universal timeless category, and needs to be understood in its context of use. This particular term has had such a long and complex history, however, that there are residues of meaning which could well be highlighted once again. Collingwood's use of 'magic', in contradistinction to the narrow reasonings of utility, was part of his broader effort to give more space to emotional experience and the felt power of human agency in an account of social life and history, and there is no *a priori* reason why we should not respond to his appeal. He has certainly made a strong case for restoring a language that recognizes the dispositions of feeling which guide so much of our behaviour, and if his use of 'magic' as a key to that language is a little bizarre on first reading, it is perhaps a necessary provocation.

I believe we can find Collingwood persuasive in his evocation of the joyful or otherwise satisfying feelings of powerfulness inhering in many of our practices, and their analogies in the ethnographic and historical evidence. The actual terms in which he expresses his case, however, and his argument for the recognition of 'magic' as such in our sports and arts and ceremonies, present some difficulty and no doubt make for confusion. He may have overdone his claims for magic *tout court*. Perhaps by recognizing the 'glorious' feeling of sailing a fine boat before the wind, we are not necessarily able to make all manner of 'magic' phenomena, such as the contents of fairy tales, more intelligible. Nevertheless, Collingwood convincingly evokes felt power as an aspect of human action, and the relevance of the idioms in which this may be conceptualized and transmitted. There is no doubt that he was right in criticizing the reductive and rationalistic explanations often given to reports of the apparently bizarre behaviour of 'savages', and in seeking to use the same kind of personal insight in interpretation that a historian would apply to those peoples and historical periods closer to us. Whether or not one is comfortable today in going along with the terminology of 'magic', his arguments are likely to appeal to today's readers, familiar as they are with the literature on phenomenology and less confident over even their own rationality than were Collingwood's contemporaries.

The fifth text I would like to discuss briefly is part of the wider survey Collingwood undertook of the literature of anthropology and folklore. It was presumably intended as a case study to illustrate his projected book, and concerns 'Cinderella'.[48] The piece is a detailed essay based on a book produced by Miss Marian Cox in 1893, which analysed 345 variants of the story. These stories are found all over Europe and in many parts of Asia including Japan, and a few are found in Africa and the New World (though these may represent relatively recent transmission). Collingwood explains how Miss Cox arranged the stories in three main classes:

1. *Cinderella 'proper'*: a girl is ill-treated by her stepmother, receives magical help, usually from an animal, so she can go to a gathering where a young man falls in love, follows her, and picks up a shoe by which he recognizes and marries her.

2. *Catskin*: the heroine leaves home in order to escape her father, who has fallen in love with her. She becomes a servant in a great house, attends a gathering, but is recognized [though sometimes disguised in a catskin] by the food she cooks for her lover.

3. *Cap o'Rushes [or King Lear]*. This resembles *catskin* except in the opening: here, the girl is driven from home by her father, angry because she does not express her love for him warmly enough; she often says in these stories that she loves him like salt. She later marries, and makes a saltless meal to convince her father of the value of salt.

Collingwood's essay on Cinderella has never been discussed in any public forum and is, I believe, quite unknown among folklorists of the present day. It is not referred to for example in Dundes' compilation of old and new essays on the Cinderella story.[49] However, Collingwood's essay not only goes beyond the standard comparative folklore analyses of his own period, but still has much to interest the reader today. The early twentieth century folklorists tended to seek out primary source areas, and original, authentic versions of tales. Collingwood follows the 'historical' methods he recommended in his first chapters, in treating all variants in a cycle as viable, and as representing the continuing creativity of 'tradition'. He pursues an 'excavation' of the modern Cinderella, revealing possible connections and patterns of change in the way elements of the story and its cognates were combined and recombined back to the medieval period. He draws attention particularly to the way in which European variants recombined elements which probably came from Asia in the first place and were then shaped by medieval European traditions, especially of romantic love culminating in marriage (giving our Cinderella) and of the Christian themes of threatened virgins and violence done to chastity, medieval story tellers 'piling on the agony' to yield, for example, the story of a father's injustice in *King Lear*. The modern paradoxes of social morality are reconstructed from the materials of an older juxtaposition of marvellous elements.

There is an overall historical coherence to the patterns Collingwood suggests, rather greater than in the extant Cinderella literature. He even pursues the discussion back to the times before written history or other evidence, here reinforcing the claims he put forward in the first chapter of the 'Fairy Tales' manuscript. However, he does seem here on more questionable ground. He draws attention to the role of wild animals, and the interaction of human and animal, in many variants of the Cinderella cycle, and suggests in a tentative way that there is no reason why we may not assume some kind of continuity with the cave art of the Upper Paleolithic. Here he invokes 'totemism'; this term is well and truly out of modern anthropology, but it is true that there is today a growing recognition of the significance of philosophical ideas about human/animal interaction as a part of the thinking of an age, and a sensitivity to ecological questions which has been dubbed a new kind of totemism.[50]

'Cinderella' is a complicated essay, though engaging and readable if one pursues the main line of argument and brackets off those passages which offer the detailed justifications. The comparison of myths across the Indo-European region has long been an important and intriguing area of study. Collingwood's treatment was ahead of his time, not only finding comparisons between India and medieval Europe but seeking a socio-cultural rationale for the changing shapes and emphases of the narratives. His work could now be seen to foreshadow aspects of Lévi-Strauss's structural analysis of myth (mainly for the native peoples of the Americas), a method designed to reveal basic principles of the formal relationship of elements in a mass of narratives. At the same time Collingwood's attempt at locating the key periods of change in the history of a cycle of tales is very much in sympathy with more recent treatments, which attempt to locate the processes of fragmentation and reconstruction substantively and historically. The essay certainly belongs with the overall argument of Collingwood's 'Fairy Tales' project, reinforcing with a specific case something of what he was there recommending in principle. It also illustrates the transference of an archaeologist's concern for detail and pattern to the kind of oral narrative with which anthropologists have always tried to deal.

The 'Fairy Tales' manuscripts of Collingwood include a few shorter pieces, of which the most substantial and polished is entitled 'The Authorship of Fairy Tales', and is the final text I would like to mention here.[51] Of particular interest in this essay is Collingwood's explicit setting of the modern arts, including plays and music, in the broader context of the traditional arts. In the modern setting, authors and composers are less 'original' than we might think, always borrowing and re-arranging each other's themes; while in the traditional sphere, story tellers are more innovative than might be imagined. There is no hard and sharp division between the two, as the scientific folklorists among others used to think; though Collingwood rather disarmingly ends with a footnote confessing that while he has always admired folk ballads, when compared with masterpieces such as Milton's *Lycidas*, they suffer, to the point that he has asked himself whether the ballads really are as beautiful as they had always appeared.

Some wider resonances

I believe the 'Fairy Tales' manuscripts, against the background of the published works, fill out several areas of Collingwood's thought and illuminate the connections between his practical, 'fieldworking' methods and his philosophical approach to history. They also demonstrate clearly that Collingwood took a lively interest in anthropology, that he saw its subject matter as within the scope of his historical method with all the implications that might carry, and that he regarded his own work as a contribution to the developments that were then taking place in anthropology. His efforts were parallel in several respects to those of Evans-Pritchard, as they both sought an alternative to the positivism of early anthropology. In the manuscripts Collingwood referred explicitly to the current state of anthropological theory, and associated himself with the reforming efforts of his contemporaries: 'A reader may ask why I say nothing of the controversies and inquiries which are occupying the minds of anthropologists today: the diffusionist controversy, for example, or the attempt to blend the functional and psychological methods into a new synthesis. If I ignore these it is not because I doubt their importance. It is because the cross-currents of a "critical period", as the present age of anthropological studies has been called . . . are of interest not for what they have achieved but for what may come of them . . . What I have to say is rather a contribution to the work of this critical period than an estimate of it.'[52]

Listening to the voices of others, including those reconstructible in part from the past, was a hallmark of Collingwood's approach to many topics, historical or philosophical. His sensitivity to language as some-thing essentially shared, transmitted between people, including parent and child, even as couching one's perception of self, is well known.[53] These are attitudes to language shared by modern anthropologists, and inform the principles which guide their field investigations. Collingwood's philosophy was not set exclusively in the abstractions of the mind, nor of that discipline's written texts. It was an exploration of the human world. Not all his philosophical readers have understood this, nor have all his archaeological readers appreciated the fact that he did represent the unearthing of the human past as a metaphysical enquiry. His genius lay in seeing how these endeavours were related; but few of his contemporaries appreciated this vision, rarely focusing their eyes beyond the apparent certainties of the printed word (in the philosopher's case) or the gritty turf and stones laid bare by the excavator's pick in the other. Even now, as there is a rising interest in Collingwood's work among the philosophers, few go up to Cumbria and take into account the connection with the practical business of digging up the earth to see who built which bits of a Roman road, when, and why, and how they lived and felt. The past of north-western Britain, and indeed north-western Europe, was a part of the imaginative world R. G. Collingwood had been brought up in, not only through archaeological digs but also through painting, textual and literary scholarship, and the writing of historical novels.[54] Within anthropology, I believe that our perspective as fieldworking scholars, especially our speciality of engaging with living societies and the transmission of spoken language, along with our subsequent reflective writing upon them, is directly in sympathy with some of the questions which R. G. Collingwood placed at the centre of the historical method as a mode of philosophical enquiry. The 'Fairy Tales' manuscripts are a transparently clear set of evidence as to Collingwood's thought in this respect.

* This paper draws on a longer text, 'Collingwood, Evans-Pritchard and Anthropology', presented to the Collingwood Conference, 1997, held at St. Catherine's College, Oxford. For some years I have been encouraged to pursue the theme of Collingwood's interest in, and influence upon, anthropology, with especial reference to his manuscripts in the Bodleian, by Jan van der Dussen, Teresa Smith, David Boucher, James Connelly and Peter Strong. In addition, I am grateful to those who have made specific comments on the conference paper, in particular W. H. Dray, James Lund, and Hidami Suganami; and also to those graduate students at the Institute of Social and Cultural Anthropology who have shared my interest and taken part in discussions of this theme.

NOTES

1   R. G. Collingwood, *The Idea of History*, revised edition with additional material edited by J. van der Dussen, Oxford, 1993, 79.

2   Collingwood, *Idea of History*, 91-2.

3   Collingwood, *Idea of History*, 155.

4   Collingwood, *Idea of History*, 224.

5   I have not traced the phrase in his published works, though it does occur in the 'Fairy Tales' manuscripts, Dep. 21/5, 42.

6   A. R. Radcliffe-Brown, 'On Social Structure', Presidential Address to the Royal Anthropological Institute, 1940, in *JRAI* LXX, 1940; reprinted as chapter 10 in *Structure and Function in Primitive Society*, London, 1952.

7   T. K. Penniman, *A Hundred Years of Anthropology*, London, 1935, 15.

8   This claim will be explained and justified in a separate essay.

9   Bodleian manuscripts, Dep. Collingwood 21 (referred to in more detail below).

10 Some of the earliest comments on these lines include, for example, Alan Donagan asking in 1962 why Collingwood claimed for history the whole province of the study of human thought and action. 'Why not say that all the sciences of human action are forms of anthropology? Economics, sociology, political science, and even human geography are by definition limited either to kinds or aspects of human action; but anthropology, like history, is not. It is important to recognize that while doubtless many reasons for preferring history weighed with him, none was compelling. He would have had no objection to the name "anthropology", provided that it were stipulated that the methods of anthropology are the same as those of history . . .' (*The Later Philosophy of R. G. Collingwood*, Chicago, 1962, 170-71). Donagan was employing a more recent vision of what anthropology is, or ought to be, than of course had been available to Collingwood.

Louis Mink a little later pointed out that Collingwood's concept of history as 'knowledge of mind by re-enactment on the evidence of action' applies, among other things, to the characteristic methods of disciplines not usually regarded as 'historical' in the empirical phase of the concept: 'some literary criticism or some fieldwork in anthropology, for example.' ('Collingwood's Historicism: A Dialectic of Process', in *Critical Essays on the Philosophy of R. G. Collingwood*, ed. Michael Krausz, Oxford, 1972, 161).

Nathan Rotenstreich, in the same volume of essays, suggested 'What actually emerges from Collingwood's *Essay on Metaphysics* is a kind of cultural anthropology of metaphysics, a study of different world views entertained in the course of history by individuals and by groups of individuals.' And further, he suggests in criticism that 'His view is formulated both from the level of his own intentionality and from the level of a historical or cultural anthropologist referring to views and revealing their disguised historicity.' ('Metaphysics and Historicism', in *Critical Essays*, ed. Krausz, 1972, 199-200).

A. J. M. Milne in the same volume refers to the work of social anthropologists on tribal communities as a kind of evidence which contradicts Collingwood's political vision of non-state communities in *The New Leviathan*, as though this is the kind of evidence he ought to have drawn on ('Collingwood's Ethics and Political theory', in *Critical Essays*, ed. Krausz, 1972, 316-17). While Collingwood himself suggests in his *Preface* to this work that it is 'best understood as an attempt to bring *The Leviathan* up-to-date in the light of the advances made since it was written, in history, psychology, and anthropology', and refers to various ethnographic accounts including the customary law of the Iceland of the Sagas, we should remember that fieldwork-based political anthropology scarcely existed in the 1930s. My point rests that here is a modern critic spontaneously thinking of the relevance of anthropological literature now available (as it was not then) on the law, politics and government of non-state communities to Collingwood's project of updating Hobbes' vision. Evans-Pritchard and Fortes told us in *African Political Systems* (OUP, London, 1940) that they had not found Hobbes and the rest very helpful in formulating a comparative empirical approach to political society, but it seems to me that they were at least asking parallel questions to those Collingwood was asking in *The New Leviathan*, and had he lived, he might have used their work.

11 Stephen Toulmin, 'Introduction' to R. G. Collingwood, *An Autobiography* [1939], Oxford, 1978, xv-xvi.

12 Isaiah Berlin, *Vico and Herder: Two Studies in the History of Ideas*, London, 1976, 4.

13 Isaiah Berlin, *The Proper Study of Mankind: An Anthology of Essays*, ed. Henry Hardy and Roger Hausheer, London, 1997, 7. It is interesting that recent commentators upon Berlin give considerable prominence to Collingwood, not only in the background, but in the characterization of Berlin's own writings. Bernard Williams suggests that his account is 'more in the spirit of Collingwood than of any analytical philosopher' in dealing with 'various models or presuppositions which men have brought to their experience, and which have helped, indeed, to form that experience' ('Introduction' to Berlin, *Concepts & Categories: Philosophical Essays*, ed. Henry Hardy, Oxford, 1980, xiii). Roger Hausheer describes Berlin as being 'led to explore and deepen the notion that a large part of the thought and experience of a period is organized by what Collingwood termed 'constellations of absolute presuppositions' ('Introduction' to Berlin, *Against the Current: Essays in the History of Ideas*, ed. Henry Hardy, Oxford, 1981, xxi). Berlin himself makes it clear that he takes these 'absolute presuppositions' to be those of 'other societies, other cultures', which contrasts with the way in which they have been assumed by some philosophical commentators to refer to formal systems of scientific thought as explicitly constructed by individual scientists. There is some ambivalence in Collingwood's own writings about this question; and my feeling is that it is partly because the socio-cultural, or anthropological, interpretation of what Collingwood meant by absolute presuppositions has come to take precedence over the formal logical or scientific definition, that modern commentators have increasingly come to appreciate the 'anthropological' character of Collingwood's vision of history. Certainly both Williams and Hausheer have assumed these absolute presuppositions to be embedded in a social and cultural sense in the thinking and unthinking practice of an age, rather than limited to the formal thought processes of individual scientists in the laboratory.

14 E. E. Evans-Pritchard, review of *Roman Britain* by R. G. Collingwood, *Man* XXXII, 1932, 220-21.

15 E. E. Evans-Pritchard, 'The Intellectualist (English) Interpretation of Magic', *Bull. of the Faculty of Arts*, University of Cairo, I, Pt. 2, 1933, 1-21. 'Lévy-Bruhl's Theory of Primitive Mentality', *Bull. of the Faculty of Arts*, University of Cairo, II, Pt. 2, 1934, 1-26, repr. in *Journal of the Anthropological Society of Oxford*, I, 1970, 39-60. 'Science and Sentiment: an Exposition and Criticism of the Writings of Pareto', *Bull. of the Faculty of Arts*, University of Cairo, III, Pt. 2, 1936, 163-92.

16 For a comprehensive listing, see T. O. Beidelman, ed., *A Bibliography of the Writings of E. E. Evans-Pritchard*, London, 1974.

17 E. E. Evans-Pritchard, *The Zande Trickster*, Oxford, 1967. The series included an influential general volume by Ruth Finnegan, *Oral Literature in Africa*, Oxford, 1966, as well as a wealth of particular studies from across the continent.

18 Dep. Collingwood 16/8.

19 Letter from W. D. Hogarth of the OUP to C. G. Seligman, ref. P.11216/WDH of 25th February 1935, OUP Archives LB 7652.

20 Radcliffe-Brown to J. Mulgan of the OUP, P.12358 of 11 December 1937, and J. Mulgan to Evans-Pritchard (in Cairo), P.12358/JM of 7 February 1938. OUP Archives, LB 8263.

21 Dep. Collingwood 19/3.

22 Dep. Collingwood 21/1-3.

23 Dep. Collingwood 21/4-13. See the manuscript catalogue of Collingwood's papers deposited at the Bodleian Library, Oxford, compiled by Ruth A. Burchnall, 1994, 12-13. Cf. W. J. van der Dussen, *History as a Science: the Philosophy of R. G. Collingwood*, The Hague, 1981, 450-51.

24 Dep. Collingwood 21/4, 18.

25 Van der Dussen, *History as a Science*, 183-91.

26 R. G. Collingwood, *Essays in Political Philosophy*, ed. David Boucher, Oxford, 1989, 39-40, with an excerpt from the manuscripts, 197-200. See also David Boucher, *The social and political thought of R. G. Collingwood*, Cambridge, 1989, 196-206.

27 Sonia Giusti, 'Collingwood's Unpublished Writings on Folklore', in *Storia, antropologia e scienze del linguaggio*, VIII, 3, 1993, 23-41.

28 Maureen E. Rudzik, 'Folklore and History: An Analysis of an Unpublished Manuscript by R. G. Collingwood', thesis submitted for the degree of Doctor of Education in the University of Toronto, 1990.

29 Dep. Collingwood 21/4, 12-14.

30 Dep. Collingwood 21/4.

31 Dep. Collingwood 21/4, 1.

32 Dep. Collingwood 21/4, 5.

33 Dep. Collingwood 21/4, 19.

34 For example, Michel Foucault, *The Birth of the Clinic: An Archaeology of Medical Perception*, London, 1973 [1963], *The Archaeology of Knowledge*, London 1972 [1969].

35 Dep. Collingwood 21/4, 16.

36 Dep. Collingwood 21/5.

37 Dep. Collingwood 21/5, 26.

38 Dep. Collingwood 21/5, 12.

39 Dep. Collingwood 21/6.

40 See R. Angus Downie, *Frazer and the Golden Bough*, London, 1970, with references to Eliot at pp. 21, 60-61; and Brian V. Street, *The Savage in Literature: Representations of 'primitive' society in English Fiction 1858-1920*, London, 1975, 177-9.

41 R. G. Collingwood, *The Principles of Art*, Oxford, 1938, 57-61.

42 R. G. Collingwood, *The Principles of Art*, Oxford, 1938, 61.

43 Dep. Collingwood 21/7.

44 See for example Keith Thomas, *Religion and the Decline of Magic*, Harmondsworth, 1972.

45 Marcel Mauss, *A General Theory of Magic* [1904 with H. Hubert], trans. R. Brain, London, 1972.

46 Claude Lévi-Strauss, *Totemism* [1962], trans. R. Needham, London, 1964; Franz Steiner, *Taboo*, London, 1956.

47 Talal Asad, *The Genealogies of Religion*, Johns Hopkins, 1993; Caroline Humphrey and James Laidlaw, *The Archetypal Actions of Ritual: A Theory of Ritual illustrated by the Jain rite of Worship*, Oxford, 1994.

48 Dep. Collingwood 21/10.

49 Alan Dundes, *Cinderella: A Casebook*, Madison, Wisconsin, 1982.

50 See for example R. G. Willis, *Signifying Animals: Human Meaning in the Natural World*, London, 1990, esp. xx-xxv, 5-7.

51 Dep. Collingwood 21/9.

52 Dep. Collingwood 21/5, 1. See T. K. Penniman, *A Hundred Years of Anthropology*, London, 1936, esp. Chapter V, 'A Critical Period: 1930-1935'.

53 *The Principles of Art*, 1938, 226-48.

54 See for example the first two articles in the first volume of *Collingwood Studies*, 1994: Douglas H. Johnson, 'W. G. Collingwood and the Beginnings of *The Idea of History*', 1-26; and Teresa Smith, 'R. G. Collingwood: "This Ring of Thought": Notes on Early Influences', 27-43.

Review Article:

R. G. Collingwood: Religion and Philosophy

LIONEL RUBINOFF
Trent University, Canada

I

Religion and Philosophy, originally published in 1916[1] and recently reprinted,[2] was the first of a series of publications which were to earn for their author a reputation as one of the most original and thoughtful philosophers of the twentieth century. The re-issue of this text is thus to be welcomed by Collingwood scholars both for its having become available to a wider audience and for the opportunity it provides for re-assessing the place of religion in Collingwood's conception of philosophy in general and the centrality of faith to his conception of reason in particular. Although known chiefly for his pioneering work in the philosophy of history, Collingwood's choice of the relation between philosophy and religion as the subject of his first book reflects an interest which was to occupy a central role in the development of his philosophy throughout the remainder of his career. But, as D. M. Mackinnon explains, since Collingwood 'never wrote (apart from the very early *Religion and Philosophy*) a sustained treatise on the philosophy of religion to compare with the later works on method, on politics, on aesthetics, on metaphysics, on nature and on history . . . one has to turn to occasional papers, and in the light of them, go back to the major treatises and extract from them confirmation and redefinition of the views suggested as the writer's own'[3] on the nature of faith. I would hasten to add that in so doing what will become evident is the extent to which *Religion and Philosophy* was not just an attempt to defend religion, and Christianity in particular, against the assault of secular rationalism, but (in Collingwood's own words) to 'treat the Christian creed . . . as a critical solution of a philosophical problem' (RP, xiii), and in so doing, prepare for himself an agenda for his later works which were devoted to the above mentioned topics. In short, the relationship between faith and reason, as expressed in the phrase *fides quaerens intellectum*, remained central to Collingwood's approach to all of the other philosophical problems to which he turned his attention from the publication of *Speculum Mentis* in 1924 to *The New Leviathan* in 1942.

This is especially true of *An Essay on Metaphysics*; for, as Mackinnon rightly observes 'the substitution of one set of presuppositions for another, or the rendering of a set of presuppositions internally consistent with itself' (which it is the purpose of metaphysical analysis to obtain) 'belongs to the world of *fides quaerens intellectum* as Collingwood regarded that world in his own writing.'[4] I would even suggest that when viewed from this perspective Collingwood's controversial characterization of presuppositional change as 'a modification not consciously devised but created by a process of unconscious thought' (EM, 48) will seem less puzzling, though not altogether unproblematic.

Notwithstanding Collingwood's continuing interest in the role of religion in the life of the mind, and indeed of civilization itself, and his unremitting conviction that *fides quaerens intellectum*, many of his commentators have nevertheless either underestimated or simply ignored the importance of his publications on religion in their overall assessment of his philosophical development.[5] Thus, for example, Louis Mink has suggested that although Collingwood was a deeply religious person he had no sympathy for the 'philosophy of religion.'[6] In support of this judgement Mink cites a passage from *Speculum Mentis* in which Collingwood refers to the philosophy of religion as a refuge for philosophers at the edge of bankruptcy (SM, 269). But what Mink fails to notice is that this statement was made about what Collingwood here calls 'religious philosophy,' and it occurs in the context of a more general discussion of 'dogmatic philosophy' which Collingwood regards as an error in self-understanding, the 'negative moment of the dialectic of experience,' or 'blind-alley' in 'the process of thought' (SM, 263).

Such philosophizing, Collingwood cautions, is not to be confused with the conception of philosophy as 'absolute knowledge,' with which *Speculum Mentis* concludes. When conducted from the standpoint of absolute philosophy, philosophy of religion takes on a character quite different from that of the 'religious philosophy' which offers itself as a refuge for philosophy at the edge of bankruptcy.

The conception of philosophy as absolute knowledge which defines the standpoint from which *Speculum Mentis* was written was subsequently exemplified by a series of publications throughout the following two decades during which Collingwood pursued the program for philosophy that was first laid down in *Speculum Mentis*. What Collingwood dismisses in *Speculum Mentis* as an error in self-understanding is just another version of the kind of philosophy criticized in *Religion and Philosophy* which attempts to philosophize about God in total abstraction from what one already believes on faith or authority. Such philosophizing begins in a state of presuppositionless scepticism and then attempts to overcome it by pure abstract, a priori, reasoning alone. Systematic scepticism, writes Collingwood in *Religion and Philosophy* is admittedly the essence of all philosophy; 'but scepticism, if it means pretending not to entertain convictions which in fact one finds inevitable, soon passes over into systematic falsehood' (RP, 69). Against this view of philosophy Collingwood argues that instead of pretending to begin with a blank sheet the true philosopher seeks, first of all, to 'discover what he actually does think, and then to find out, if he can, whether his first idea was just or not; that is, to prove it or disprove it' (RP, 69).

Although Collingwood is not entirely clear about what is meant by 'proof' here, we are given some clue to its meaning in his further observation that the kind of thinking that is involved in 'believing,' or in accepting some truths 'on authority,' is not entirely 'passive' or uncritical. 'The authority is not accepted without some reason, and the fact that it is accepted does not incapacitate us from analyzing the reasons for acceptance and from discovering further reasons.' (RP, 69) Philosophy, in other words, is an attempt to render explicit in the form of a *logos* what is already implicit in the form of belief (*doxa*). Or, as Collingwood was eventually to explain, philosophy is 'faith cultivating itself.' *Fides quaerens intellectum.*[7] This is precisely the theory of knowledge – thoroughly idealist in nature – that underlies Collingwood's philosophy throughout his career, and his explication and defence of this doctrine in *Religion and Philosophy* is a clear anticipation of the approach taken to the analysis of absolute presuppositions in *An Essay on Metaphysics*.

Mink also remarks that for him *Religion and Philosophy* is the least interesting of Collingwood's books for the reason that it is the least dialectical of his works.[8] Other commentators, notably T. M. Knox and Alan Donagan, regard Collingwood's later philosophy as a radical departure from and repudiation of the doctrines of *Religion and Philosophy* and *Speculum Mentis*, referred to by Collingwood himself as juvenilia. The same view was held by Croce. But while Collingwood himself acknowledged the errors in his early writings, his own view was that rather than repudiating his earlier doctrines his later writings render explicit in a more coherent form what is already implicit, which is precisely what is required of dialectical reasoning. It could be argued further that given Collingwood's own conception of dialectic, *Religion and Philosophy* represents a necessary stage in the career of his philosophy which develops as a process of dialectical criticism of errors (SM, 289).

In *Speculum Mentis* the process of self-understanding and self-making is described as the life of absolute mind, the knowledge of which is the province of absolute philosophy. Absolute philosophy is nothing more than mind knowing itself through the history of its changes, and '[a] mind which knows its own change is by that very knowledge lifted above change.' (SM, 301). It is precisely this theory of mind which finds expression in both *The Idea of History*, in which the mind makes itself through the self-knowledge achieved through the study of history, and *An Essay on Metaphysics*, in which the process of self-making is described as a history of changes at the level of absolute presuppositions.

An early version of the theory of mind as a dialectical process of self-making is clearly present in *Religion and Philosophy*; although I must confess to having failed to realize the extent to which this is so in some of my own previously published assessments of Collingwood's philosophical development. Consider, for example, his frequent references to the conception of mind as pure act:

> [the] idea of the mind as a thing distinguishable from its own activities does not seem to be really tenable; the mind *is* what it *does*; it is not a thing which thinks, but a consciousness; not a thing that wills but an activity (RP, 34; cf., also, 100, 164-165).

Among other things, the activity of mind consists in a critical examination of beliefs, with a view to either proving or disproving them (RP, 69). The transition from a belief in materialism, with its implied dualism between mind and matter, to a type of idealism in which the dualism is overcome, without, as in crude subjective idealism, cancelling all differences between them, represents one of the more important chapters in the actual history of mind (RP, 93-95).

In this actual history the passage from materialism to idealism is represented as if it were also a logical sequence, the outcome of what Collingwood was eventually to call a 'logic of question and answer.' Precisely this question and answer process is illustrated in *Religion and Philosophy* in the critique of erroneous interpretations of the mind's relationship to matter, of man's relationship to God, of philosophy's relationship to religion, and so on. In the course of this critique, the actual nature of mind is revealed as a phenomenon which is strikingly similar to what in *An Essay on Philosophical Method* is described as a scale of forms to be comprehended by means of a logic of overlapping classes. The logic of overlap of classes is an alternative to what in *Religion and Philosophy* is referred to as 'the logic of things and qualities,' which Collingwood rejects as an appropriate model for the understanding of mind, whether the finite mind of man or the infinite mind of God (RP, 165).

It is through the question and answer process as employed by Collingwood in *Religion and Philosophy* that erroneous interpretations of the nature of mind and its relations are overcome and truth is revealed. The falling into and overcoming of error is the essence of the self-making process. Properly understood, the search for truth, as revealed through the study of history, presents itself as a history of successive attempts to reach truth by correcting previous errors which not only eliminates error but sums up whatever truths were contained in those errors (RP, 138-9). Accordingly, Collingwood characterizes the life of mind as a self-making process whose finitude and infinity consists merely in its failure or success in the attainment of its desire to know itself and the limits of its power to know Reality, especially the Reality of God (RP, 152).

From the perspective of Collingwood's theory of philosophy as a dialectical critique of error, which we have every reason to believe his own philosophy was intended to exemplify, *Religion and Philosophy* occupies an important place in Collingwood's philosophical development, and rather than being the least interesting and least dialectical, it is in many respects the most interesting for the reason that it is here that the questions and problems to which the remainder of his philosophy is addressed were first articulated: and where, as the evidence of the text clearly indicates, Collingwood first experimented with a dialectical style of criticism – the making explicit of a truth already implicit in error by exploring every problem as a dialogue between truth and contradiction. It is also the place where he first introduced the theory of the dialectical nature of reality, or scale of forms, which is a variation of the idealist doctrine of internal relations.

II

Collingwood's stated purpose in *Religion and Philosophy* is to rescue religion from all forms of reductionism, as represented for example by such claims as that it is nothing more than an evolutionary mechanism designed to enhance the survival of the species, or that it originates from a fear of nature combined with an unconscious need for an all powerful protector and is thus essentially a matter of temperament, emotion, and ritual, rather than of intellect.[9] In his *Essay on Metaphysics* Collingwood regarded the tendency to so inferiorize religion as a symptom of what he called 'the propaganda of irrationalism' in which the distinction between reason and unreason, science and pseudo-science, breaks down. Collingwood was particularly annoyed by the claim that the function traditionally performed by religion can be served better by knowledge gained from common sense and science. Typical of these tendencies is the philosophy of logical positivism which, to the extent that it has fallen victim to the propaganda of irrationalism, has the paradoxical if not ironical effect of undermining the very practices of science and reason that it purports to protect.

Against these views Collingwood seeks to demonstrate the centrality of religiosity both to how we conceive reality, on the one hand – and this in all of its modes, including art, science, history, and even philosophy itself – and to how we actually live our lives and make our moral choices, on the other. This objective is realized, in part, by demonstrating, first of all, that religion is not the activity of one faculty alone, but a combined activity of all elements of the mind (RP, xvi), and secondly that religion is also a life, or practice; a performance or willing of duty and not simply an intellectual acknowledgement of the existence of such duties as we are commanded by reason to obey. Indeed, argues Collingwood, the very likelihood of our being able to live up to the ideals of morality and civility that underlie the theory and practice of western democracy depends upon the strength of the emotions deriving from the religious convictions that comprise the creed of Christianity. These are the emotions that activate the will to obey or live by what the intellect provides as a canon for democracy and the practice of liberty. Religion is a system of conduct in the sense that it both prescribes definite convictions and inculcates certain definite modes of action.

> . . . religion never exists apart from conduct. Just as all religion involves thought, as every religion teaches doctrine and a true religion teaches true doctrine, so all religion involves conduct; and whereas a good religion teaches good conduct, a bad religion teaches bad. (RP, 29)

Collingwood's doctrine here is that in religion the love of God implies both knowing God on the one hand and doing his will on the other (RP, 10-11). Philosophy as a love of wisdom implies a similar identity between knowledge and will. For both religion and philosophy 'no moment of thought is conceivable which is not also a volition, and no moment of will is possible which is not also an act of knowledge' (RP, 31). For both the religious and the philosophic life 'there is no dualism at all between knowing and acting' (RP, 33).

The doctrine defended in *Religion and Philosophy* is not just that religion and philosophy lead parallel lives in which the dualism between thought and action has been abolished. While it certainly can be argued that in religion the love of God is synonymous with doing His will and in philosophy the love of wisdom (knowledge) is synonymous with willing to act by that knowledge, the more interesting and philosophically significant doctrine argued by Collingwood is that thought or reason is *inherently* religious and it is the religious dimension of thought that provides the emotional and conative impetus to action; whether political, social, or moral. Religion, in other words, provides the bridge from philosophical realism, according to which knowledge and action are not only distinct but separate, to philosophical idealism, in which knowledge and action are identical, and knowing makes a difference both to the knower and to the object known. Not only does this doctrine affirm the identity of knowledge and action, for both religion and philosophy – with the implication that to know the true and the good is to will this knowledge into action – it affirms as well the doctrine that all wrong doing results from ignorance mistaking itself for knowledge.

Finally, in keeping with the spirit of this doctrine, Collingwood argues that it is not just the institutionalization of religion in the Church but the day to day practice of religion that sustains the life of mind and morality. The practice of Christianity derives from the Christian faith, which for Collingwood means the genuine or true love or knowledge of God as expressed through the creed or doctrines of Christianity. Were this faith to be lost, even though the institution remained intact it is unlikely, on Collingwood's view, that philosophical reasoning alone would be able to inspire the practice of morality. Of even greater concern, for Collingwood, is the prospect of a faith based on a false knowledge of God's will, in which case, the doctrines of the creed will be spoken not *in nomine dei* but *in nomine diaboli*.

Nearly 25 years later, towards the end of his life, Collingwood applied this very doctrine to his explanation for the rise of Fascism and Nazism in Europe. In 'Fascism and Nazism,'[10] he traces the success of these political aberrations to their ability to fill the emotional vacuum created by the eclipse of God and the gradual disappearance of the religious practices associated with Christianity. Not only had the latter shaped European civilization it was the chief source of the emotions that give men the power to sustain the principles of liberal democracy which lie at the basis of that civilization. As a result of the withering away of religiosity the practice of democracy has been reduced to a mere habit; a habit devoid of 'punch.' In one striking passage from 'Fascism and Nazism' Collingwood's recapitulation of the perspective on religion which was first presented in *Religion and Philosophy*, and consistently maintained throughout the rest of his life, takes the form of a prophetic and eloquent tribute to the awesome power of religion as a civilizing agent.

> The vital warmth at the heart of a civilization is what we call a religion. Religion is the passion which inspires a society to persevere in a certain way of life and to obey the rules which define it. Without a conviction that this way of life is a thing of absolute value, and that its rules must be obeyed at all costs, the rules become dead letters and the way of life a thing of the past. The civilization dies because the people to whom it belonged have lost faith in it. They have lost heart to keep it going. They no longer feel it as a thing of absolute value. They no longer have a religious sense of its rules as things which at all costs must be obeyed. Obedience degenerates into habit and by degrees habit withers away (187) . . . Liberal or democratic principles, I have argued [consistently since the publication of *Religion and Philosophy*] are a function of Christianity (195) . . . the emotional force, the 'drive' or 'punch,' that once made them victorious was due to Christianity . . . as a system of religious practice rich in the superstitious or magical elements which, in Christianity, as in every other religion, generate the emotion that gives men the power to obey a set of rules and thus bring into existence a specific form of life (194). Fascism and Nazism, then, are successful because they have the power of arousing emotion in their support (192) . . . in Germany, as in Italy, . . .

the new political movement contains ideas drawn from the sur-
vivals of an unextinguished pre-Christian religion, and derives
its 'punch' from the emotional appeal of that religion (196).[11]

So long as the Christian faith remained alive as a source of inspiration
for the practice of democracy it was a 'good religion' teaching 'good
conduct.' But when the German and Italian peoples lost faith in the
religious convictions of Christianity the vacuum created was filled by
'bad religion' teaching 'bad conduct.' Under some conditions, 'bad
religion' might take the form of a perverted understanding or profound
misunderstanding of what is believed to be the Christian creed, and
were Collingwood still alive he would very likely be tempted to apply
this analysis to the rise of the 'religious right' and would no doubt agree
with those who argue that the problem with the religious right is that
they are neither. For Collingwood the chief explanation for the
resurgence of the pagan emotions which have remained incapsulated
throughout the history of the western culture that was shaped by
Christianity lies with the breakdown of the Christian faith as a formidable influence on the life of Europeans and its replacement by the ethic
of rational humanism and the metaphysics of materialism—both of
which come under attack in *Religion and Philosophy*. The anti-religious
movements of rationalism and materialism have exhausted liberalism
and democracy of the emotional force of Christianity and reduced it to
a mere matter of habit which lacks the 'punch' to resist or stand up to
the destructive forces operating upon it.

The principles appealed to in this historical/causal explanation are
essentially the same as those referred to in Collingwood's explanation of
the Celtic revival in his *Roman Britain* and *An Autobiography* in which
the problem posed by the celtic revival is solved by appeal to what he
refers to as the principle of incapsulation.[12] It is this analysis of the
principle of incapsulation which lends authority to Collingwood's
diagnosis of the pathology that infects a civilization, and allows it to fall
under the spell of the 'propaganda of irrationalism.'[13] This phenomenon
takes hold whenever a society loses the religious emotions that lie at its
heart, or when it loses faith in its absolute presuppositions, which for
Collingwood amounts to the same thing. In short, while religion with-

out philosophy (faith without reason) is blind, philosophy (reason) without religion (faith) is but an empty abstraction lacking the ability to resist the resurgence of the pagan passions which like viruses lie dormant or incapsulated within any given culture until such time as the conditions which provide a source of immunity from infection collapse. This diagnosis begins with the publication of *Religion and Philosophy* and culminates in the prophetic warning with which he concludes 'Fascism and Nazism.'

> The time has long gone by when anyone who claims the title of philosopher can think of religion as a superfluity for the educated and an 'opiate for the masses.' It is the only known explosive in the economy of that delicate internal-combustion engine, the human mind. Peoples rich in religious energy can overcome all obstacles and attain any height in the scale of civilization. Peoples that have reached the top of a hill by the wise use of religious energy may then decide to do without it; they can still move, but they can only move downhill, and when they come to the bottom of the hill they stop (196).

Much the same conclusions were reached in *An Essay on Metaphysics* with respect to the 'guardianship of the European 'scientific frame of mind' which Collingwood believed is invested in the religious institutions of European civilization. From these institutions humanity derives the will 'to retain the presuppositions by whose aid he reduces such experience as he enjoys to such science as he can compass; and it is by dint of these same religious institutions that he transmits these same presuppositions to his children' (EM, 198). The science referred to in this passage is metaphysics, whose fate as a genuine science depends upon the strength of the religious institutions which support the act of presupposing and maintaining fidelity to our most cherished beliefs, an act which for Collingwood is synonymous with religious faith (EM, 216). At the same time, he argues, metaphysical analysis is an integral part of scientific thought and the scientific frame of mind upon which liberalism and democracy depends for its viability. The attack upon both religion and metaphysics which has gradually infected European civilization is thus an attack upon the very foundations of science and liberal democratic civilization.

But why has this attack upon the foundations of liberal democracy been so successful? How is it that the propaganda of irrationalism and the cult of pseudo-science has taken hold of modern civilization without serious challenge? The answer given in *An Essay on Metaphysics* rests upon the same convictions that were originally expressed in *Religion and Philosophy*. Because religion, science and metaphysics stand together, an obstinate error in metaphysical analysis is fatal to the integrity and viability of the science and civilization which depend upon the analysis being conducted properly; which means, being conducted in a manner which keeps alive, or maintains faith with, the fundamental convictions or presuppositions comprising the moral code from which civilization draws its strength, and upon which it therefore depends for its survival. The fundamental error which has brought European civilization under the spell of the propaganda of irrationalism is the substitution for the Christian creed of the metaphysics of materialism and reductionism, which are the prime targets of attack in *Religion and Philosophy*, and the pseudo-sciences of experimental psychology and the metaphysics of positivism, which are the primary targets of attack in *An Essay on Metaphysics*. In short, European civilization succumbed to the propaganda of irrationalism, as represented by Fascism and Nazism, because of its own failure to keep alive the fundamental convictions from which it originally derived.

III

Religion and Philosophy marks Collingwood's first attempt to argue the case for religion in a way that will explain the important role that it plays in the life of mind and the practice of morality and liberal democracy. He does this by means of an argument which in the first instance establishes an identity between religion and philosophy, which in turn provides the basis for an identity between religion and morality, and eventually between religious belief and historical understanding. In the case of morality the argument is not simply that religion reinforces a morality that can be independently established by reason and common sense. It is rather that without religion morality, like philosophy, to repeat, is merely an empty abstraction. These considerations apply to philosophy in general, conceived as a theory of the universe (RP, 17), and may explain why, under certain conditions, individuals and even entire societies, seem unable, no matter how advanced their knowledge, to 'keep the faith.' In subsequent publications, as we have already noted, Collingwood will make similar claims with respect to the relationship between science and metaphysics, which represent truth and reality as a progressive series of belief systems including the beliefs that support science. *Religion and Philosophy* marks the beginning of Collingwood's lifelong search for a rapprochement philosophy that will reunite the forms of experience in the life of mind and thus establish the foundation for a rapprochement between thought and action. For, as he argues in *Speculum Mentis*,

> We now recognize the nature of our disease. What is wrong with us is precisely the detachment of [the] forms of experience – art, religion, and the rest – from one another; and our cure can only be their reunion in a complete and undivided life. Our task is to seek for that life, to build up the conception of an activity which is at once art, and religion, and science, and the rest.[14]

This task began with *Religion and Philosophy*, in which Collingwood first attempted to establish the identity of religion, philosophy, history and morality. The importance of the doctrine of identity is illustrated by his discussion of the centrality of the historical Jesus to the Christian faith and the life of morality. In claiming that religion is a philosophy in whose truths it is necessary to believe as a condition of being rational, that the ultimate questions of philosophy are those of religion as well, and may be the more easily answered in a life which is at one and the same time both religious and philosophical (RP, 38), Collingwood emphasizes the importance of coming to know, by means of historical thinking, the mind of Jesus from whom the creed of Christianity is derived. For Collingwood, this means believing in the *historical* reality as distinct from the *myth* of Jesus. In rethinking the mind of the actual Jesus the philosopher is re-living a life which serves as an example of how a human life may satisfy the highest possible moral standards. Only then can a person be expected to imitate that life. The historical life of Jesus, which only history can establish, is thus the guarantee that man can be perfect if he will (RP, 53).

Here in essence is an early version of the doctrine of history as the self-knowledge of mind which occupies such a central role in Collingwood's later philosophy. In rethinking what someone else thought, as expressed through their actions, we think it ourselves. In knowing what someone else thought and how they acted we know that we ourselves are able to think and to act in that way. And finding out what we are able to do is finding out what kinds of persons we are (A, 114-115; IH, 85, 209, 218, 226; NL, 61-2). What is more, acquiring the ability to perform certain determinate operations is the acquisition of a determinate human nature. Thus the historical process 'is a process in which man creates for himself this or that kind of human nature by re-creating in his own thought the past to which he is heir' (IH, 226). The Christian faith, like history, to the extent that it performs the same determinate operations whenever it re-thinks or identifies with the mind of Christ, is therefore the acquisition of a determinate human nature, which in the case of Christians, is the ability to imitate the life of Christ.

From the standpoint of religion the belief that Christ really lived, whether it is true or false, colours the whole consciousness of the believer (RP, 54). We must know that a thing has happened before we can believe and act according to its teachings. So stated, the question arises whether Collingwood's doctrine comes close to exemplifying the psychology and fallaciousness of the doctrine of the will to believe to which William James drew attention; the fallacy of assuming the existence of something on the strength of one's convictions, as in Pascal's famous wager over the existence of God. Is it in this sense that Collingwood is arguing for the identity of faith and reason? Even in his later writings Collingwood stresses the importance of recognizing that the ontological argument is convincing only for those who already believe on faith what the argument seeks to demonstrate by reason.[15] Hume argued that reason is and ought always to be the slave of the passions. Is Collingwood arguing the similar doctrine that reason is and ought always to be the slave of faith and the feelings inspired by that faith?

In fact, Collingwood here and elsewhere denies that he is arguing to the reality of the historicity of Christ on the strength of feeling alone. He is rather determined to show that Christianity and its ability to inspire 'right conduct,' would not be absolutely unchanged by the demonstration that those things are mythical (RP, 54), in the same sense that the conduct of science would not be unchanged by a demonstration that there is no universal law of the uniformity of nature, no whole of which the fragments studied by science are parts.[16]

The same argument applies to the existence of God. The determination of what anyone believes about God is not a different thing from the question whether that belief is true (RP, 62). Collingwood does not, in any of his writings, accept any of the traditional proofs for the existence of God as rational or logical demonstrations. In the language of his later philosophy, what Collingwood is arguing here is that believing in the historical reality of Jesus is an absolute presupposition of the system of morality derived from his teachings, in the same sense in which he later argues, in *An Essay on Metaphysics*, that the proposition 'God Exists' is an absolute presupposition of the practice of natural science.

Yet the question remains; to be answered not by means of a priori demonstrations but by examining certain beliefs concerning God and the world which are central to Christian theology together with objections alleged against them, which, to the extent that they can be taken care of, lend credibility and authority to the beliefs. Here Collingwood appears to subscribe to a doctrine similar to Kierkegaard's doctrine of 'immediacy after reflection,' and J. S. Mill's doctrine that Truth is a function of the effort to refute it.[17] In both cases it is necessary to step outside the framework of belief and expose it to criticism as a condition of preserving its integrity as a belief system. Finally, these beliefs – having, to Collingwood's satisfaction, survived criticism – are applied to the solution of an interesting range of problems, such as, the incarnation, the atonement, miracle, and evil. The foundation of this inquiry, which occupies the remaining sections of *Religion and Philosophy*, is the conception of God as spirit (the antithesis of materialism), as person in relation to other persons (the antithesis of radical individualism), and as omniscient, omnipotent and perfectly good – which, of course raises the paradox of the co-existence of God and evil.

Collingwood's approach to the analysis and defence of the creed of Christianity takes shape within the wider context of a confrontation and debate between materialism and realism, on the one hand, and idealism and theism, on the other. In the final analysis Collingwood arrives at the theory of mind as pure act, previously referred to, in which the self-identity of mind is achieved by means of the self-dedication of the individual will with the will of God. While this might appear to mark the end of individuality, as in quietism and mysticism, it is, in reality but the beginning of a new and indeed more active life of self-realization (RP, 29; 65-66), in the same sense in which through the study of history the individual mind acquires its identity and makes itself through knowledge of the whole.

In Part Two, chapter III, which deals with personality, Collingwood defines and analyses the meaning of the self-identity of the individual person in the context of a bond between individuals and their community. The basis of this bonding is the sharing of the same knowledge and will to pursue the same ideals (RP, 98). According to this account and its implied epistemology, the relationship between mind and its object is not, as realism argues, the relationship of an independent subject thinking about objects. The mind, to repeat, is not so much that which thinks as the thinking itself; it is not an active thing but an activity. Its essence is not *res cogitans* but *cogitare*. It is not however a merely abstract power of thinking but the consciousness of something definite; particular thoughts about particular things. The *esse* of mind is not *cogitare* simply but *de hac re cogitare*.

In order to infer the identity of minds from the fact that they are thinking the same thought it is necessary, according to Collingwood, to distinguish between thinking and imagining, or between the thought and its image. Only in thinking does the mind achieve identity with its object such that two minds thinking the same object become one and the same mind. But merely to distinguish thinking from imagining does not yet provide the analysis of thinking which accounts for the identity in difference which Collingwood claims defines the relationship between thought and its object and which in the *Autobiography* he cites as the most difficult problem that he had to come to terms with – the answer to which took years to work out (A, 112-113).

What precisely is the problem with which Collingwood will be forced to wrestle in subsequent publications? The outlines of the problem are made clear by the doctrines which Collingwood hopes to establish with the theory of knowledge put forward in *Religion and Philosophy*. In the first place, as we have already noted, there is the doctrine of the identity of minds knowing the same object. Secondly, Collingwood insists that the identity of mind with its object which obtains in the act of knowing does not preclude progress in knowledge through which more and more of the object's nature is disclosed to the knowing mind.

By means of such progress, which takes the form of a progressive increase in knowledge of objects, the knowing mind itself comes to know itself better and is thereby able to make itself into a more and more adequate expression of its inherent potentialities. Thirdly, the relationship of identity between mind and its object does not preclude either the independent existence of a *rerum naturam* or the uniqueness of each person's individual self-consciousness. The community of individuals which is brought into existence by their all having knowledge of the same objects is a community of unique individuals; a unity in difference (RP, 101). Collingwood makes a point of emphasizing the difference between his position and that of subjective idealism in a footnote in which he declares that the argument of *Religion and Philosophy* 'contains little if anything which contradicts the principles of either Realism or Idealism in their more satisfactory forms,' and he cites Joachim's *The Nature of Truth*, Pritchard's *Kant's Theory of Knowledge*, and Carritt's *Theory of Beauty*, as examples (RP, 101).

The doctrine set forth in the chapter on personality is intended to set the stage for an analysis of religious consciousness as a knowledge of God (of whom we have knowledge but not images) in which, rather than the individual disappearing it is reborn (RP, 29). It thus becomes important for Collingwood to explain how this is possible. Once again the question arises, Whereupon does the uniqueness or individuality of each person's consciousness of the same thing consist? And once again Collingwood takes refuge in the doctrine of the concrete universal, or principle of identity-in-difference, without actually accounting for the conditions under which the terms of the doctrine are fulfilled. The best that Collingwood can offer at this stage is a description of the main tenets of the theory of truth that follows from the doctrine of the concrete universal – which is, that Truth, Reality or the Universal, expresses itself under infinitely various aspects, each of which is both identical with the rest (hence warranting being called by the same name) and yet different in ways which are significant. Neither does the difference destroy the identity nor does the identity destroy the difference (RP, 106). Conceived as an abstract universal, Reality, by contrast, consists of a series or collection of identical parts or species. Collingwood proceeds to apply this doctrine to the solution of the problems which comprise the creed of Christianity, without first having provided a satisfactory justification for the doctrine in the first place. This is finally accomplished, however, in *An Essay on Philosophical Method*, in the account given there of the logic of the overlap of classes and the scale of forms.

In *Religion and Philosophy* the doctrine of the concrete universal is applied to the task of accounting for the self-identity of individuals both as individuals and as members of a community, whose self-identity as a community – whether it is a genuine *Gemeinschaft* or a mere *Gesellschaft* – depends upon the individuals comprising it. The individuality of individuals is achieved not *in spite of* but *through* their identity with the community. Just as the community comes into existence gradually, through the acts of willing of its individual members, as if travelling through the spiral tunnel of an alpine railway, so that it ends not where it began, but in a beginning raised to a higher level, so the life of an individual person may similarly be construed as a self-making process in which the same relation of parts to whole obtains. The community, according to this analysis, is not simply an aggregate of externally related individuals (*Gesellschaft*) but a dynamic synthesis of internally related individuals (*Gemeinschaft*).

In such a community the individual members become a community by virtue of willing the same ends or ideals, thus producing a cooperation of wills, each of which is identical with the things which it does; which, to the extent that they are the outcome of willing the same things (goals, ideals, purposes) gives way to an identity in virtue of which the plurality of wills can be described as one, single, self-identical activity of willing (104). This conception of the community finds its parallel in the contemporary ecological conception of nature as an organic system of interdependent and interacting forces which complement each other in their mutual effort to sustain the web of life.

By the terms of Collingwood's social ecology, notwithstanding the fact that each person has his or her own peculiar duties and desires as dictated by his or her peculiar situation, there is a community of aims and desires which consists in the fact that what each person wants is something which he or she cannot have except with the help of everyone else. Or, each person desires the existence of a whole to which he or she can only contribute one among many parts. The other parts must be contributed by other people. And therefore, 'in willing my part I will theirs also' (RP, 106). The character or selfhood of the individual cannot be distinguished from its relations to other selves (RP, 112).

The model upon which the chapter on personality is based is the relationship of the individual to God. I suspect that for Collingwood this is also the basis upon which he has interpreted the meaning of the concrete universal as both transcendent, a Reality greater than what any finite mind can comprehend, yet immanent, the actual source of the ideals and goals whose pursuit by individuals becomes the basis of community. The love of God is what inspires the enterprise of co-operatively willing the same goals and provides an answer to the question which cannot be handled by pure reason, 'Why ought I to be moral?' To love God and believe in his existence is to affirm the moral law as an absolute presupposition to which we are committed as members of the community of persons, in the same sense in which, as Collingwood argues in *An Essay on Metaphysics*, the community of natural scientists are committed to the principle of the uniformity of nature – the affirmation of which is also an affirmation of the existence of God.

IV

One of the primary objectives of *Religion and Philosophy*, as it is for *An Essay on Metaphysics*, is to dethrone the abstract universal from its exalted place in the tradition of metaphysics and theology. In its place we find the concrete identity of activity. A mind is self-identical if it thinks and wills the same thing constantly; it is identical with another if it wills the same thing as that other. Both self-identity and identity with others persist through change, and indeed are presupposed by change. It is the property of truth to present itself under the aspect of innumerable differences; and yet within these differences it is still one. I have already suggested that in *An Essay on Philosophical Method* this conception of identity in difference is explained with reference to the doctrine of the scale of forms and the logic of the overlap of classes in which rather than the generic essence transcending entirely the variable element or aggregate of species, as in the case of the abstract universal, it is qua reality identical with its progressively changing appearances in time.

Precisely this kind of relationship between universal and particular applies both to the self-identity of God and his identity with the human mind. Keeping in mind that at this stage of his career the influence of idealism on Collingwood's thought is quite strong it would not be surprising to find that his theory of mind incorporates some version of the idealist doctrine of innate ideas as a foundation for the doctrine of the identity of God and man(RP, 119). To be human is thus to be inherently in communion with the divine mind of God. Why then, if this identity between God and the human mind exists is the history of humanity one of error and evil? What is the nature of the divine presence in a mind that wills evil? Or, what is the nature of God that his implicit identity with all finite minds can be superseded by an explicit affirmation of error and evil?

The answer depends upon a clarification of the meaning of immanence/transcendence with respect both to God and to community. God is first of all the knowledge of all things true; a knowledge not limited by ignorance, and capable therefore of existing side by side with a knowledge of all possible errors. He is secondly the active willing of all things good as well as the understanding of the possible willing of evil. The mind of God remains transcendent against the minds of finite human persons who out of ignorance are mired in error and is the ground of the possibility of overcoming error. To the extent that other minds share the thoughts and volitions of God – so far, that is, as they know any truth or will any good – they have become one with each other and with God. This unity is not simply the abstract identity of the co-existence of the mind of god and the minds of individual persons whose minds are the moving images of eternity. The unity in question is the concrete immanent unity of minds co-operating with each other in their active pursuit of common goals.

> Thus God is at once immanent and transcendent and man can be regarded as, on the one hand, a part of the universal divine spirit, and on the other, as a person separate from God and capable of opposition to him. God is immanent because all human knowledge and goodness are the indwelling of his spirit in the mind of man; transcendent because, whether or not man attains to these things, God has attained to them; his being does not depend upon the success of human endeavour (RP, 119).

In *Speculum Mentis* precisely this characterization is shown to apply to the Absolute, and in *The Idea of History* the doctrine of immanence/transcendence reappears as the model by means of which Collingwood explains the self-making life of the a priori idea of history which develops throughout time as a transcendent truth whose finite expressions comprise the history of historiography. It is by means of the same self-making process of immanence-transcendence that the ideas of nature, the state, and even philosophy itself have come into existence.

What Collingwood puts forward as a defensible case for theism could be regarded as a mere apologia for a humanism arrived at by experience and common sense. As Bertrand Russell has argued, Christians are persuaded that to love one's neighbour (and all that this entails) is a good thing because it is how God and Christ would wish us to behave. In truth it is only because people already hold such views that they regard Christ's teachings as evidence of his divinity. 'They have, that is to say, not an ethic based on theology but a theology based on their ethic. They apparently hold, however, that the non-theological grounds which make them think it a good thing to love your neighbour are not likely to make a wide appeal, and they therefore proceed to invent other arguments which they hope will be more effective.' This, according to Russell, is a very dangerous procedure.[18] So far as Russell is concerned, notwithstanding the fact that the members of the Christian community explicitly recognize that their conduct is an affirmation of the existence of God, God remains a mere unproven hypothesis.

Collingwood's response to this observation, while implicit in *Religion and Philosophy*, is not fully articulated until *An Essay on Metaphysics* in which he provides an alternative analysis of the proposition 'God Exists' to that of empiricism and positivism. Collingwood might argue against Russell that not only has he (Russell) committed the category mistake of confusing the belief in the existence of God with beliefs about the world of empirical facts which are subject to empirical verification, he has failed to recognize that uncertainty about the authority of the moral rules derived from common sense and experience is in fact well grounded, given the inability of reason to provide an answer to the question, 'Why ought I to be Moral?'

Rather than proving the existence of God Collingwood attempts in both *Religion and Philosophy* and *An Essay on Metaphysics* to explain what it means to believe in a God whose existence is not the conclusion of an argument but an absolute presupposition of the form of life which such a belief makes possible.

> Every good man, and every seeker after truth is really, even if unconsciously, co-operating with every other in the ideal of a complete science or a perfect world; and if co-operating, then identified with the other and with an all-embracing purpose of perfection. There really is such a purpose, which lives in the lives of all good men wherever they are found, and unifies them all into a life of its own. *This is God immanent*; [my italics] and it is no mere hypothesis (RP, 119).

The question remains, however, whether God is more than the will to believe, more than a useful fiction; whether it is equally certain that he also exists as transcendent, whose transcendence is not merely a projection of subjective certainty. The difficulty of answering this question, explains Collingwood in *Religion and Philosophy*, is bound up with the central problem of idealism, which is how to prove the existence of anything except as present to the mind. The arguments for pure immanence are at bottom identical with the philosophical creed of subjective idealism, and with that creed they stand or fall (RP, 120). But fall they must, if any sense is to be made of the doctrine of the incarnation and the problem of the co-existence of God and evil resolved. Only a transcendent God can be perfectly wise and good. And yet an immanent God must embrace evil as well as good, error as well as truth. How can the existence of a perfectly good God be reconciled with the reality of minds whose will is the very antithesis of his own? (RP, 121).

These are the questions to which the remainder of *Religion and Philosophy* are addressed. The burden of the chapter on evil is to show how the character of the perfect or ideal mind is implicit even in the imperfections of mind as we know it (RP, 124). This is accomplished by conceiving God not as imposing his will on the world from without, but as himself sharing in all the experiences of other minds (RP, 125) which collectively comprise a process of progressively overcoming error and evil by the truth and the good which contradicts it. To argue that in this process God is immanent does not mean that he shares the false opinions and evil wills of those who express them. He shares rather the suffering of those who recognizing the error of their ways choose to direct their will toward the good rather than evil or toward the truth rather than error in full knowledge that the evils and errors already committed remain. The problem of evil now reappears as follows:

> God is the absolute good will: his will includes all good actions and nothing else. How then can we identify him with a universe which includes both good and bad? The answer will be that within the same totality of will there cannot be both good and bad motives bearing on the same action or situation. Just so far as totality is attained, the good will must eliminate the bad, and therefore the universe conceived as a totality of will must be entirely good. Nor is this argument dependent on the hypothesis, if it is a hypothesis, of a perfectly good God; for it follows from the conception of the universe as containing both good and evil, without any assumption except that the parts of the universe are in relation to one another (RP, 142).

To the question, 'Why does God permit evil?' Collingwood's answer is,

> He does not permit it. His omnipotence is not restricted by it. He conquers it. But there is only one way in which it can be

conquered: not by the sinner's destruction, which would mean
the triumph of evil over good, but by his repentance (RP, 144).

It is the idea of repentance that lies at the basis of the doctrine of the
atonement for which the duty to punish rests on the same basis as the
duty to forgive; it is a pronouncement of the moral consciousness (RP,
171), and the foundation of justice, both secular and divine. The aim
of punishment, according to the doctrine of Atonement, is to bring the
criminal to accept his wrongdoing, to accept his condemnation by
society as just and deserved, and so punish himself, that is, inflict on
himself the pain of remorse and conversion from his evil past to a
better present (RP, 187).

There is only one way of destroying sin; namely to convert the sinner
(RP, 192). The condemnation of the criminal or sinner by men and
women of good will is also God's punishment and condemnation – the
act of a transcendent God. Through condemnation and punishment,
the minds of God and mankind are identical. But God is also present
in the act of repentance. God's punishment of man is man's own self-
punishment, and man's repentance is also God's repentance (RP, 187).
Atonement is thus the re-indwelling of divine spirit in a person who
has previously been alienated from it – an alienation which God per-
mits and suffers through in the act of repentance as well as suffering
through the pain of self-punishment and remorse.

In this doctrine, the omnipotence of God is not limited by his
willingness to permit sin but is rather reaffirmed by the fact of the possibility inherent in the consciousness and will of the criminal/sinner for
remorse and repentance. God's purpose of redemption is powerless apart
from man's will to be redeemed, yet only in a universe in which God
exists is such a conversion of will possible or even conceivable. But
because such a decision on the part of a person is not forced or determined in any causal sense by the will of God, it can be considered a
miracle. And because the possibility of conversion is always inherent in
the universe, the universe, it might be said, exists in a state of perfection. For while the perfection of the universe depends upon its being
a totality of all things good, it is a totality *in posse* not *in esse* (RP, 142),
and the goodness of the universe is therefore manifest, even in the will

to evil. Vice always exists in a will which is not only potentially but actually to some extent virtuous (RP, 143).

> Evil can exist only in an environment of good. No society is ever utterly depraved, and crime owes its existence to the fact that it is exceptional . . . It seems then that there cannot be . . . a totally bad person, and *a fortiori* a totally bad society or universe. If coherence and totality are to be attained at all, they must be attained by complete goodness. And, if we are right, they can be thus attained. A will can be absolutely good; not in the sense that it is ignorant of evil, but in the sense that it knows the evil and rejects it, just as a sound intellect is not ignorant of possible errors, but sees through them to the truth. This state is equally perfection, whether it has been won through error and sin, or without them; for the mind is not in bondage to its own past, but may use it as the means either of good or evil (RP, 144).

In subsequent publications Collingwood takes up many of the issues raised in *Religion and Philosophy*. Although the techniques of analysis may change, and the doctrines espoused fall more and more under the influence of the kind of historicism expressed in *The Idea of History* and *An Essay on Metaphysics,* the fundamental convictions from which the earlier work draws its inspiration remain intact. Among the concerns which occupied him in his later philosophy the relationship between religion, metaphysics, science and civilization, was of primary importance. But as the later half of *Religion and Philosophy* makes clear he had a great interest in the kinds of topics which are today taken up in the areas of moral issues and applied ethics – or what might more generally be regarded as social philosophy. Much of what he might have contributed in these areas can be gleaned from his chapters on personality, evil and redemption. Its a pity that he did not live to develop his thoughts on these topics in ways which might have thrown an interesting perspective on the fundamental moral issues of our time. There is nothing however to prevent those interested in Collingwood's thought to pursue this project on their own. And for this purpose, a serious re-examination of *Religion and Philosophy* will prove most rewarding.

NOTES

1 London, Macmillan & Co., Ltd.

2 Bristol, Thoemmes Press, 1994, in the series *Key Texts: Classic Studies in the History of Ideas*.

3 'Faith and Reason in the Philosophy of Religion,' in David Boucher, James Connelly and Tariq Modood, eds., *Philosophy, History and Civilization* (Cardiff, University of Wales Press, 1995), p. 79.

4 Boucher, Connelly, Modood (eds.), *Philosophy, History and Civilization*, 87.

5 Some exceptions to this tendency are John P. Hogan's *Collingwood and Theological Hermeneutics* (University Press of America, 1989); D. M. MacKinnon's 'Faith and Reason in the Philosophy of Religion,' in Boucher, Connelly and Modood, (eds.), *Philosophy, History and Civilization* and David Bates' 'Rediscovering Collingwood's Spiritual History,' *History and Theory*, 35 (1996).

6 *Mind History and Dialectic: The Philosophy of R. G. Collingwood* (Bloomington, Indiana University Press, 1969), 260, n. 7.

7 See, *Faith and Reason* (Ernest Benn, 1928), and 'Reason is Faith Cultivating Itself,' *Hibbert Journal*, 1927. Both are reprinted in Lionel Rubinoff, ed., *Faith and Reason: Essays in the Philosophy of Religion by R. G. Collingwood* (Chicago, Quadrangle Press, 1968).

8 Rubinoff (ed.), *Faith and Reason*, 20.

9 In *An Essay on Metaphysics*, written in 1940, Collingwood describes the 'tendency of late years, even in theological circles, to . . . regard religion as an affair of the emotions,' as a symptom of what he calls 'The progaganda of irrationalism.' This tendecy, he continues, has the effect of substituting for the worship of universal truth and goodness the worship of a sectional or tribal god personifying the mass-emotions of a particular people.' (Oxford, At The Clarendon Press, ch. XIII, 137.) This is precisely, according to Collingwood, what explains the rise of Fascism and Nazism in Europe, which he regarded as a resurgence of pagan emotions made possible by the collapse of the Christian Faith.

10 *Philosophy*, 15 (1940). Reprinted in R. G. Collingwood, *Essays in Political Philosophy*, ed. David Boucher (Oxford, The Clarendon Press, 1989).

11 All page references are to the reprinted version in David Boucher's edition of Collingwood's *Essays in Political Philosophy* (Oxford, Clarendon Press, 1989).

12 Oxford University Press, 1939, ch. X1, pp. 137 ff. Cf. also, pp. 97-99.

13 *An Essay on Metaphysics* (Oxford, Clarendon Press, 1940), ch. VIII.

14 Oxford, Clarendon Press, 1924, p. 36

15 See in this regard 'Faith and Reason,' in L. Rubinoff (ed.), *Faith and Reason*, p.135.

16 The relationship between religion and science which is explored at length in *An Essay on Metaphysics* (esp. in Part III), was first raised in ch.I of *Religion and Philosophy* and in 'Religion, Science and Philosophy,' *Truth and Freedom*, II, 1926; reprinted in Rubinoff (ed.), 89 ff.

17 *On Liberty*, ch. 2. Thus Mill writes, 'The beliefs which we have the most warrant for have no safeguard to rest on but a standing invitation to the whole world to prove them unfounded.'

18 'Can Religion Cure Our Troubles,' in *Why I am Not a Christian* (New York, Simon & Schuster, 1957), 200.

COLLINGWOOD
CORNER

Art, History and Science: The Contrasting Worlds of Collingwood and Oakeshott

Complied and Introduced by
JAMES CONNELLY
Southampton Institute

Consideration of the relationship between the forms or modes of human experience, a concern with understanding the character of different ways of knowing the world, was central to the philosophical work of both R. G. Collingwood and Michael Oakeshott. They were near contemporaries, Collingwood being the older man by twelve years. It might be said of both that they kept philosophical idealism alive, although both would probably have disclaimed both the intention and achievement. In many respects their philosophical approach was convergent; but in others ways it was strikingly divergent.[1]

In addition to their writings developing a general account of the modes of experience, both also wrote extensively on art, history, politics, education and religion as subjects in their own right. Collingwood wrote about science at greater length than Oakeshott who, in turn, wrote at greater length about politics. The characterisation each gave of the forms or modes of experience displayed a certain general similarity; but this broad similarity of approach masked an equally significant dissimilarity. For example, in *Speculum Mentis* Collingwood conceived the forms of experience as forming an overlapping scale. For Oakeshott, by contrast, modes did not overlap and did not form a hierarchy of any sort: the profoundest intellectual error was to confuse modes or speak of one in terms appropriate only to another.

Neither philosopher wrote extensively about the other, although where they did there was generally a high degree of mutual esteem. Collingwood wrote that 'Oakeshott's work . . . represents the high-water mark of English thought upon history', (*Idea of History*, p. 159), and Oakeshott wrote that 'Collingwood happened to possess in large measure the genius both of the historian and the philosopher.' Collingwood wrote directly about Oakeshott in the review reprinted below and also in Part IV of *The Idea of History*. Oakeshott wrote two reviews of Collingwood – of *The Principles of Art* and on *The Idea of History*. His other comments, such as they were, were both more oblique and more critical. He rarely mentioned Collingwood by name, even where it is clear that he was controverting him. For example, in 'The Activity of being an Historian' he writes that:

> The 'historian' adores the past; but the world today has perhaps less place for those who love the past than ever before. Indeed, it is determined not to allow events to remove themselves securely into the past; it is determined to keep them alive by a process of artificial respiration or (if need be) to recall them from the dead so that they may deliver their messages. For it wishes only to learn from the past and it constructs a 'living past' which repeats with spurious authority the utterances put into its mouth. But to the 'historian' this is a piece of obscene necromancy: the past he adores is dead.
> (*Rationalism in Politics*, London: Methuen, 1962, p. 166.)

With a polemical stroke of his pen Oakeshott thus dismisses Collingwood's conception of the living past as well as the suggestion that historical knowledge has or ought to have any practical import. And here Oakeshott is returning to an old battleground. In *The Idea of History* Collingwood suggests that Oakeshott finds himself in a dilemma in which the past has to be conceived of as either dead or as not past at all but simply present. The only escape from this dilemma, he suggests, lies in the conception of the living past, living because re-enacted in the present. Oakeshott will have none of this: the past is past; there is an historical past and a practical past; a practical past might conceivably be called a living past, but such a past has nothing to do with the historical past. There is thus, for Oakeshott, no genuine overlap between history and practice, although in the practical world we might use the past for our own purposes. His earlier rejection of the practical value of history ran as follows:

> Whenever history finds itself joined with practical experience, the result can only be the destruction of both. No guidance for practical life can be expected to follow from the organisation of the totality of experience *sub specie praeteritorum*. The world of history has no data to offer of which practical experience can make use; and to conceive it as offering such data is to misconceive its character. This does not mean that in matters of practice any form of appeal to any past is always irrelevant . . . What it means is that this practical appeal to a practical past is not even an abuse (much less a 'use') of history, it is merely not history at all . . . Neither the truth nor the character of history depend, in any way, upon its having some lesson to teach us. And if ever we persuade ourselves that the past has taught us something, we may be certain that it is not the historical past which has been our teacher.
>
> (*Experience and its Modes*, 1933, pp. 157-8)

Oakeshott will clearly have no truck with either Collingwood's scale of forms nor with his view that history can provide insight and practical wisdom. This was stated explicitly in *An Autobiography*:

> So long as the past and present are outside one another, knowledge of the past is not of much use in the problems of the present. But suppose the past lives on in the present; suppose, though incapsulated in it, and at first sight hidden beneath the present's contradictory and more prominent features, it is still alive and active; then the historian may very well be related to the non-historian as the trained woodsman is to the ignorant traveller. 'Nothing here but trees and grass', thinks the traveller, and marches on. 'Look,' says the woodsman, 'there is a tiger in that grass.' The historian's business is to reveal the less obvious features hidden from a careless eye in the present situation. What history can bring to moral and political life is a trained eye for the situation in which one has to act.
>
> (*An Autobiography*, p. 100)

Oakeshott's distinction between the practical past and the historical past would be alien to Collingwood, and Collingwood's view that we study history to study how we came to be where we are and are thereby enabled to act would therefore be alien to Oakeshott. Where Collingwood found overlap, unity in diversity, and dialectical development, Oakeshott found separation, diversity and an absence of dialectic.

Elsewhere, as in, for instance, their writings on art, Oakeshott and Collingwood also show interesting divergences. In 'The Voice of Poetry in the Conversation of Mankind' Oakeshott adopts a position close in many respects to Collingwood's. The greatest difference appears, again, in their respective views on the relation of art with practice. Hence, whatever in Collingwood's philosophy of art he was disposed to accept, Oakeshott was certainly not disposed to accept the idea of the artist's role in the community as curing corruption of consciousness (*Rationalism in Politics*, p. 240). For Oakeshott, art was to be delighted in for its own sake and it had (and would be foolish to seek) any sort of practical import; for Collingwood the position is different. His view is that art should be pursued for its own sake, but that in being pursued for its own sake it nonetheless succeeds in having profound practical value.

In addition to the three Oakeshott-Collingwood pieces, we reprint two pieces by Collingwood dealing with, respectively, *The Principles of Art* and the relationship between science and history. Collingwood's views on the relationship between science and history are expressed in many different places, both in books such as *Speculum Mentis* and in articles and other books. The piece reprinted below dates from 1923 when he was writing *Speculum Mentis*. The piece on *The Principles of Art* is taken from the *Transactions of the Cumberland and Westmoreland Antiquarian and Archaeological Society* where it appeared anonymously. It seem probable, however, bearing in mind both the tone of the piece, its implicit claiming of a privileged standpoint, that it was written by Collingwood himself. It is interesting to note the claim that one of the aims of the book is 'to illustrate the author's doctrine concerning the relation between philosophy and history by focusing attention on contemporary art and its problems, and treating these as part of the problem of contemporary civilisation.'

OAKESHOTT AND THE MODES OF EXPERIENCE

(A review of Michael Oakeshott, *Experience and its Modes. Cambridge Review*, February 16th, 1934).

'*Experience* stands for the concrete whole which analysis divides into *experiencing* and *what is experienced*: and experience is not mere consciousness, it is also and always thought, judgement, assertion of reality: there is no sensation which is not also thought, no intuition which is not also judgement, no volition which is not cognition: these, like the subject-object distinction, are distinctions valid in themselves but erroneous if taken as implying a real division between the elements distinguished. Experience, thus conceived, may be pictured as an infinite ocean or endlessly-flowing river; and to navigate its waters, conscious of their infinity, is to philosophise; for philosophy, alone among forms of experience, is identical with experience itself, 'experience without reservation or arrest, without presupposition or postulate, without limit or category.'

But experience may be 'modified' by arresting it at this or that point, and there, using the point of arrest as an inviolable postulate, constructing a 'world of ideas' in terms of this postulate. Such a world of ideas is not a constituent element in experience, not a reach of the river, but a backwater of the river, a digression from the unreserved flow of experience; but it is not a 'world of mere ideas' it is not only coherent in itself but is a special way of representing experience as a whole; not a world, but *the* world as seen from that point of view, and, subject to that qualification, rightly seen. Such a world is a 'mode' of experience. There are many such modes; theoretically their number is infinite; but none is inevitable; every one of them, in so far as the arrest of experience at that point is unjustified, rests on a foundation of error, and the concrete world of experience is achieved by avoiding them all.

Such, though sadly travestied by this clumsy compression of his statement, is Mr Oakeshott's main conception; from which he proceeds to examples by a survey of three modes: history, science and practice. Each of these is a complete and self-contained world; not a part of experience, but experience itself as organised and envisaged under one particular category. History is the world *sub specie praeteritorum*: its differentia is the attempt to organise the whole world of experience in the form of the past. Science is the world *sub specie quantitatis*: its differentia is the attempt to organise the world of experience as a system of measurements. Practice is the world *sub specie voluntatis*: the world as a system of acts, each modifying 'what is' so as to bring it into harmony with what ought to be.

I have tried to expound Mr Oakeshott's thesis rather than criticise it, because it is so original, so important, and so profound that criticism must be silent until his meaning has been long pondered. Nor is the thesis an essay in system-building copied (as his modest expressions of indebtedness might possibly suggest) from Hegel and Bradley. It has been arrived at, I suspect, mainly from an intense effort to understand the nature of historical knowledge. Mr Oakeshott writes of history like an accomplished historian who, driven into philosophy by the problems of his own work, has found the current philosophies impotent to cope with their philosophical implications; and in that sense the chapter on history seems to me the real nucleus of his book. Of this chapter, I can, in this brief notice, only say that it is the most penetrating analysis of historical though that has ever been written, and will remain a classic in that hitherto almost unexplored branch of philosophical research. But the whole book shows Mr Oakeshott to possess philosophical gifts of a very high order, coupled with an admirable command of language; his writing is as clear as his though is profound, and all students of philosophy should be grateful to him for his brilliant contribution to philosophical literature.

COLLINGWOOD'S PHILOSOPHY OF ART

Review by Michael Oakeshott of *The Principles of Art. Cambridge Review*, June 9th, 1938.

Since I doubt my capacity to give in this review any adequate and convincing impression of the value and importance of this book, I can do no better than state at once that it is the most profound and stimulating discussion I have ever read of the question, What is art? The field of aesthetic enquiry has not, indeed, been barren up till now, but this book gives us so much that it is difficult for us to persuade ourselves of the value to what we had before. It is the work of an artist and a philosopher; it is written with a charm and a vigour which matches the subtlety and sanity of its doctrine; and it leaves the reader with the impression that he has been in touch with a mind of altogether exceptional learning, tact and penetration. All these are qualities that we have learned to expect from the work of Professor Collingwood; anyone who had read *Speculum Mentis* or *An Essay on Philosophical Method* would open this book anticipating a brilliant performance, but here is something even better than he could have expected. It is a delight to witness the masterly unfolding of its argument; it is equally a delight to follow the author when he steps aside from the exposition of his main thesis to reinterpret Plato's remarks on art, to expose the 'quibbles and sophistries' of Freud's views on magic or to give us his reflections on the condition of art yesterday and to-day.

'The business of this book is to answer the question: What is art?' It is not, however, an attempt 'to investigate and expound eternal verities concerning the nature of an eternal object called Art,' but an attempt to deal with the problems which force themselves upon anyone 'who looks around at the present condition of the arts in our own civilisation.' It is the attempt of an artist and an historian, fortified by the critical mind of a philosopher, to make clear to himself the nature of art and the conditions of its life in the world to-day. Anyone who begins to cultivate this field will find in it a luxuriant growth of weeds, and there is plenty of hard hitting in his book; but of carping criticism the reader will find nothing.

The method of exposition, which is also a method of thought, which Professor Collingwood pursues, may be called a Socratic method. First, without any suggestion of a theory, he tries to disentangle what, as a matter of fact, we all know about art, in the belief that the truth is to be found *in* what we all know about it, though often that truth is not exactly what we at first take it to be. This leaves us with a number of philosophical questions to be investigated, because in stating what we all know about art we make use of words and expressions – sensation, thought, emotion, language – which call for analysis. Lastly, there comes the construction of a Theory of Art, a synthesis of the truths which have emerged and established themselves in the earlier discussions. And it may be said that not the least of the delights of this book is its masterly handling of this method.

The argument begins, then, with an attempt to distinguish Art from not Art, to make certain that we know how to apply the word 'art' where it ought to be applied and refuse where it ought to be refused. And it leads to the rejection of certain things which, though they are often confused with art, have a character different from that of art. These are craft or skill, magic and amusement. The confusion of these things with art is dangerous because it has led, in each case, to a false aesthetic theory and to the perversion of art itself. These opening chapters admirably display Professor Collingwood's acute critical mind and are among the best in the book. But destruction is followed by construction, and art proper is shown to have two characteristics: expression of emotion and imagination. And the conclusion of this first inspection of the subject is that 'by creating for ourselves an imaginary experience or activity we express our emotions; and this is what we call art.'

But 'what this formula means, we do not yet know.' And in order to find out we must penetrate a world of philosophical analysis, consider the nature of sensation, feeling, thought and emotion and the nature of language. This, for the ordinary reader, will be the most difficult part of the book; but he need not be afraid of it, for the doctrines are expounded so lucidly that all but the absolutely unavoidable difficulties are absent.

The last part of the book, consisting of three chapters – Art as Language, Art and Truth, and The Artist and the Community – contains the final expression of his theory of art. It would be stupid here to attempt any exposition of the doctrine, and worse to offer any criticism of matters of detail. The value of the book does not depend upon our being convinced by the doctrine (though I myself find it singularly convincing); it lies in the experience it offers of following a masterly discussion of all the fundamental questions which any doctrine must consider. And Professor Collingwood's concluding reflections on the condition and future of art in England are of exceptional interest.

This is not the sort of book that has to be recommended with the qualification that the hard labour entailed in reading it will be rewarded in the end; the reader is rewarded on every page. If there is anyone who, because of the nonsense he has been obliged to read, doubts whether a philosopher can talk sense about art, let him read this book. It has something to offer anyone interested in literature or art; it is a book in which, for example, anyone engaged in the study of literature in a University will find illumination. And it is a book which anyone who can take pleasure in a profound and critical piece of philosophical thinking will find a delight.

Notice of *The Principles of Art, Transactions of
the Cumberland and Westmorland Antiquarian
and Archaeological Society*.
New Series, Vol. XXXVIII, p. 314. This is unsigned,
but appears to be by Collingwood himself.

This, the author's chief work down to the present time, is a treatise on aesthetic. Its aim is not simply to add one more to the many extant 'theories of art,' but to illustrate the author's doctrine concerning the relation between philosophy and history by focusing attention on contemporary art and its problems, and treating these as part of the problem of contemporary civilisation.

It is divided into three parts. Book 1 is devoted to establishing the distinction between 'art proper' and certain other things which are habitually confused with it: namely amusement, understood as the technique of arousing emotions for the sake of their own pleasurable-ness, and magic, or the arousing of emotions for the sake of their practical value in the affairs of life. The theories of amusement and magic are worked out in detail, and an analysis is made of the parts they play in modern European civilisation. Art proper is shown to have two leading characteristics: (1) it is expression of emotion, as distinct from excitation of emotion, (2) it is an exercise of the imagination, as distinct from a technique of manufacturing bodily or perceptible objects.

Book II works out these distinctions by propounding a theory of knowledge with special reference to imagination. This faculty is com-monly ignored by the schools of philosophy now fashionable, which habitually confuse its work with that of sensation. To correct this error it is necessary to criticise the doctrine of these schools and make contact with the classical tradition of European thought, in particular with Hume, whose work has never been more neglected than by those contemporary philosophers who profess themselves his disciples.

In Book III the results of this theoretical discussion are brought to bear on the special problems of contemporary art. Our traditional pictures of 'the artist' and of his work are shown to be in many respects false and an attempt is made to build up a new picture, which may help to show artists what they should aim at doing and to show others what they should require artists to do for them.

HISTORY

Review by Michael Oakeshott of *The Idea of History* in the *English Historical Review*, LXII, 1947, pp. 84-6.

No small part of the native genius of a philosopher lies in the perception of where in the world of contemporary speculation is the point from which advance may best be made; for such perception (coming as it must early in life) springs less from a profound study of history of philosophy than from an intuitive apprehension of what is opportune. Collingwood's genius led him to perceive that, while for three centuries philosophy had concerned itself primarily with the logical and epistemological problems thrown up by natural science, little discussion had been given to the no less difficult problem of the character and possibility of historical knowledge. And it may be said that, with the single exception of Croce, he is the only philosopher of first-class ability to give prolonged and concentrated attention to this problem. *The Idea of History* contains all that is recoverable of his achievement in this direction. But, unfinished and scrappy though it is, it is enough to show that if he had been unhindered by ill-health and early death he could have done for historical knowledge something like what Kant did for natural science.

Collingwood died before he was able to put into final form his reflections on historical knowledge. What we have here has been selected and edited by Professor T. M. Knox from the considerable body of manuscripts which Collingwood left behind. The only previously published writing reprinted here is his Inaugural Lecture as Waynflete Professor of

Metaphysical Philosophy on *Human Nature and Human History* (1935) and the British Academy lecture on *The Historical Imagination* (1936). The editor's admirable preface explains the character of the manuscripts with which he has had to deal and the circumstances in which they were written, and contains besides an appreciation, at once moving and critical, of Collingwood as a man and as a philosopher, for which all friends and students of Collingwood will be grateful.

About two-thirds of the book is based upon lectures on the philosophy of history, originally composed in 1936, which trace the changing character of the conception of the historians' subject matter, method and aim from the emergence of historical thinking in Greco-Roman civilisation to the present time. Much of this account, particularly the early part, is written with Collingwood's accustomed subtlety and brilliance; all of it exemplifies his remarkable powers of critical sympathy. As an historian of ideas his outstanding quality was imaginative appreciation of the mind and purposes of writers whom he considers. The peculiar generosity of his appreciation sprang, not from any lack of ideas on his own account, but from an ability to detect the condition and difficulties that produce the limitations of a writer's achievement; it sprang from the conviction that everything which comes to the historian has value and meaning if only the imagination can detect it and the intellect grasp it. The task of the historian of ideas, as he saw it, was precisely to understand a writer more profoundly than the writer understood himself, just as the task of the historian of feudal society (for example) is to understand that society more profoundly than anyone who merely enjoyed it could understand it. But I think the reader of this account of the history of historical thinking will suffer some disappointment as he proceeds. For, while the earlier part consists of an examination of how the historical writers of the ancient world went about their business and the presuppositions that lie behind their achievement, the later part comes to consist more and more of an examination of the ideas of philosophical writers about the nature of historical knowledge, and the historian himself is less and less called upon for evidence. And the final chapter on scientific history contains scarcely any examination of modern historical writing, though it does call upon the philosophical reflections of such historians as had any to offer. No doubt

Collingwood saw that a study of the eighteenth and nineteenth centuries of the same kind as his study of Greek historiography was impossible, and indeed less necessary, on account of the growth of what may be called the self-consciousness of historical thought. There are, of course gaps in this account of historical thinking, caused mainly by the scale on which it is conceived, and often the treatment of important periods is very slight, but the only serious gap is the absence of a discussion of the importance of the study of Christian origins in raising the problems of the nature and possibility of historical knowledge during the last two hundred years, an importance that makes, for example, Schweitzer's *Von Reimarus su Wrede* a classic in the history of historiography.

The last hundred pages of *The Idea of History* is all that remains of Collingwood's projected work on the principles of historical knowledge, but it is enough to put him ahead of every other writer on the subject. He discerned that history had come to take its place beside natural science as a presumptive form of knowledge, and conceiving it to one of the tasks of philosophy to reflect the dominant interest of a time, he concluded that the contemporary philosopher had a special obligation to examine the nature of historical knowledge. His first concern was to distinguish historical from scientific knowledge, and establishing its autonomy in its own field, he enquired into its character and possibility. History is knowledge of the actions of human beings that have been done in the past, acquired by the interpretation of evidence. Since it is concerned with human actions it is always a history of thoughts and ideas, and, in the end, it consists in an imaginative entry into the minds of people now dead. Its purpose is: self-knowledge: historical knowledge is knowledge of what man has done and thus of what man is. It is impossible to follow Collingwood into all the subtle detail of his conception, but brief (and owing to the occasions of its exposition, somewhat disconnected and repetitive) though the argument is, it is profoundly thought out and brilliantly expounded. But is must be observed that, almost imperceptibly, Collingwood's philosophy of history turned into a philosophy in which all knowledge is assimilated to historical knowledge, and consequently into a radically sceptical philosophy. In which direction he would have gone from this position, for it is not likely that he could have stayed there, it is impossible to guess.

The important thing is that he had made a notable contribution to the philosophy of history before he sheered off on this fresh tack.

The question that the historian as such no doubt will ask is, what is the bearing of this or any analysis of the epistemological problems involved in historical knowledge upon the task of writing history? At every point in his philosophy of history Collingwood drew upon his actual experience as an historian, and there is no doubt that he considered himself to be a better historian for having thought out an answer to the question: How is historical knowledge possible? But what he says of natural science he knew to be no less true of history: 'Long before Bacon and Descartes revolutionised natural science by expounding publicly the principles on which its method was based, people here and there had been using these same methods, some more often, some more rarely. As Bacon and Descartes so justly pointed out, the effect of their work was to put these same methods within the grasp of quite ordinary intellectuals.' The true historian is not necessarily a self-conscious historical thinker. Historical imagination belongs to his genius, and he uses it as a native faculty which is as much a natural gift as an aptitude for mathematics or music, escaping the errors of positivists and others, not by a reflective knowledge of the philosophical principles of historical thought, but by means of his intuitive grasp of his own subject, and without knowing in detail what he is escaping. The problems of the philosopher, though real, are of his own making, arising from the question he, but not the historian, must ask himself. Collingwood happened to possess in large measure the genius both of the historian and the philosopher.

NOTE

1 It is impossible to do full justice here to the relationship between the philosophies of Collingwood and Oakeshott. The following are valuable for anyone wishing to explore further: D. Boucher, 'Overlap and Autonomy: The Different Worlds of Collingwood and Oakeshott', *Storia, Antropologia e scienze del linguaggio*, Anno IV, fascicolo 2-3, 1989, pp. 69-89; D. Boucher 'Human conduct, history, and social science in the works of R. G. Collingwood and Michael Oakeshott', *New Literary History*, Summer 1993, vol. 24, no 3, pp. 697-717; P. Franco *The Political Philosophy of Michael Oakeshott*, Yale U.P. 1990; W. H. Greenleaf, *Oakeshott's Philosophical Politics*. London: Longmans Green, 1966.

Science and History

R. G. COLLINGWOOD

The Vasculum. Vol. 9, No. 2, 1923, pp. 52-59.

The tramp that underlies the civilised surface of an Englishman wakes up in August, and drives him afield to face the rain and the sun and his thoughts. He lodges in lonely inns, the lonelier the better, and these he will revisit till he begins to fancy they are growing fashionable, when he abandons them for yet remoter haunts. My inn, on the evening of which I write, must have reached the second phase of this cycle. It stood bleakly, wrapped in mist, near the edge of a cliff, on an unfrequented road. There was no village within a mile, nor town within ten; and the only sounds about it were the voice of the sea against the cliff and the rushing of winds. But inside I found two other temporary tramps, drinking tea and eating bacon; and when they had finished they seemed to resume a long-standing argument, to which, after the first of my hunger was allayed, I began to pay attention.

"Your scientific methods are all right for stars and electrons and prime numbers," the younger man was saying, "but they don't seem to fit when you come to men and women. You can tell exactly what a planet will do when it comes into a gravitational field, and you gain nothing by watching to see whether it does it or not. If you do watch, and it doesn't do it, you only conclude that the gravitational field wasn't there. But if you expose a man to a temptation, there is no rule that tells you how he will react. If he resists the temptation, that does not prove it wasn't there. Every fresh person is a fresh fact, and you have to study him afresh from the very beginning. A planet isn't a fresh fact in that sense, it is just another instance of a known law. But there aren't any laws of human conduct; or if there are, they have so many exceptions that they aren't any use."

The other man had been elaborately cleaning his pipe, and was filling it. When it was alight, he said, "Then you don't think there is any science of man?"

"No," said the younger, "no science, only history. Anthropology and psychology and economics aren't real sciences – their laws are only rough generalisations, not the least like the laws of chemistry and physics, which are absolutely true. I suppose matter is subject to really uniform laws; but when you get to human beings you get to mind, and every mind is unique and unlike every other. So types disappear – or at least, if they exist, they are quite unimportant – and there are only individuals. And where everything is individual, science has no foothold: you can only observe the fresh facts, and that is history."

There was a moment's silence, and then the older man asked, "But you think the astronomer does understand the motions of a planet?"

"Oh yes: he understands it by seeing that it merely exemplifies a physical law."

"But in that case the historian doesn't understand human actions at all."

"Why do you say that?"

"Because he doesn't reduce them to examples of a law, and that is what you say understanding means."

"Yes, I suppose that is true. The historian doesn't understand human actions: he simply records them as facts."

"As unintelligible facts, that is to say. But all facts aren't unintelligible. The astronomer records facts, and so does every scientist. But he goes on to discover their laws, and when he is done that he understands them. So far as each records facts, I suppose there is no difference between a historian and a scientist. The difference is that one stops short at the bare fact, while the other goes on to try and understand it. You say human actions can't be understood, because they are unintelligible. But isn't that the severest condemnation of history? We have the faculty of reason; and if history doesn't give us a field for exercising it, so much the worse for history. If you are right, history is no fit study for a grown man, who wants above all to think, to understand, to see reason in things, not just to note them down."

"But do you really think that human action is unintelligible?"

"I don't think so: it is you who think that. I am only a poor scientist and I think psychology and economics and so on really can explain human actions. The historian, as I look at him, is only a harmless necessary drudge collecting facts for the scientist. When he has got the facts, the scientist will produce the theory which makes them intelligible. Meantime, please go on with your history: it will all come in handy one day – like butterfly-collecting, you know."

The younger man seemed a little ruffled. "That's all nonsense," he said. You talk about this fine future science that is going to be brewed and somehow out of historical facts, when it is settled what the facts are: but there are heaps of historical facts settled, quite enough to form the basis of any science. Newton wanted some celestial motions accurately observed before he could work out his theory of gravitation, but he didn't say to the astronomers 'first discover every fact about every heavenly body, and then I'll tell you why it all happens.' The moon was good enough for him. Why isn't Julius Caesar good enough for the sociologist, or whatever you are going to call your scientist of human life? I'll tell you: it is because the moon faithfully exemplifies the general rule about bodies, but there isn't any general rule about people, so Julius Caesar can't exemplify it – and neither would all the facts of all history, past, present and to come."

"I don't think so," said the scientist. The laws of human conduct are more complex than those of gravitating bodies, that is all: and it follows that one needs more data for discovering them."

What you are really asking for," said the other, "is an infinity of data, which means that the laws are infinitely complex, which is as good as to say there aren't any."

The scientist thought it over, and broke slowly into a smile. "Do you know, I believe you are right about that," he said. "I have often thought that people who talked big about the future were trying to cover their inability to do anything about the present; and now I've fallen into the same pit myself. Of course this idea of a future sociological science which will absorb history is just a case in point. But I still say that understanding is a higher thing than observation: and if we can't hope to understand human action, that doesn't absolve history from the charge of being a low type of thought, because it is exercised on an object which obstructs thought by being unintelligible."

"I wonder," said the younger man, "whether understanding is everything. Aren't there puzzles in science? and doesn't all research imply something unknown, something in the dark, so to speak, some mystery?"

"Now it's you that are talking nonsense," said the other. "Puzzles – mysteries if you like – are all very well so long as you regard them as having an answer. A question that hasn't an answer is one that isn't worth asking. And by your own showing the problem of human conduct is one without an answer. It is a nonsense question."

"Then why not stop asking it?" the younger replied. "If there just isn't any 'why' for human conduct, history has the last word: for history just finds out what happened, and leaves it there."

There was a pause, and I heard the wind howling in the chimney. "I sometimes wonder," said the older man at last, rather drowsily, "whether even science does any more than that. After all, the scientist moves among facts just like the historian. I've been collecting fossils here; and when I say I understand the geology of the country I mean I can tell you to what horizons these formations belong, when they are laid down, and what has happened to them since. Isn't that the whole of geology – discovering or rather guessing at historical facts?

"Yes, there's a lot in that, and of course geology in that sense is just history. But surely a scientist does try to see why things happen."

"Well, doesn't a historian? I'm not one; but I know they always go on about the causes of things. We had quite a row the other day in our common-room because two of them lost their tempers over the cause of – I think it was the Peloponnesian War. I pointed out that the real cause of their disagreement was that they had both been correcting examination papers for the last ten days: but that only made them worse."

The younger man got up, and knocked his pipe out. On the hearth-rug he turned and faced us. "I believe we've been going on the wrong track," he said. "We both try to find out the why of things, and we are both more interested in facts than in anything else. It is all nonsense to say that what a scientist cares for is mere generalities, and what a historian cares for is mere facts. Neither is any use by itself. Generalisations are ways of grouping facts, and facts aren't facts at all until they are grouped. All the ordinary talk about the difference between science and history is on the wrong lines. Still, I do think there's an important difference somewhere, but I'm too sleepy to think of it tonight. I've walked thirty miles, and I'm going to bed. You had better go too: you've been half asleep for the last ten minutes."

I hadn't walked thirty miles, and their talk had interested me. I sat up and had another pipe. There is a real difference between the scientific and historical points of view, I thought, if only one could grasp it: and I felt sure that it was the clue to a right understanding of human life. The average scientist thinks of a man as a complex machine, evolved by degrees out of other machines as the universe dances its unceasing and unmeaning dance. Here is a machine which by some specialised adaptation has become conscious of itself, only to find itself a machine, to know that its consciousness is a mechanical product doomed to mechanical extinction. Man is an atom in nature, all his passion and aspiration is a mere iridescence on the surface of matter – product perhaps of a peculiar chemical combination, but first and last a product, and a by-product at that. Lizard or lemur, whatever our immediate parentage, our ancestry goes back to the dust, and man, who returns to the dust, is at bottom dust throughout – dust blown into fantastic forms by the desert wind.

History, I thought, valued man differently. Its concern is with seeing man as he is, in the full flush of his momentary existence; conscious of the universe and of himself, acting and reacting in a world that is not dust at all but mind, a world of moral ideals, political systems, scientific discoveries, hopes and fears. So seen, man is at times dignified, at times contemptible: good or bad, inspired or deceived. But nature is none of these things, and has no place for any of them. Except in a fit of idiotic temper or idiotic idolatry, no one regards molecular motion as either a bad thing or a good. Man, regarded as a part of nature, a product of evolution, is equally devoid of anything good or bad, admirable or despicable. He is just a fact, to be accepted without emotion like any other fact.

But man as the historian sees him is quite a different thing. He is not a mere fact but a drama; by which I mean that he and the things he does are not merely fresh examples of established laws, but have a unique importance of their own. It is not that the historian regards man as having a "free will," while the scientist denies it; neither of these statements is necessarily true. It is rather that, questions of free-will apart the historian regards every man, every act, as having an individual nature and a value not to be compensated or replaced by the substitution of anything else. The scientist only cares for facts so far as they exemplify laws, and if one fact were annihilated he would be perfectly content with another that served as well; he would feel no deprivation. But for the historian nothing will serve as well. His business is one in which there is no substitution, because nothing stands for anything except itself. If Queen Elizabeth lost her temper on a given occasion, that fact to the psychologist is just an example; to the historian it is a unique and irreplaceable possession, infinitely precious because nothing can atone for its loss. Its value lies in its individuality, its distinctness from every other fact of the same kind. If the scientist tells the historian that Queen Elizabeth's fit of temper was merely one form -of that consciousness which itself is merely one form of physical energy, the historian will reply, "Well, but what form? You boil everything down to its elements, as if all that mattered was what a thing was made of; now to me, all that matters is what the thing is. Man, you say, is merely a product of nature. Well, I ask, what sort of a product? What is he like when you come to him?"

The scientist may reply to that "Of course he has a nature of his own. Just as I can offer you a distinct scientific account of carbon, and do not merely say that carbon is a kind of matter, so in psychology I offer you a specific account of man as a special kind of natural being." But this will not satisfy the historian; for though he may be told that man has this or that faculty, his problem remains the same: how have these faculties actually been used on special occasions? And you may subdivide species for ever without getting to the individual.

The historian is concerned with the individual, with the wholly real. All generalisation is abstract, and to that extent arbitrary and partly untrue; the concrete individual alone is real. Queen Elizabeth's fit of temper is ultimate reality, and we travel further and further from the truth when we progressively generalise it into a fit of temper, a state of consciousness, a thing that happened. Thus, the least true thing that can be said about a man is that he is a product of nature, the latest fruit of evolution, a fleeting shape in the dust. "Is it true?" Yes, it is true: but it is so little of the truth that if it is presented as the whole truth it turns into a great bouncing lie. "What then is the whole truth about man?" Well, a truer truth would be to describe what this natural product, man, is in general like: to leave vague metaphysics and plunge into comparative anatomy, physiology, psychology. But that would still be mere abstraction, truth mutilated and falsified. At most it would be about ten per cent, instead of about one per cent of the facts. The whole, final and ultimate truth about man is this or that historical fact. Here, in the concrete acts and achievements of man, we really for the first time know him as he is, and in knowing, understand. My friends, I reflected, had agreed that historical fact was unintelligible, yet at the end of their argument they found that history and science both dealt with historical fact and both in some sense understood it. As I now saw their conclusion its meaning became plain. History and science both deal with reality – the only reality is existence – concrete fact. Now to understand a fact is simply to see it in its true perspective, in its connexion with other facts: and this is what both history and science attempt to do. But the scientist tries to understand the facts by building up round them a network of abstractions and generalisations, which come between him and the facts, and lead him to fancy that what he is really studying is not the facts at all but the generalisation. Hence he misunderstands his own purpose, and comes to believe that the object which he is investigating is the "system of laws of nature," a system that does not exist at all in the real world and is only a metaphysical name for an error in logical analysis.

Now the historian is really doing the same thing as the scientist, that is, trying to understand the facts. But he differs from the scientist in realising what he is doing. He knows that the object of his investigation is no abstract "law of nature," but the facts, and that the generalisations which he uses are only a scaffolding of thought round the object, not the object itself. But this difference of point of view has important consequences. It leads the scientist to think that he has given us the ultimate truth when he has really given us the ultimate abstraction: to aim at exhausting all the reality from the object and reducing it to a mere formula, which, as a half-truth masquerading as a whole truth, becomes a positive falsehood. The general formula, the law of nature, which is indifferently true of a number of things, is not adequately true of any one of them; and a formula that applies to all reality, if one could be found, would have precisely no meaning at all. A really adequate, really true account of anything cannot be an account of anything else except that.

Hence, I concluded, science, even at its best, always falls short of understanding the facts as they really are; for it treats them as mere examples of a law, which implies leaving out of them some of their concrete reality, and taking account, for example, of those features in Queen Elizabeth's fit of temper which are common to all fits of temper, thus passing over what makes it unique and giving up the attempt to understand the whole fact. Now when this abstraction, this killing and dissection of the facts, is consciously done, it need not bring us into positive error: it merely precludes us from reaching the positive truth: but if we think we are understanding the fact as it really is, instead of the fact as we have distorted it, then our science becomes a tissue of errors, approximations to the truth which can never reach the truth and are naively taken for the whole truth. This is a familiar thought, and has led people into saying that truth is unknowable and that all thought is falsification. But that is the wrong conclusion. The right conclusion is that there must be, in existence or to be discovered, a method of thought which does not falsify, because it does not treat the facts in this arbitrary way; a method which recognises every fact to be no mere instance of a law, but a unique individual reality, to be studied in its unimpaired concreteness. And this method can only be history.

So the historian is in the right about man. To call him the product of nature, the toy of time, is at best a half-truth, at worst a lie. The final, ultimate truth about him is that historical truth which shows him as he was and is at the various unique moments of his single history, triumphant over nature in his action and over time in his thought; no mere figure tracked in the dust but a living spirit, immortal even, if the absolute and irreplaceable value of the individual fact can be called immortality.

I began to wonder in a sleepy way whether mankind was not beginning to show some sort of corporate realisation of this truth, the relation of science to history. I remembered that modern science was the creation of the sixteenth and seventeenth centuries, while modern historical method was not born till late in the eighteenth. And was not the greatest scientific discovery of the nineteenth century a discovery which tended to remove biology from the sphere of science altogether and hand it over to history? What was the doctrine of evolution except the discovery that the method of history gave the true solution of problems which had baffled the methods of science? I seemed to see the human mind wandering in its search for knowledge from one resting-place, to another, from magic to religion, from theology to science, and now, its latest immigration, from science to history.

It struck me that the house was very quiet. My pipe was out, and the first had burnt low. As I creaked upstairs to bed, I saw that the mist had gone and the sky was full of stars.

Recent Publications

Compiled by
SUSAN DANIEL
Western Oregon University*

Armour, Leslie. 'F. H. Bradley and Later Idealism: From Disarray to Reconstruction.' In *Philosophy After F. H. Bradley*, edited by James Bradley, 1-29. Bristol: Thoemmes Press, 1996.

Bates, David. 'Rediscovering Collingwood's Spiritual History: In and Out of Context.' *History and Theory*, 35 no. 1 (1996): 29-55.

Boucher, David. 'The Significance of R. G. Collingwood's Principles of History.' *Journal of the History of Ideas*, 58 no. 2 (1997): 309-30.

Boucher, David, and Bruce Haddock, editors. *Collingwood Studies: Letters from Iceland and other essays*. Wales: Dinefwr Press, 1996.

Ciocco, Gary. Review of *Essays in Political Philosophy*, by R. G. Collingwood, edited with an introduction by David Boucher. *The Review of Metaphysics*, 50 no. 2 (1996): 395-96.

Collingwood, R. G. 'Aesthetic and the Mind,' introduced by James Connelly. *Collingwood Studies,* 3 (1996): 194-215.

Review of *Collingwood Studies: The Life and Thought of R. G. Collingwood*, edited by David Boucher. *History and Theory*, 35 no. 3 (1996): 412.

Review of *Collingwood Studies: Perspectives*, edited by David Boucher and Bruce Haddock. *History and Theory*, 35 no. 3 (1996): 412.

Collingwood, W. G. 'Letters from Iceland,' introduced by Janet Gnosspelius. *Collingwood Studies*, 3 (1996): 1-75.

Connelly, James. Review of *Creation, Nature, and Political Order in the Philosophy of Michael Foster*, edited by Cameron Wybrow. *Collingwood Studies*, 3 (1996): 228-31.

Croce, Benedetto. 'In Commemoration of an English Friend, a Companion in Thought and Faith, R. G. Collingwood,' translated by Lionel Rubinoff and Alan Franklin. *Collingwood Studies*, 3 (1996): 174-87.

———. 'Review of R. G. Collingwood, *Seculum Mentis*,' translated by Lionel Rubinoff and Alan Franklin. *Collingwood Studies*, 3 (1996): 188-93.

Deutsch, Eliot. Review of *Art and Philosophy: Seven Aestheticians, Croce, Dewey, Collingwood, Santayana, Ducasse, Langer, Reid*, by Sushil Kumar Saxena. *The Journal of Aesthetics and Art Criticism*, 54 no. 2 (1996): 188-89.

Dray, William H. *History as Re-Enactment: R. G. Collingwood's Idea of History*. New York: Oxford University Press, 1996.

Franco, Eli. Review of *Collingwood Studies* vols. One and Two, *Australasian Journal of Philosophy* 75, no. 2 (1977): 255-57.

Farrelly-Jackson, Steven. Review of *Art and Philosophy: Seven Aestheticians, Croce, Dewey, Collingwood, Santayana, Ducasse, Langer, Reid*, by Sushil Kumar Saxena. *The British Journal of Aesthetics*, 36 no. 4 (1996): 441-43.

Gardiner, Patrick. 'Interpretation in History: Collingwood and Historical Understanding.' *'Verstehen' and Human Understanding: Royal Institute of Philosophy Supplement*, 41 vol. 72 no. 279 (1997): 109-19.

Hughes-Warrington, Marnie. 'How Good an Historian Shall I Be? R. G. Collingwood on Education.' *Oxford Review of Education*, 22 no. 2 (1996): 217-35.

———. 'History, Education and the Conversation of Mankind.' *Collingwood Studies* 3 (1996): 96-116.

———. 'Collingwood and the Early Paul Hirst on the Forms of Experience: Knowledge and Education.' *British Journal of Educational Studies*, 45 no. 2 (1997): 156-73.

Ingram, P. G. 'Craft and Communication: the Distinction between Art and Craft in R. G. Collingwood's *The Principles of Art.' Journal of Value Inquiry*, 30 no. 4 (1996): 501-14.

Levine, Joseph M. Review of *History as Re-Enactment: R. G. Collingwood's Idea of History*, by William H. Dray. *Canadian Journal of History*, 32 no. 1 (1997): 145-47.

Mann, Doug. 'The Body as an 'Object' of Historical Knowledge.' *Dialogue*, 35 no. 4 (1996): 753-76.

McIntyre, K. B. 'Collingwood, Oakeshott and the Social Contract.' *Collingwood Studies*, 3 (1996): 117-36.

Ramachandra, G. P. 'Re-Experiencing Past Thoughts: Some Reflections on Collingwood's Theory of History.' *Journal of Indian Council of Philosophical Research*, special issue (1996): 67-82.

Rubinoff, Lionel. 'The Autonomy of History: Collingwood's Critique of F. H. Bradley's Copernican Revolution in Historical Knowledge.' In *Philosophy After F. H. Bradley*, edited by James Bradley. Bristol: Thoemmes Press, 1996: 30-45.

———. 'The Relation Between Philosophy and History in the Thought of R. G. Collingwood.' *Collingwood Studies*, 3 (1996): 137-72.

Simpson, Grace. 'Collingwood's Philosophy of History: Observations of an Archaeologist.' *Collingwood Studies*, 3 (1996): 217-25.

Tucker, Aviezer. Review of *History as Re-Enactment: R. G. Collingwood's Idea of History*, by William H. Dray. *Philosophy of the Social Sciences*, 27 no. 1 (1997): 102-29.

Van der Dussen, Jan. 'Collingwood's "Lost" Manuscript of the Principles of History.' *History and Theory*, 36 no. 1 (1997): 32-62.

Vanheeswijck, Guido. 'Metaphysics as a "Science of Absolute Presuppositions": Another Look at R. G. Collingwood: A Reply to Rosmary Flanigan.' *The Modern Schoolman*, 73 no. 4 (1996): 333-50.

———. Review of *Philosophy, History and Civilization: Interdisciplinary Perspectives on R. G. Collingwood*, edited by David Boucher, James Connelly, and Tariq Modood. *Tijdschrift Voor Filosofie*, 58 no. 4 (1996): 771-73.

---

* Notification of additional items would be welcome. Please send to Dr Susan Daniel, Philosophy and Religious Studies Department, Division of Humanities, Western Oregon University, Monmouth, OR 97361, USA.

Obituary

R. W. BEARDSMORE
8 July, 1944 – 13 June, 1997

by

D. Z. PHILLIPS
University of Wales Swansea[1]

Dick Beardsmore was born on 8th July 1944 and received his early education at Purley County Grammar School, Surrey. He graduated in philosophy from what was then University College, Cardiff in 1965. He stayed on there to do research. His MA thesis would, without doubt, be a PhD today. It became his book, *Moral Reasoning* published in 1969, which quickly established itself as one of the most incisive critiques of the then prevailing trends in contemporary ethics. Aesthetics was his other major research field, and his book, *Art and Morality*, published in 1972, remains one of the best discussions of this topic. Given the course Anglo-American philosophy has taken, it is not surprising that the challenges in his work have gone unanswered.

After completing his research at Cardiff, Dick held an assistant lectureship at University College, Lampeter before securing a lectureship at University College, Bangor in 1968. He taught there for nineteen years. Dick, very quickly, established himself as the backbone of the department, both as a teacher and as an administrator, strengths which were recognised, along with his publications, when he was promoted to a senior lectureship in 1987.

It took some time to get used to the geographical change coming to

Swansea involved in 1987 after the sudden close of the department at Bangor, but no philosophical acclimatisation was necessary. H. O. Mounce, at Cardiff, when Dick was his student, had already introduced him to philosophical views long associated with Swansea's philosophers, but he had made these his own in a distinctive way. Through the Welsh Philosophical Society at Gregynog, which Dick served as secretary from 1972-1982, a close philosophical affinity had developed between Swansea and Bangor.

It did not take us long to discover how fortunate Swansea had been in persuading Dick to join its Department of Philosophy. The same virtues as teacher and administrator soon became evident, and it was obvious to me as head of department, that he had a right hand man on whom he could rely absolutely. Dick's courage, integrity and respect for truth never wavered. When others were downcast, his was an encouraging voice. It seemed as though he could ride any storm, but this was not true. He felt stress in his own way.

In 1992 he was the obvious person to succeed me as head of department. He had the virtue of never taking himself too seriously and he was amazed, and amused, when he saw others taking themselves in this way in academic life. Students held him in the highest regard. This regard was due in no small measure to the fact that he was a first class teacher, conveying his enthusiasm for philosophy with an ability to express the most difficult problem in a straightforward way. His door was always open to students when others urged him to close it and put his own interests first.

There is no doubt that he put commitment to the department before his own advancement. There is much he was on the verge of accomplishing. He had become engrossed in a book on Philosophers and Animals, and was working on a book on Collingwood's *Principles of Art*, and a second edition of his own *Art and Morality*.

Dick's value in the philosophical community had been recognised in a number of ways. He has served on the Council of the Royal Institute of Philosophy, and was a Senior Fellow of the Collingwood Centre at Swansea and had been a Visiting Professor at the University of Mississippi and spent three terms at the University of Texas, Dallas. His scholarly judgement was sought widely. He had written twenty-six scholarly reviews in leading journals, many of them gems of philosophical analysis and insight, and given over 80 public lectures.

Dick Beardsmore's world was not confined to philosophy. He was a man of many abilities. He was an accomplished water-colourist, and had exhibited with success in the Ceri Richards Gallery at the Taliesin Arts Centre in the University. Perhaps he was at his most relaxed stripping and reassembling old cars which he sometimes drove at speeds which made those cars complain. Music was also an extremely important part of his life. He had a deep appreciation of jazz, rock-and-roll, and country and western music. Every week he played mandolin and banjo and sometimes guitar in a dedicated group of musicians in the department, and he had become accomplished in latter years in making mandolins and banjos.

If there is one quality that stood out among his many qualities, it was his generosity. As his colleague Ieuan Lloyd has said, "Dick had a unique kind of generosity. It was pure and spontaneous. An expressed wish was hardly out of one's mouth when Dick would say he could help. We all have many stories we could relate: brakes repaired at weekends, lifts at unearthly hours, and even accommodation for students who had no digs. (It is doubtful if Pam his wife was always consulted first.)"

It should be obvious from what has been said how great a loss his passing is to those in the Department of Philosophy and the Collingwood Centre at Swansea – colleagues, secretaries and students and to a far wider circle of friends. But that loss is nothing compared to the loss which has come upon his wife Pam and his daughter Anna. Pam and Dick met in their very first week as students at Cardiff and throughout their marriage his life has also been hers. Latterly she tried, without success, to get her husband to put himself before others when his health declined. As for his daughter Anna, Dick idolised her. His last evening at home had been a happy occasion with her and Pam – the most important people in his life. To them and to his mother and sister Val, who had lost a son and brother, and to his parents-in-law, and other members of his family, our sympathy is extended at this time.

---

1 This obituary is a revised version of D. Z. Phillips's appreciation of Dick Beardsmore read at the memorial service.

LIFE MEMBERS OF THE COLLINGWOOD SOCIETY

Dr Michael Beaney, David Blatchford, Dr David Boucher, Professor George Boyce, Dr Jonathan Bradbury, Professor R. Bradley, Melvyn Bragg, Rt. Hon. Lord Callaghan, Dr O. Caraiani, Anna Castriota, Mrs Mary Clapinson, Mr Bruce Coffin, Professor Janet Coleman, Mrs Vera Collingwood, Rev. Jeremy Collingwood, Professor Conal Condren, Dr James Connelly, Dr Susan Daniel, Professor William Debbins, Mr Robin Denniston, Professor William Dray, Professor John Dunn, Professor David Eastwood, Dr Albert Fell, Dr Joe Femia, Mr Peter Foden, Rt. Hon. Michael Foot, Dr Elizabeth Frazer, Professor Frank Gilliard, Miss Janet Gnosspelius, Professor Leon Goldstein, David A. Griffiths, Margit Hurup Grove, Professor Knud Haakonssen, Dr Bruce Haddock, Professor H. S. Harris, Dr Stein Helgeby, Professor Michael Hinz, Professor Martin Hollis, Mr Sinclair Hood, John Horton, Dr John Hospers, Dr Marnie Hughes-Warrington, Sue Irving, Professor Wendy James, Dr Jeremy Jennings, Dr Douglas Johnson, Dr Peter Johnson, Susie Johnston, Professor William Johnston, Dr Norman Jones, Dr Maurice Keens-Soper, Professor Donald Kelley, Dr Paul Kelly, Professor Kenneth Ketner, Professor Michael Krausz, Julian Lethbridge, Peter Lewis, George Livadas, Florin Lobont, Professor Alasdair MacIntyre, Dr Maria Markoczy, Professor Rex Martin, Neville Masterman, Wayne Mastin, Donald Matthews, Dr C. Behan McCullagh, Dr Graham McFee, Ken McIntyre, Hugh McLean, Iain Miller, Professor Alan Milne, Professor Kenneth Minogue, Dr Ivan Molloy, Timothy Morgan, Professor Myra Moss, Professor Terry Nardin, Professor Jay Newman, Peter Nicholson, Dr Francis O'Gorman, Dr Robert Orr, Elizabeth Pakis, Professor Carole Pateman, Roy Pateman, Dr Zbigniew Pelczynski, Rik Peters, Lord Professor Raymond Plant, Professor Clementina Gily Reda, Dr Angela Requate, Dr Dwaine Richins, William Rieckmann, Peri Roberts, Professor Lionel Rubinoff, Professor Alan Ryan, Mrs Brigit Sanders, H. Simissen, Dr Grace Simpson, Professor Quentin Skinner, Mrs Teresa Smith, Robert Stevens, Guy Stock, Peter Strong, Dr Hidemi Suganami, Sherwood Sugden, Peter Sutch, Professor Donald S. Taylor, Professor Richard Taylor, Leo Ten Hag, Rt. Hon. The Baroness Thatcher, Dr Julian Thomas, Dr Martyn P. Thompson, Professor Jan van der Dussen, Naomi van Loo, Professor Guido Vanheeswijck, Professor Donald Verene, Professor Andrew Vincent, Dr Kallistes Ware, Dr Lawrence Wilde, Professor Howard Williams, Andrew Wilson, Dr Adrian Wilson, Dr Ian Winchester, Professor David Wood, Dr Elizabeth Wright.

CARFAX PUBLISHING LIMITED

Journal of Political Ideologies

EDITOR
Michael Freeden, *Mansfield College, Oxford, UK*

Supported by an International Editorial Board

Launched in 1996, the *Journal of Political Ideologies* is dedicated to the analysis of political ideology in its theoretical and conceptual aspects, as well as with reference to the nature and forms of concrete ideological phenomena within social, temporal and spatial contexts. It encourages the exploration of the impact of political ideologies on political processes and institutions and vice versa. Significant attention is devoted to investigating ideologies in terms of their actual histories, geographical and cultural expressions and to interpreting the idea-patterns of particular ideological variants.

The *Journal of Political Ideologies* wishes to advance the scholarly study of ideologies as a major field of political theory, while drawing in to the study of ideologies work from related disciplines, in particular the history of ideas, sociology, area studies, cultural studies, discourse analysis, international relations, policy studies and political psychology. It welcomes qualitative and quantitative analysis, and theoretical and methodological insights from a range of different perspectives.

SUBSCRIPTION RATES
Volume 3, 1998, 3 issues. ISSN 1356-9317.
Institutional rate: £104.00; North America US$158.00.
Personal rate: £27.00; North America US$42.00.

ORDER FORM
Please send a completed copy of this form, with the appropriate payment, to the address below.

Name
Address

CARFAX

Visit the Carfax Home Page at	UK Tel: +44 (0)1235 401000
http://www.carfax.co.uk	UK Fax: +44 (0)1235 401550
	E-mail: sales@carfax.co.uk

Carfax Publishing Limited • PO Box 25 • Abingdon • Oxfordshire OX14 3UE • UK